ISBN 978-1-331-69596-7
PIBN 10222685

This book is a reproduction of an important historical work. Forgotten Books uses
state-of-the-art technology to digitally reconstruct the work, preserving the original format
whilst repairing imperfections present in the aged copy. In rare cases, an imperfection in
the original, such as a blemish or missing page, may be replicated in our edition. We do,
however, repair the vast majority of imperfections successfully; any imperfections that
remain are intentionally left to preserve the state of such historical works.

1 MONTH OF
FREE
READING

at

www.ForgottenBooks.com

By purchasing this book you are eligible for one month membership to ForgottenBooks.com, giving you unlimited access to our entire collection of over 700,000 titles via our web site and mobile apps.

To claim your free month visit:

www.forgottenbooks.com/free222685

Similar Books Are Available from
www.forgottenbooks.com

JACOBITE CORRESPONDENCE

OF

THE ATHOLL FAMILY,

DURING THE REBELLION,

M.DCC.XLV.—M.DCC.XLVI.

FROM THE ORIGINALS IN THE POSSESSION OF

JAMES ERSKINE OF ABERDONA, ESQ.

EDINBURGH:

PRINTED FOR THE ABBOTSFORD CLUB.

M.DCCC.XL.

EDINBURGH: PRINTED BY T. CONSTABLE,
PRINTER TO HER MAJESTY.

20 David Irving Esquire, LL.D.

James Ivory, Esquire, Solicitor General.

Hon. Francis Jeffrey, Lord Jeffrey.

James Kinnear, Esquire.

George Ritchie Kinloch, Esquire.

25 David Laing, Esquire.

Rev. John Lee, D.D.

William Hugh Logan, Esquire.

James Lucas, Esquire.

William Macdowall, Esquire.

30 James Macknight, Esquire.

James Maidment, Esquire.

Theodore Martin, Esquire.

John Miller, Esquire, M.D.

William Henry Miller, Esquire, M.P.

35 Rev. James Morton, B.D.

Robert Nasmyth, Esquire.

Edward Piper, Esquire.

Robert Pitcairn, Esquire.

John Robertson, Esquire.

40 Right Hon. Andrew Rutherfurd, Lord Advocate.

Andrew Shortrede, Esquire.

John Smith, Youngest, Esquire.

Edward Vernon Utterson, Esquire.

Right Hon. Sir George Warrender, Bart.

Treasurer.

45 John Whitefoord Mackenzie, Esquire.

Secretary.

William B. D. D. Turnbull, Esquire.

At a Meeting of the ABBOTSFORD CLUB, held at Edinburgh the 26th day of November 1838,

" Mr. LAING having stated that JAMES ERSKINE OF ABERDONA, Esq., had, through the medium of JOHN HILL BURTON, Esq. Advocate, kindly offered to the CLUB for publication, the " CORRESPONDENCE OF THE MARQUIS OF TULLIBARDINE, (assuming the title of DUKE OF ATHOLL,) during the Rebellion in 1745"—the originals of which are preserved among the Family papers at Aberdona,—the Meeting directed the thanks of the Members to be returned to Mr. ERSKINE,—accepted his obliging offer, and instructed the Secretary to order transcripts to be immediately made for press. At the same time the editing of the Work, for the use of the Members of the ABBOTSFORD CLUB, was confided to Mr. BURTON and Mr. LAING."

INTRODUCTORY NOTICE.

THE ABBOTSFORD CLUB is indebted for the following series of Letters to the politeness of JAMES ERSKINE of Aberdona, Esq., among whose family papers they have for many years been deposited. On the manner in which they may have come into the hands of one of Mr. Erskine's ancestors, neither the documents themselves, nor any extraneous information, traditionary or written, throw any light. It might be natural to presume, from the evidence they were calculated to supply against the leaders of the Rebellion, that they came officially into the hands of Charles Erskine, Lord Justice-Clerk, (the lineal ancestor of the present proprietor of the papers,) who, at the period to which they refer, was a Senator of the College of Justice, under the title of Lord Tinwald. As they bear no evidence, however, of having passed through any public office, a more plausible theory, as to the mode in which they had been acquired, seems to be the following:—In 1748, Lord Tinwald's son, James Erskine, Esq., was appointed sheriff-depute of Perthshire, and in the same year his father was elevated to the dignity of Lord Justice-Clerk, in the room of Lord Milton. About this period, the new sheriff had, in all probability, by some means or other, discovered and obtained possession of these documents; which,—at a date so long after the Rebellion, the punishment of many of the individuals compromised by the correspondence, and the death of others,[1]—he conceived that he would better aid the returning tranquillity of the country by suppressing altogether, than by using them as

[1] Among these was the unfortunate Marquis of Tullibardine himself, who died in the Tower of London on the 9th July 1746.

the means of further vengeance against those whose misdeeds he probably thought had been already sufficiently atoned for. With this view of the matter, he had, in all likelihood, deposited these " cold ashes of rebellion" in his private archives, where they have since remained, along with other more harmless correspondence and family papers. That there cannot be a doubt of their authenticity, an inspection of the Letters, even in their printed form, will at once establish; and the Editor may add, on the information of the proprietor, that the late Duke of Atholl, many years ago, expressed to a mutual friend of Mr. Erskine and his Grace, his knowledge of this correspondence being in Mr. Erskine's hands, and his desire that it should not be made public, at least in his lifetime,—probably not caring to have the misguided, though gallant exertions of his grandfather, brought back to the recollection of the public, although his Grace's known loyalty and national spirit might well have expiated the failings of a far more misguided ancestor, and had long afforded a guarantee to the public, in regard to himself, that

> In him the savage virtues of his race,
> Revenge, and all ferocious thoughts, were dead.

The reader may perhaps be disappointed who expects in these letters much additional information relative to the more public transactions of the insurrection. The large body of evidence already laid before the public would seem to have well nigh exhausted that branch of the subject; and the utmost that can be now looked for, is the corroboration of any points that may have been made the ground of discussion, or considered as standing in need of farther evidence. Among these points is the conduct of Lord George Murray; and it is to be regretted that the gap in the present series, embracing the whole period from the army's entering England, until it reached Falkirk on its retreat northward, renders it impossible to draw from it any additional particulars regarding the coolness that took place between Lord George' and Charles Edward, or the part which the former took in regard to that retreat, which, without doubt, tended greatly to abate the sanguine hope and spirit that had hitherto attended the enterprise. The numerous letters of Lord George, at other dates, show sufficiently that he acted throughout with the utmost energy and zeal, nor is there any allusion made to his having experienced injury or withdrawal of confidence at the hands of Charles Edward or any of his councillors; from the beginning to the end of the campaign, his letters breathe the same language of unwearied and ungrudging devotion to the cause; but it is evident, from the accounts given in his and other letters of the continual desertion of the Highlanders, and the difficulty of keeping them together, that the retreat from England was a measure of absolute necessity. No means had been left unused, (and it is chiefly on this head that these letters constitute a new body of evidence,) to raise men for the service and to keep them from leaving it. The enthusiastic loyalty of the Clans, regarding which so much has been said and sung, may hereafter, with propriety, disappear from the pages, at least of history. More perfect evidence of quite as arbitrary an exercise of coercion as Napoleon's conscript scheme, and certainly much more indiscriminate, cannot be required, than what is afforded by the letters of the Marquis of Tullibardine and his agents in the following pages.

It has not been considered necessary to prefix a systematic account of the parties who figure in this correspondence. The principal actors in the events which it serves to record, have been long familiar to the world both in history and .romance; and any peerage will at once give all the necessary information regarding the births, marriages, and deaths of the Marquis of Tullibardine, Lord G. Murray, The Earl of Kilmarnock, Lord Strathallan, Lord Nairne, &c. &c., while the principal chieftains and landed proprietors are in like manner chronicled in Douglas' Baronage and other works of a similar nature. With regard to the inferior agents, the numerous Robertsons, Spaldings, &c., the "*fortes Gyae fortesque Cloanthi*" of Atholl, it would doubtless require a knowledge of Gaelic, and a pilgrimage to the scene of their career, to acquire any competent information; and it is not probable that the result would repay the pains taken to arrive at it

There is, however, one individual who makes a rather prominent figure in this correspondence, whose name has not hitherto, (so far at least as is known to the Editor,) been connected with the events of the period. The Doctor Colvill, who so frequently corresponds with the Marquis and his satellites regarding all the measures which they had the task of carrying into operation, was undoubtedly the Honourable George Colvill, fourth son of the eighth Lord Colvill of Culross, who is said by Wood to have been a physician in Dundee, and to have died unmarried in 1755. It is worthy of remark that his elder brother, (who had distinguished himself at the battle of Dettingen,) commanded the North British Fusileers at the victory of Culloden; and a nephew, of the same name, son of the ninth Lord Colvill, is also mentioned by Wood as having "pursued the rebels into Scotland under the Duke of Cumberland." Such divided politics in families were, as is well known, far from uncommon in Scotland at the period.

The style employed by most of these correspondents is neither better nor worse than the usual language of their time. The Marquis of Tulli bardine, having lived much abroad, seems to have lost any facility of composition in his native language that he may have ever possessed, and in one letter printed in the Appendix, (No. V.) he appears to have found it so difficult a task to express his own meaning, that it may be doubted whether the illustrious individual to whom it is addressed could be much edified by its perusal. Lord George Murray's letters, on the other hand, are plain and decided in their language. Robertson of Strowan's effusions are so characteristic of that very eccentric genius, that it has been thought right to subjoin a lithographic facsimile of one of his most extravagant productions. Much bad spelling generally prevails, especially among the Highland gentry, but it cannot be denied that the palm in this respect is borne away by the heroine of the Rout of Moy,—the Lady of Mackintosh, —than whom, writes the *gallant* General Stewart, " of all the fine ladies, few were more *accomplished*, more beautiful, or more enthusiastic." Her enthusiasm is undisputed, nor would it be courteous to question her beauty, but it must be owned, that whatever accomplishments she may have possessed, they do not appear to have been of a literary nature.

The proof sheets have been rigidly compared with the original letters, which are thus *verbatim et literatim* put into the hands of the Club. In many instances the facility of perusal might have been assisted by slight emendations, but it was considered that even mistakes and peculiarities, whether in spelling or grammar, were traits of character and habits which it would be improper to suppress.[1]

These papers may be considered as constituted of two distinct elements, —the original communications which the Marquis of Tullibardine received, and the scrolls of his own letters. On only two occasions does the signature of "Atholl" occur in the course of the series; in one of these instances it is partially torn off, in the other so nearly obliterated that it was with some difficulty that the original autograph could be traced for the purpose of a facsimile. The scrolls are, in general, written by the Marquis's successive secretaries; some of those so penned are corrected by himself, and others are entirely in his own handwriting. The letters received by the Marquis have been indorsed with punctilious accuracy, displaying the name of the writer, with the place and date of writing and receipt. This is generally in the handwriting of a secretary, but occasionally in that of the Marquis, who has also, in some of the scrolls of his own letters, supplied deficiencies and corrected mistakes. These indorsations afforded to the Editor the best possible authority for heading and titling the letters for the press, and he has therefore thought it right to adhere to them on every occasion, at some slight sacrifice of technical precision to virtual accuracy of designation. This circumstance will readily account to the reader for the Jacobite phraseology which pervades the table of contents. The convenience of this arrangement will readily present itself to the reader; it would have been, for instance, productive of perpetually recurring confusion, and cousequent necessity of explanation, to have given the title " To the Marquis of Tullibardine," to a letter beginning " My Lord Duke."

[1] The following errors have escaped correction during the passage of the volume through the press. Lady George Murray's signature, at pages 23 and 51, ought to have been printed Æmilia: the title of No. XXIV. at page 27, should have been " The Duke of Atholl to Sr Alex^r McDonald [and] McLeod;" and Cluny's signature throughout, should have been " Ev. McPherson."

Each letter is twice numbered on the back, one of the sets of numbers showing a collective, the other an individual reference. It at first occurred to the Editor, that one at least of these numerations might have been appended as a means of arranging the correspondence for the purpose of prosecution, but further examination showed that all markings of any kind in the series were made for the convenience of the Marquis himself. It appears that he numbered his letters in the order in which he received them, until he came to number 50, when he commenced a new series of a like number, distinguishing the fifties from each other, by No. 1. on each letter of the first series of 50, No. 2. on each letter of the second, and so on. It is perhaps worth noticing, as characteristic of the minute precision of the great Jacobite leader, that the Editor has seen several specimens of the domestic correspondence of the Marquis, at an early period of his life, consisting of invitations to dinner, and other communications of like importance, in which the same business-like system of indorsation is rigidly followed.

The Appendix is composed of two distinguishable sets of documents. The one (from No. 1. to No. 6. inclusive) consists of letters, which have evidently originally formed part of the Atholl correspondence, but which have apparently been for some time separated from the collection in the possession of Mr. Erskine. With the use of these documents, for the purpose of illustration, the Editor has been kindly furnished by their proprietor. The other series of documents consists of papers not connected with the Atholl correspondence, and which have no further claim to be associated with it than their reference to the same series of political events, and the circumstance that they have been found among the papers of the same family. Should the reader be inclined to think that the latter portion of these add unnecessarily to the bulk of the volume, it is hoped that the censure will not apply to the three letters from Lord Lovat—productions which the editor cannot help considering so intrinsically interesting, that there is no occasion to make any apology for their introduction. These three letters are all deeply tinged with the qualities and characteristics of their remarkable author;—the insinuating address—the deep guile—and the calm assumption of stainless integrity which enabled him to end his black career with the unabashed application to his fate of the " *dulce et decorum est pro patria mori*," of Horace. Of these letters, the signature only is in the handwriting of their author, the services of a secretary having been employed on each occasion; and it may be noticed that the second and third, six years distant from each other in date, and written under such different circumstances, are in the same handwriting, showing apparently that even Lovat had some retainer in his service, who would not desert him in his last day of danger and distress,—an indication of devoted attachment, which appears somewhat unaccountable, if the following anecdote regarding him from Burt's letters from the North of Scotland is to be relied on, as furnishing fair data on which to form a general judgment of the estimation in which he was held by his dependents.

" As this chief was walking alone in his garden, with his dirk and pistol by his side, and a gun in his hand, as if he feared to be assassinated; and as I was reading in his parlour, there came to me, by stealth, (as I soon perceived,) a young fellow, who accosted me with such an accent, as made me conclude he was a native of Middlesex, and every now and then he turned about as if he feared to be observed by any of the family. He told me, that when his master was in London, he had made him promises of great advantage, if he would serve him as his gentleman; but though he had been there two years, he could not obtain either his wages or a discharge. And, says he, when I ask for either of them, he tells me I know I have robbed him, and nothing is more easy for him than to find among these Highlanders abundant evidence against me, innocent as I am, and then my fate must be a perpetual jail or transportation, and there is no means for me to make my escape, being here in the midst of his clan, and never suffered to go far from home. You will believe I was much affected with the melancholy circumstance of the poor young man; but told him that my speaking for him would discover his complaint to me, which might enrage his master, and in that case I did not know what might be the consequence to him. Then with a sorrowful look he left me."

7, HOWARD PLACE, EDINBURGH,
7th March 1840.

CONTENTS.

CONTENTS.

CONTENTS.

APPENDIX.

I need not p.
a man to be
who makes nu
science of wrong
the King. few pe
scruple in th
I have been ca
nt by your Gra
lations tho   a

JACOBITE CORRESPONDENCE

OF

WILLIAM, MARQUIS OF TULLIBARDINE.[1]

I.

CIRCULAR LETTER—TO THE LAIRD OF ASSHENTILLY AND OTHER GENTLEMEN IN ATHOLL.

GENTILMEN,

THE King, for the recovery of his rights and puting ane end to the deftructive procidings of unlafull government, has conftitut The Prince, Regent of His Majefty's dominions, as you will fee by a coppy of his Comiffion and Declaration inclofed. His Royal Highnefs in this condition has brought me with him for the better accomplifhment of his intention of freeing thefe Nations from the ufurpation of foreigners and the impofing practifes of thofe that adheres to them; therefore, according to the Prince's comands, this is requiring my Brothers, or any other of my near relations who are capable and well inclin'd, to make themfelves

---

[1] It will be remarked that in the following correspondence the title of DUKE OF ATHOLL is assumed by William Marquis of Tullibardine, who would have succeeded to the family honours and estates, had he not been excluded by an Act of forfeiture, on account of his connection with the Rebellion of 1715. The title was, by the same act, made to devolve on his younger brother James; but the forfeiture of the elder brother was never acknowledged by the Jacobites.

the Royall Standard; of which time and place you fhall be more fully acquainted by

GENTILMEN,

From the Camp at LOCHIEL,   Your moft Affectionat
Agust 22*nd*, 1745.   and very Humble Servant.[1]

To the Laird of Asshentilley,
Mr. Stewart of Kennichan,
and the other honest Gentill-
men in Atholl, to the care of
Mr. Stewart of Glenbucke.

II.

CIRCULAR LETTER FROM THE DUKE OF ATHOLL.

It is not above an hour fince I had the honour to arrive here, in Company with his royall Highnefs the Prince, to affert his Majefty's right; and as you have ever continued to act as Loyall Subjects and Lovers of your Country, it leaves me no room to doubt that you will on this occafion manifeft to the world your zeall and attachment to the royall family by appearing immediatly in Arms, with all the men you can get together, to join the royall Standard. I fhall be heartily forry that your delay to appear fhould oblidge me, by his Highnefs orders, to ufe more difagreable methods, therefore I hope you'll by no means faill to join our Army here to morrow or Munday, and I am,

Your affect. hu^ble Servt.
ATHOLL.[2]

From the CAMP at BLAIR, }
the 31*st Aug^t.* 1745.   }

[1] This letter has no signature, but was evidently written by the Marquis of Tullibardine.
[2] The Signature has been partially torn off.

III.

SCROLLS OF LETTERS FROM THE DUKE OF ATHOLL, WITH A LIST
OF THE PERSONS TO WHOM THEY WERE SENT.

SIR,

I have informed the Prince of your ſtedfaſt adherence and good
ſervice done the King in the 1715, when you was ſo good as join your
brother's men to mine in the regiment commanded by my brother Lord
George. I perſuade myſelf that the ſame good principles do ſtill remain
in you, and that you'll furthwith raiſe all the men living upon the
Barronys of Aſſhuntly and Balmacruchy, with thoſe on your own intereſt,
and join the army commanded by the Prince, wherever the royall ſtandard
is, as moſt convenient for you. I am well informed, that ſince you have
left the country you have always confidered your intereſt joined wᵗ my
family at all occaſions; and therefore I hope you'll do the ſame at this
junᢉure. You ſerved as Lieut. Coll. laſt, and now deſervedly you need
not doubt of having yᵉ Coll.'s command, and of all other ſervice I can
render you, being, wᵗ perfeᢉ eſteem and confideration,

SIR, &c.

It is not above an hour ſince[1] I had the honour to arrive here in
company with his Royall Highneſs the Prince, to aſſert his Majeſty's undoubted right; and as you have ever continued to aᢉ as loyall ſubjeᢉs
and lovers of your country, it leaves me no room to doubt that you will
on this ſo much wiſhed for occaſion manifeſt to the world your zeall and

---

[1] This Letter is nearly the same, and is followed by another copy, almost *verbatim* with the
one marked No. II.

attachment to the royall family, by appearing immediatly in arms, with all the men you can get together, to join the royall ſtandard. I ſhall be heartly ſorry that your delay to appear ſhould oblidge me, by his Highneſs' orders, to uſe more diſagreable methods. The army proceeds to-morrow to Blair, where I hope you will by no means faill to join on Sunday.

Your moſt affect hu^{le} Servt

DALNACAIRDICH,
30 *Aug*^{t.} 1745.

STRATH TAY.

Robert Steuart of Kilchaffie.
Duncan Steuart of Blackhill.
Mr. George Robertſon, Min^{r.}
Robert Steuart of Derghullich.
James Menzies of Bofracks.
John Reid of Pitnairie.
Chas. Steuart of Ballechan.
John Robertſon of Eaſter Tyre.

BELOW Y^E PASS.

Finlay Ferguſon of Baladmin.
Henry Balnevis of Edderadour.
Thos. & Robert Fleeming, Elder and Y^{r.} of Muneſs.

STRATHERDAILL.

Daniel Robertſon of Balnacraig.
William Small of Kindruggin.

John Robertſon of Strathloch.
Patrick Small of Dirnanean.
Baron Reid.
Alex^{r.} Rattry of Tullichcarran.
Alex^{r.} Rattry of Balinault.
Don^{d.} Robertſon of Cultalonie.
Spalding and M'Intoſh, Portioners of Strommuck.
Alex^{r.} Murray of Arns.
Ja^{s.} Ferguſon of Weſtercallie.
Alex^{r.} Kay Corridon.
John M'Kenzie of Borlunt.
Duncan Steuart of Milton.
David Spalding of Whithouſe.
Steuart, &c. Portioners of Corlarich.
Chas. Spalding of Drimfork.
David Robertſon of Eaſterbleton.
Alex^{r.} Rattry of Dalruillean.

IV.

FROM W. MURRAY, TAYMOUNT, TO THE DUKE OF ATHOLL.

My Lord,

The kindnefs you was pleafed to fhew me in my younger days, encourages me ftill to hope for your patronage and friendfhip, which I flatter myfelf I have never done any thing to forfeit; but, as I hope to have the honour of waiting of you foon at Dunkeld, I will trouble you no further, only to affure you I always have been, and ftill am,

My Dear Lord, your Grace's afectionate
Coufin and obedient humble Servt.
W. MURRAY.

Taymount, Septbr. 2nd 1745.

When I have the honour to fee you, I will give my reafon for not writing fooner.

V.

FROM WILLIAM DAVIDSON, TO HIS GRACE THE DUKE OF ATHOLL AT BLAIR.

May it please your Grace,

I prefume to acquaint you that I am William Davidfon of Auchterarder, near to your Grace's caftle of Tullibardin, who had the honour to fit next you in the elafs at St. Andrews during the whole courfe of your ftudys under Pringle and Vilant, Regents. I had the miffortune to be the greateft fufferer when our 5 villages were burned, in the fatall January 1716, when your Grace went beyond fea, as you will fee by the royall declaration enclofed. Having then loft all, and a numerous family to fupport by my daily induftry, I could never recover my former eftate.

I am not accuftomed to arms, but can be ane able faithful penman, if your Grace think fit to employ me; I fhal take fhare of any fortune, and never leave you til death part us, being now free, a Widower, and all my children in bufinefs.

Otherways, may it pleafe your Grace, in my favours to apply his Royal Highnefs Charles Prince of Wales, Regent, and onely Righteous Heir to the Croun of thefe long oppreffed Kingdoms, that I may have fome fubfiftence to live by til God fbal enable him to make full reparation, conform to Juftice and his Father's Royal Promife. I pray God may cronn your arms with fuccefs,—*Ferrea jam pereant, redeant Saturnia regna,* and am, with the moft profound refpect,

May it pleafe your Grace,

Your Grace's moft humble petitioner,

Moft obedient fervant,

WILLIAM DAVIDSON.

Blair, 7*ber* 2, 1745.

Refpice famelicum, Maecenas digne Poetam
  Bis captum Martis Mulciberique dolis;
Intulit, ah, mifero flammas Montana Juventus.
  Trux Iber in tumidis me fpoliavit aquis.
Filius ante diem patrios inquirit in annos.
  Accipe nunc humiles mente favente preces.

An Dom
1716.
1740.

PARAPHRASED.

Buru'd by the CLANNS in furious ire,
  Stripp'd by fierce Spaniards on the fea,
Efcaped twice thro' fword and fire,
  My cruel fon hath robbed me.

VI.

MEMORIAL HUMBLY OFFERED TO HIS GRACE THE DUKE OF ATHOLL
ANENT THE ARMY'S ROUT IN THE LOW COUNTRY, TO THE ONELY
SURE PASSES UPON FORTH, BY DOUN AND THE FORD OF FREW;
ALSO, THE ROUT FROM THENCE TO LINLITHGOW, A MOST CON-
VENIENT QUARTERS, OR TO GLASGOW, A WEALTHY OPEN CITY;
ALSO, OF THE STRENGTH AND INCLINATIONS OF THE SEVERAL
NOBLEMEN AND GENTLEMEN OF THESE COUNTRYS, AND HOW
THEY STAND AFFECTED TO THE ROYAL CAUSE, BY

WILLIAM DAVIDSON.

Ου χρη παννυχιον ιυδειν βuλnφoρον ανδρα.—Homer.
At pater in ripa gelidique sub ætheris axe
Æneas, tristi turbatus pectora bello,
Atque animum nunc huc celerem, nunc dividit illuc,
In partesque rapit varias, perque omnia versat.

Virgil.

Nam priusquam inceperis consulto, et ubi consulueris mature facto opus est.—Sallust.

MAY IT PLEASE YOUR GRACE,

To glance over the following advices given by a fincere well-wifher, anent your rout from Perth, if you pafs by the heads of Forth; containing ane accompt of all Gentlemen how they ftand affected or difaffected to the Royal Caufe.

DISAFFECTED.		WELL-AFFECTED.
1. Craigie of Kilgrafftoun, wealthy.	From Perth to Ochterarder and Tullibardin. —10 Miles.	1. Smyth of Methven, wealthy, but not much to be depended upon.
2. Belfhes of Innermay, wealthy.		2. Graham of Balgowan, very wealthy and firm.
3. Fenton of Milnearn, poor.		3. Moray of Abercairny, very wealthy and firm.
		4. Oliphant of Gafk, pretty wealthy and firm.

DISAFFECTED.		WELL-AFFECTED.
		5. Vifcount of Strathallan, firm.
		6. Lord George Murray, wealthy, *non liquet*.
		7. Lord Rollo, poor, *non liquet*.
		8. Lord Ruthven, *non liquet*.
		9. Old Regent Craigie of Dumbarny, wealthy, *non liquet*.
		10. Moncrief, wealthy, *non liquet*.
1. Haldane of Gleneagles, wealthy.	From Ochterarder to Dumblane. —10 Miles.	1. Sir Henry Sterling of Ardoch, firm.
		2. Drummond M^crigor of Balhaldie, who, with Glengyle, can raife 400 M^cgrigors, firm.
		3. Kippendavie, firm.
		4. Linton of Pittendrich, firm.
		5. Braco Graham's relict widow, a ftrong houfe, but the heir abfent in Dutch fervice.
		6. Son-in-law to Burdon of Fedals, firm.
		7. Duke of Perth, moft firm.
1. Campbel of Aberuchil at Kilbride.	From Dumblane to Doun, where	1. Newtoun Edmonftoun, firm.

DISAFFECTED.

1. Lady Kilcroich, a widow.
2. Bontein of Mildovan, poor.

1. The City of Glafgow, wealthy and powerful.
2. Campbel of Shawfield, wealthy.
3. The Toun of Paifly.
4. Port-Glafgow.
5. Sʳ John Shaw with the toun of Greenock.
Store of iron cannon at thefe two harbours.

there is a ftrong old caftle, which commands the bridge and pafs upon the rapid river Taith.—4 Miles.

From Doun to theFoordofFrew upon Forth.—3 or 4 Miles.

If you take your rout to Glafgow, a wealthy open city, where there is a good magazine of arms, and ftore of ammunition.—14 Miles.

WELL-AFFECTED.

2. Hume of Argatie, wealthy and firm.
3. Edmonftoun of Cambs. Wallace, *non liquet.*
4. Stuart of Ballachallan, firm.

1. Blair Drummond, very wealthy and firm.
2. Haldane of Lenrick, *non liquet.*
3. Graham's of Monteith, with Gartmore, and David Graham of Orchil, Doer for the Duke of Montrofe, generally firm.
4. Buchanan of Drumakill, able and firm.
5. Givan of Buchaple, firm.
6. Two Cunninghams upon Enrick-water, *non liquet.*

1. Earl of Wigtoun at Cumbernauld, firm and rich.
2. Stirling of Keir, at Calderhoufe, rich and firm.
3. Duke of Hamiltoun powerfull and well-affected.
4. Sʳ James Hamiltoun of Rofehall, very wealthy.
5. Sʳ Archibald Stuart of Caftlemilk.

B

1. Toun of Stirling.
2. Sʳ James Campbel of Ardkinlaſs.
3. Sʳ James Livingſton, his Grandſon and Heir.

If you take your rout from the paſſago of Forth towards Linlithgow, where is a moſt convenient encampment, defended by a rapid river, with impaſſable banks on the weſt, on the north and caſt by a loch, which almoſt ſurrounds the palace, in a plentiful country, midway betwixt Edinburgh and Stirling, where his Royal Highnes may expeⒸ powerful aſſiſtance, and may command a paſſage upon Forth to keep a free communication by Alloa, Airth, Borrowſtouneſs, or Queensferry, it

1. Seaton of Touch.
2. Paterſon of Bannockburn.
3. Murray of Powmeaths.

DISAFFECTED.

WELL-AFFECTED.

being within 5 miles of any of thefe. From the foord of Frew to St. Ninians.—7 Miles.

1. Lord Napier.
2. The greater part of the Low Country common people, of the Prefbyterian party, but the whole Epifcopal party are firm to the Royal caufe.

From St. Ninians to Linlithgow.—11 Miles.

1. Graham of Airth, a wealthy learned Lawyer I fuppofe firm.
2. Boyd Earl of Kilmarnock, at Callendar Houfe, at Falkirk, I think firm.
3. Lord Elphingfton, firm.
4. Earl of Hoptoun, immenfly rich, within 3 miles of Linlithgow, who to preferve his beautiful feat of Abercorn, will not fail to contribute largely.
5. Lord Erfkin, *alias* E. of Mar, at Alloa.
6. Earl of Traquair, moft firm.
7. Stuart Lord Blantire, moft firm.
8. Hay of Drummellior, moft firm.
9. The body of the city of Edinburgh, and many Hays of Eaft Lothian, moft firm.

Done by **WILLIAM DAVIDSON,**
BLAIR, *September* 3d. 1745.

VII.

ROBERT MERCER OF ALDIE, TO THE DUKE OF ATHOLL.

MY LORD DUKE,

As Mr. Murray tolde me Lord George faid I was to fee the in-clofed, I judged there might be orders for me, which, finding there is, I have ordered the men of the Property lands to meet me on Thurfday at ten in the morning, to execute your furder orders. I expeﬅed to have met fome of the Strathardl Vaffels, who are not yet arrived, and was this day with Stenton, with whom I left orders about them; what elfe I had to fay have tolde your Servant, and am,

Your Grace's moﬅ obedient humble Servant,

R°. MERCER.

NAIRNE, *Sept. 8ᵗʰ 1745.*

VIII.

THE DUKE OF ATHOLL TO COMMISSARY BISSET.

BLAIR, *Septʳ. 9ᵗʰ 1745.*

SIR,

By your upright and carefull diligence, authority, and influence with the young Commiffary your fon, to whom I join my good friend Mr. James Scot, as you'l acquaint him, I expeﬅ, demand, and pofitively re-quire that the Dunkeld company of men, formerly confiﬅing of fixty good men, come up here againﬅ to-morrow night, without farther delay, as you and your Son will be anfwerable to me at your peril, fince our King and Country's caufe can allow of no further idle excufes or impofing pretences, to fruﬅrate my juﬅ expeﬅations, which I expeﬅ will be readily comply'd with as you regaird your own honour and fafety. Therefore, don't imagine that people of honour are to be ﬅham'd off with pitifull ﬅories. You muﬅ be here to-morrow morning, and be fure your Son come

Royial Highnefs. As formerly, he has thought fit to give me the command on this fide of the river Forth, I cannot but think it's proper that you fhould march what men your Lodp. has readie to Dunkeld, to Joyn me to-morrow night, or as foon as poffible, where you may mett fome of the clans who are coming up, and allfo be ufefull in helping me to raife more men than I have as yet got out of that countrey; befides, it does not feem as yet fafe for your Lordfhip to march after the Prince, unlefs you cou'd have met with the above detatchment this night; therefore, I believe you will do very good fervice to the King by coming to Dunkeld or Blair.

As your Lo. lyics near to get Intelagence of the Enemy, I hope you will lay yourfelf out for fure information of them from time to time. Pray let me heare from you fo foon as poffible; in the meantime, I am.

XVI.

DUKE OF ATHOLL TO LORD GEORGE MURRAY.

TULLIBARDIN, 16ᵗʰ Septʳ 1745.
Ten o'clock in the morning.

DEAR BROTHER,

Juft now I had the pleafure of yours, dated yefterday morning, from Lithgow, and am glad to find by it that H. R. H. and his armie is well and hearty. I went to Dumblain with my Lord Nairn and about a thoufand men he brings up to the Prince, who were to pafs the Forth laft night; I am perfwaded they will be no plunderers, being honeft brave men, tho difhertned for want of armes. I am much furprifed that Secretary Murray has omitted to fend me, as he promifed, the Regent's pour to command in the moft regular manner; I hope you'll get it foon fent me by fome trufty perfonne, with money to defray the charges of a confiderable number of men, who, I prefume, will yet be quickly got together in thefe parts to follow H. R. H. with the reft of the clans, who,

it 's faid will foon be with us; and Lord Ogilvie, he and all with me,
God willing, may ere long be able to join you effectually, but armes and
money is much wanted, of which I defired Lo. Nairn, Kynochan, and
Blairfaite to fully inform our young mafter.—I am, &c.

This night I am to be at Dunkeld on my way to Blair, adieu.

XVII.

DUKE OF ATHOLL TO LORD OGILVY.

DUNKELD, *Sept*[r] 19th 1745.

MY LORD,

I wrote your LoP. on the fifteenth from Tullibardin, to which I
have the anfwer by your exprefs, who left your LoP. this morning at
Cortochy.   I thank you kindely for your Lordfhip's good will towards
helping me in raifing more men, which I hope may be done without com-
pultion.   The letter your LoP. fends me is from the Prince Regent's
Secretary, Mr. J. Murray, dated the 15th inftant, who informs me that
his Royal Highnefs defires you fhou'd march forward to joyn him with
all expedition, believing that you and the Mar men were 800 ftrong,
therefor I intreat your LoP. will make no delay in fetting out for that
end, as I fhall likeways do, as foon as it is poffible to get any confiderable
number of men together who may be fitt for his fervice, to which I can
add no more, being, with perfect refpect, my Lord,

Your moft obedient

and moft humble Servant.

XVIII.

DUKE OF ATHOL TO Mr. MURRAY, SECRETARY TO THE PRINCE REGENT.

DUNKELD, *Septbr*. 20*th* 1745.

SIR,

Late laſt night I had the honour of your's, dated the fifteenth, under Lord Ogilvy's Cover ; there is here incloſed a copey of my anſwer to his LoP's letter, with a copey of the anſwer to my brother George's Letter of the ſame date with your's, for I am afraid it came not to hand, tho' ſent by him who brought the accounts he ſent me. I hope his R. H.'s ſituation is mutch changed to the better from what it was then, ſince we are rejoyſing here on repeted, tho' indireƈt accounts, that the Prince is in Poceſſion of the Capitoll of his Antient Kingdom. I heartily wiſh we cou'd frequently have ſure Intelagence of your Situation, by which it wou'd be mutch eaſier for us to direƈt our motions. Pray, with my moſt humble denty to his R. H., let him know that nothing ſhall be ne-glcƈted can poſſibly be done by me for his ſervice, and ſhall loſe no time in Joyning him when any ſufficient number of men can ſoon be got together. I am told that ſome of the Clans are ſoon to be in theſe partes, ſo pray remember nothing can be done with them nor others to purpoſe without Armes, Amunition, and Money, which is principally wanted. Above a third of what you ſent me was given to the detachment paſſed Forth with my Lord Nairne ; if the earneſt deſire I have to be with you is conſidered, one mnſt be ſupported in unavoidable charges, beſides on Verbal Orders I cannot ſhew ſufſitient Power to aƈt in ſutch a manner as is regularly fitt for his Highneſs' Service ; ſince that's my only Veu, I would rather receive Poſative Orders, than be forced to aƈt without a Perfeƈt Concert. I am, SIR,

Your moſt humble and
moſt obedient Servᵗ.

XIX.

My Lord,

I am juſt now inform'd by a Gentleman who came from Stirling at eleven laſt night, that, ſome hours before he left that place, there were certain accounts come of an Engagement betwixt His Royal Highneſs's Army and Cope's, near to Cockeny, about ſeven miles from Edr. The Highlanders lay encamp'd the night before half a mile from the regular Troops, and at break of day attack'd them both Front and Flanks. The enemy's Horſe very ſoon gave way, but the foot fought reſolutely. There are three Companys of the firſt taken Priſoners, five hundred of the laſt kill'd, and they ſay the reſt taken. Cope run away, and got aboard of a man of war which was lying near to Cokeny. Colonel Gardiner is mortally wounded; and Colonel Hackit, Laird of Pitkellony, and ſeveral Officers taken Priſoners. The Battle laſted but about half an hour, and the Highlanders behaved moſt bravely. The Gentleman who brought the above accounts into Stirling was preſent the time of the action, and ſtay'd there two hours after all was over; he tells that the Prince was well; that he ſee'd the Duke of Perth and Ld. George after the Battle; and heard of nobody of any note being either kill'd or wounded on our ſide; and but a few of the Private men.

I pray God continue to proſper His Royal Highneſs' Arms, and congratulates your Grace upon this Happy ſucceſs. Tho' 'tis like your Grace may have a more particular account of what has happened before this comes to your hands, yet in caſe you had not, thought it my duty to acquaint you of what I heard, imagining that your Friends wou'd not find time for writing imediately after the Engagement.

As I have a very great concern about your Grace's Health, I beg to know how you have kept it ſince I had the Honour of ſeeing you here;

and if you have gót quite rid of your Cough. I am, with the greateſt
eſteem and regard,

MY LORD,

Your Grace's moſt affectionate

ſiſter, and moſt Hum^{le} Servant,

AMILIA MURRAY.

TULLIBARDIN, 22nd *Septr.*
seven in ye morning, 1745.

I hear that there is lying at Alloa 16 piece of Cannon, which Cope
cauſ'd ſhip at Aberdeen, beſides a good deal of his baggage.

XX.

DUKE OF ATHOL TO LADY GEORGE MURRAY.

DUNKELD, *Sep^{r.}* 22, 1745.

MADAM,

About mid-day I was moſt agreeably ſurprized with your Ladyſhip's
delightfull letter, giving the only diſtinct Account has yet come here of
the victory gain'd by his Royal Highneſs's army, for which all honeſt men
in theſe parts are in the utmoſt joy. All friends with me are very thank-
full for your obligeing and carefull diligence in letting us know the certainty of ſuch valuable and important news. Pray, Madam, be ſo good as
to continue your uſeful endeavours towards acquainting us with what you
hear is paſſing of Conſequence, which may be very ſerviceable to the
Loyal Cauſe, and moſt obligeing to one who is, with perfect Eſteem,

MADAM,

Your moſt affectionat Brother

and humble Servant,

ATHOLL.⁽¹⁾

(1) The Signature is scored out.

I beg you'll excufe my writing you by another hand than my own, being really a very flow writer, and at prefent has very little time to employ as wifh'd.   I hope your lovely children are ftill in good health, pray remember me in the moft affectionat manner to them.   I thank you kindly for your Ladyfhip's concern about my health, which is better than it was. I have repeted affurances of what you write, about Cope's baggage and Cannon at Alloa, and wifhes we may be able to find fome effectual means for timeoufly feizing of them, fo that they may be made ufeful to the publick Service.

XXI.

LORD GEORGE MURRAY TO THE DUKE OF ATHOLL.

EDINBURGH, 24th Septr 1745, *six at night.*

DR BROTHER,

I'm fure you would not blame me for not writeing, did you know the fatigue and various Dutys I have been oblig'd to undergoe, and am ftill fubjected to.   I thought fending a perfon off the Field to tell you by word of mouth was better than any accounts I could write of our Batle. I can now tell you for certain there can never be 500 men affembled of Mr. Copp's armie again, perhaps fcarce the half.   Our lofs may be about 36 kill'd, and 50 wounded; theirs, 600 killed, as many wounded, and 12 hundred prifoners befides, for of whole and wounded, we have actually from 16 to 18 hundred prifoners, of which above 80 officers.   The inclofd print is not very correct, and take it altogether is pretty tolerable. I fend you a lift of his Highnefs' Privy Councile, we expect money and every thing elfe will be got ready now, and thofe of the Councile who will act for ordinary are pretty well verfed in affairs, and quite ftaunch.

Balgowen and Abercairney and others in our country will furnifh you with all the money can be got by them, and I expe&t fome may be fent you foon from hence. Nothing vexes me at prefent fo much as that your men are much fewer in number than was expe&ted, and of thefe few, feverals have deferted fince they paffed the Forth; I fhall fend lifts of thofe by my next, and intreat, if poffible, you may make up our two batalions 500 each, and wifh Mr. Mercer, (who will foon have a commiffion fent him,) had one of the fame number, in which cafe you could go to Perth for your head quarters, and take up the cefs and other taxes of Perth, Angus, and Fyfefhire; this I write as my own fentiment. We have got above 1000 ftand of more arms more then we want at prefent; 2000 targets and 500 tents are furnifhed by the Town of Edinburgh, which, with what we have got from Cope's armie, will ferve near duble our number. Being vaftly wearied and fleepy, I conclude with my hearty wifhes that the latter parte of your life may be as fortunate as the former was crofs. Adieu. I am, unalterably, yours,

GEORGE MURRAY.

LIST OF HIS ROYAL HIGHNESS' PRIVY COUNCIL.

Duke of Atholl, Prefident.
Earl of Wemyfs.
Lord George Murray.
Vifcount of Strathallan.
Vifcount of Arbuthnot.
Lord Kenmuir.
Lord Nairn.
Lord Elcho.
Lord Ogilvie.

Lord Cardrofs.
Sir James Stewart of Goodtrees.
Mr. Wauchop Niddery.
Mr. Hugh Hamilton of Bogg.
Mr. John M'Leod of Moravenfide.
Mr. John Stirling of Keir.
Mr. Archibald Stewart, L.P.
Mr. James Graham of Airth.
Mr. John Murray of Broughton.

XXII.

DUKE OF ATHOL TO LORD LOVAT, THE EARL OF SEAFORTH, AND THE EARL OF CROMARTY.

My Lord,

Being perfwaded of your Lod^p's inclinations to ferve the King for the delivery of your country from oppreffion, his Royal Highnefs having conftituted me Commander-in-Chief of his Majeftie's Forces benorth the River of Forth, I cannot but hereby defire your Lo^p may raife all your men in arms, and with the outmoft expedition, march them with me to join his Royal Highnefs.

I hope your Lo^p. will, without delay, fhould not your health allow you to come yourfelf, appoint and direct your men, with fuch officers as you think proper, to fet out foon. And as doubtlefs you are informed of his Highnefs' complete victory, you will alfo encourage your neighbours quickly to fecond his glorious undertaking.

Pray let me have your return as foon as poffible, that I may acquaint His Royal Highnefs of your Lo^p's refolution, who expects you are ready to fhow your Loyalty on fo happy ane occafion.

I beg your Lo^p. will excufe the not writing with mine own hand, having really fo much adoe as renders it almoft impoffible.—I am,

My Lord,

Your Lo^p's moft obedient humble Servt.

Blair Castle, *September 25th*, 1745.

XXIII.

DUKE OF ATHOL TO THE DUKE OF GORDON.

Blair Castle, 25 *Sept^{br}*, 1745.

My Lord,

As His Royal Heighnefs the Regent has been pleafed to confirm the Commition formerly given me by the King, to be Comander-in-Chief on this fide the Forth, allow me to fay here I fhould be glad to fee your Grace will quickly Joyn with all your folowers to affift in Reftoring him to his Crown.

The former Loyalty of your Prediceffors gives me no room to doubte your cheerfull and readie inclinations to fecond the defires of our Royal Mafter; and as I have the honour to be nearly allied and related to your Grace, hopes you'll have fome regaird for the requeft of a well-wifher that entreats he may foon have the pleafure of feeing you appeare as is neceffary for advancing our King and Countrey's fervice on this happy occafion, whereby you'll give much fatiffaction.

I hope your Grace will be fo good as to communicat this to my Nephew the Earle of Aberdeen, to whom I had writte had not I heard that you are together at Kelly. I beg your Grace will moft affectionatly remember me to my Lady Duchefs.

XXIV.

DUKE OF ATHOL TO Sʀ ALEXʀ MᶜDONALD, MᶜLEOD.

BLAIR CASTLE, *Septʰʳ 25ᵗʰ*, 1745.

SIR,

Being perfwaded of your good Intentions to ferve the King and deliver your Country from oppreffion, his Royal Highnefs having Conftituted me Commander-in-Chief of his Majeftie's Forces benorth the River of Forth, do hereby defire you'l raife all your men in arms, and with the outmoft expedition march with me to join his Royal Highnefs.

I am fenfible it was more your miffortune than fault that you have not already had a fhare in the late victory obtained by His Highnefs, the moft compleat that has been known, all the enemy's foot being either killed or taken prifoners; and a great number of the horfe alfo either kill'd or taken ; and that with a handfull of brave Highlanders, 1500 of them only having been engaged. I hope after the example of your pre-deceffors, you will endeavour to bring up not only your own followers, but your neighbours, who I expect will excufe me from not writing to every one, hoping you'l be fo good as communicat this to them. Pray let me have your return as quick as poffible, that I may acquaint his Highnefs of your refolution, who expects you are ready to fhow your Loyalty on fo happy ane occafion.

XXV.

CLUNY MᶜPHERSON TO THE DUKE OF ATHOLL.

MAY IT PLEASE YOUR GRACE,

I have the honour to receive both your Grace's letters, and would will-ingly fend the number of men you defire, but I find it abfolutely neceffary to keep all the men I can make together untill we march wholly. As one reafou, I find we muft ufe force before we can bring all we intend from thefe quarters ; and by the enclof'd your Grace will fee that it will not be difagreeable to others, that we doe not hurry a movement till they have time to be at us ; and befides, I know by the difpofition of people here, it will be difpleafing to them not to be allowed to march from the country in one body ; for which reafons, and fome more I cou'd adduce, I hope your Grace will exenfe me.

I give thanks to Almighty God for the glorious victory His Royal Highnefs has obtained, and wifhes our dear Countrymen who had the honour firft to join in the caufe, and have been active, all joy. Pray God we may all foon congratulate one another on the finifhing of the great and glorious work. I beg your Grace may pleafe to fend me as parti-cnlar accounts as poffible of the action, the kill'd, wounded, and prifoners taken, and return ye enclofed. I am, with great fincerity, and all imaginable refpe&,

> MAY IT PLEASE Y^R GRACE,
>> Your Grace's moft faithfull and moft
>>> ob^t humble Servant,
>>>> C. M^cPHERSON.

CLUNY, 26th Septr 1745.

XXVI.

DUKE OF ATHOL TO CLUNY M^cPHERSON.

BLAIR CASTLE, *Sept^r*. 26th 1745.

SIR,

I received yours and the Gentleman's letter you inclofed, who I believe means very well, and gives his Opinion for the beft. I am perfwaded that the greater body of men appears foon to go out together it would be the better; but as it's uncertain when fome of our neighbours can pofitively joyn us, we fhould not lofe time for ane uncertainty. It is not fhew of numbers can do the bufinefs, therefor am ftill very mutch of opinion you fhou'd come up hither without delay, and rather give than take the Example of being forward in the King and Countrey's Service: one is not to account for others, if they do well themfelves. Believe me, the Prince expe&s every particular body of men will come up to him as faft as they can, without waiting the motions of any other people who are flow, or at a more remote diftance.

As I am very fenfible of your hearty good will for the public caufe, and concern for what regairds me, fo you may be fatiffied of the affe&ion and efteem with which

I am, &c.

XXVII.

LORD GEORGE MURRAY TO THE DUKE OF ATHOLL.

Eᴰ^ʳ 26th Sepʳ 1745.

Dᴿ BROTHER,

This goes by Sheen Menzies, who, with a hundred men, gaurds fo many of our prifoners to Loŭgaret, which is the place thought moſt proper for gaurding them for the prefent. As they know if any of them ſhould atempt to make their efcape, the prifoner being retaken after fuch atempt, will imediatly fuffer death, it will make them in my aprehention be upon their good behavior and under abfolute comand. There muſt be an exa�&ct; liſt of their names, and the different regiments they belong to, and tho' they be quartered thro' all the toun of Logerate, yet twice a day they muſt be revew'd. The gaurd you place at Laugaret may be in your Houfe, and the court room will hold a confiderable number of the prifoners, and the jaile is at hand if any of them ſhould be obſtreperous. Tho' there be no arms but Lochaber axes it will fufice; and all the country to be warned if any of the prifoners ſhould be found any where half a mile from Logaret, to be looked upon as endeavouring to make their efcape. You will pleafe give direᏆ&tions to provide meal, for it is thought that two pecks o' meall in the weak to each prifouer is a full allowance; but, if you think it proper, for one of the pecks, you may order fo much mutton a-week to each as will anfwer to the other peck. Of all things, you muſt find a proper perfon to have the charge of the prifoners, and be cap. of the gaurd, and one to be provifor. You can order in meal from any part of the country where it can be gott, and give recepts for it in his Highnefs' name.

I told you, in one of my former, that fome Gentlemen had promifed more money in loan to his R. H. befides what they already gave, but it is to their Ladys you will pleafe to write, as they appear to do the thing, and not the Hufbands. It is alfo expeᏆ&ted you will give the requifite orders for levying the Land tax and Excife, &c. I have in the meantime procured £200 Sterling, which Shian will deliver to you from his R. H. for the moft urgent occafions in which you are judge.

For God's fake caufe fome effectual method be taken about the deferters; I would have their houfes and crop deftroyed for an example to others, and themfelves punifhed in a moft rigorous manner.

What I have wrote is by his R. H. exprefs Commands, and he further bids me tell you, that by Letters taken and otherways, Commiffary Biffet appears to be a noted Spy, and his Highnefs defires you if poffible to fecure him in clofe confinement, that he may not have the ufe of pen, paper, and ink.

I know you want armes, but tho' we can fpare fome, I do not know how to get them fent. I ever am,

DR BROTHER,

Your moft affec^{t.} Brother, and

Faithful Humble Servt.

GEORGE MURRAY.

His Highnefs defires the Sergeants and Corporals may be quite feperate from the private men, and have no communication with them. All Highlanders that have not a pafs fhould be fecured, if going homeward through your Country.

XXVIII.

LORD GEORGE MURRAY TO THE DUKE OF ATHOLL.

Ed^r, *26th Sept^r.* 1745.

D^R. BROTHER,

I have wrote to you juft now by Sheen, who goes with the prifoners (afleep a great many of them) to Logierat, where they are to be kept. I muft refer you to what I have faid in that letter, but thought it beft, acquainting you before hand, that all things may be in readinefs by the time they come there. They talk of fome Dutch being landed, but they are not above 1000 men, near Newcaftle or Berwick. I can promife you we have a vaft defire to be in hands with the Dutch, and are refolved not to be cumbered with Dutch prifoners as we are with our own Country-men. Mr. Mercer's Commiffion fhall be fent as foon as poffible; fuch is the hurry, that we have not time to fleep or eat.

I ever am your's,

GEORGE MURRAY.

XXIX.

LORD GEORGE MURRAY TO THE DUKE OF ATHOLL.

Dᴿ Brother,

As this goes by Fafcaly, who is fent to bring up the men to com-pleat your two Batalions, I need not fay much, but refer you to him. Some feveritys muft be ufed (to prevent greater evils) againft thofe who have deferted, and you fhould even take all their armes from them, and give them to others, for upon their coming back to us they will get armes. Could we keep our men together, and prevent depredations on the Country, I firmly believe we would be able to go thro' all the Ifland.

I ever am your's,

GEORGE MURRAY.

Eᴅᴿ. 27ᵗʰ *Septʳ.* 1745.

XXX.

LADY GEORGE MURRAY TO THE DUKE OF ATHOLL.

My Lord,

The enclof'd having come to my hands to-night, I take the occa-fion of writing your Grace a few lines along with it, to return my thanks for the Honour of your kind and obliging Letter of the 22ᵈ, and as your Grace defires in it, I fhall be fure to inform you of any thing I hear that 's worth while to acquaint you off. I was told to-day that Mʳ. Forbefs, the Prefident, had wrote a Manifefto, Counter to the Prince's, where in the ftrongeft terms he difwades his country men from joining His Royal Highnefs; tho' tis very like this ftory may be entirely without foundation, for the authority I had it from was not good, however writes it to your Grace as I happened to hear it. My intelligence was wrong about part of Cope's Baggage, &c. being at Alloa, for a Gentleman told me, who came from that place on Tuefday, that it was lying in a Ship at Boriftounefs, with a man-of-war hard by to guard it. There pafs'd laft week through Ochterarder, feven of the Atholl men, deferters from the Army (two of them was nam'd Stewart, and lives in Glenqueath), and the people there took from them fix guns and a fword, which was brought here next day, where they ftill are. Wifhing for good accounts of your Grace's Health, I have the honour to be, with great regard,

MY LORD,

Your Grace's moft affecᵗᵉ Sifter,

and moft humble Servant,

ÆMILIA MURRAY.

TULLIBARDIN, 27ᵗʰ *Septʳ* 1745.

I'd fain hope your Grace has by this time heard of Sʳ· Alexʳ· MᶜDonald and MᶜLoid's being to join the Prince.

XXXI.

CLUNY MᶜPHERSON TO THE DUKE OF ATHOLL.

MAY IT PLEASE Yᴿ GRACE,

I have from the Bearer Twelve Letters, which I fhall take care duly to forward. I wifh my Exprefs, fent to your Grace yefterday, may

E

bring me particular accounts of the Battle, the numbers and names, as far as can be got, of the Dead and wounded.   I fhall be with your Grace as foon as poffible, and with all Due Refpeĉt, moft faithfully am,

MAY IT PLEASE YR GRACE,

Your Grace's moft obedient humble Servant,

C. MᶜPHERSON.

CLUNY, 27ᵗʰ *Septʳ* 1745.

XXXII.

GEO. STIRLING TO THE DUKE OF ATHOLL.

MY LORD,

I was honoured with your Grace's of the 25ᵗʰ curt. laft night, and communicat it to Glenbucket, who had appointed me to levy the Excife and Stent of this place, which he's to take with him, having run fhort of monnie.   He defires me to offer your Grace his humble Compliments, and would have writ you himfelf, had he not been much hurried ; he marches this day by Crief to p a the Forth.   Lord Ogilvie's men were laft night at Couper, and are to joyu Glenbucket about Dumblane.   There's a great many horfe coming with Lord Pitfligo ; Glenbucket had given Commif-fion to Mʳ· Fergefon to colleĉt the Excife of that Colleĉtion, but I believe he muft have affiftance of a Party.   There's at leaft half-a-year's cefs due. I doe think your Grace fhould appoint a Colleĉtor to levy it.   We have nothing new from the Prince's Armie, only they are all in top fpirits, and wants to be furder fouth.   A perticullar of the Glorious Viĉtory was print-ed in the Munday's Mercury, which I make no doubt your Grace has feen. With all deutifull Refpeĉt and Efteem, I am,

MY LORD,

Your Grace's moft obedient

and very humble Servant,

GEO. STIRLING.

PERTH, 27ᵗʰ *Septʳ* 1745.

XXXIII.

GEO. STIRLING TO Mr. MERCER OF ALDIE.

Sir,

Yours to Glenbucket of the 27th, cam here yefterday, Lord Ogilvie made it open, as the Generall had marched the day before; I forwarded it to him by Mr. Da. Fothergham, who was to be at Dumblaine laft night. Lord Ogilvie marched this day for Crief with 400 men, more are following him, and fome feu of the Brae of Mar men, with Monaltrie. There's a good many from Dundee, and Angus Gentilmen, with Lord Ogilvie. I fend this Exprefs to acquaint you, there's £32 fterling here, in Mr. Carmichall of Beglie's hands, collected fince Glenie went off, and a good dale more to collect of the Excife and Stent; but I am afrayed it will not be payed, except his Grace of Atholl fend down a few men here, and at the fame time ane order upon Carmichael the Collector, to pay in what he has collected to any body his Grace fends, who's to give a receipt for what he receives. It's a pitie we had not a few men here to keep the countrie in awe, and raife the publick monnie. I faw a fervant of the D. of Perth's here yefterday, who left the Prince and all his Armie, to the number of 8000, in top fpirits, Thurfday's Evening. There's a detachment of Horfe and Foot fent to Glafgow to raife monnie. Pleafe offer my moft humble Deuty to my Lord Duke, and, with all efteem, I am,

Your moft humble obedt Servant,

GEO. STIRLING.

Perth, 29th Septr 1745, one afternoon.

Remember me to the honeft Doctor. They have elected a Dundie Magiftrat, and are to doe it here to-morrow. As all the men are to leave this to-night, in order to meet Lord Ogilvie at Dumblaine to-morrow, I expected you would have fent a Detachment here to prevented this, as I told you.—Adeu in beaft.

XXXIV.

Honᴰ. Sir,

I juſt now had the incloſed from Mr. Stirling, p. exprefs, which I thought would be yᵉ ſteadieſt man I could get to go forward, which he willingly undertook. I ſuppoſe Mr. Stirling has wrote you that Glenbucket and his men left Perth on Friday, Ld. Ogilvie this day, Lord Pitſligo is coming up, he ſays, with 300 Horſe, Monaltry croſſed at Bridgend this afternoon with 70 or 80. Your Strathardale party is not yet arrived here ; I hear a great many Atholl people that went out are returned, eſpecially ſome men at Logyreat that got money. Our Collection of Exciſe ſhould be to-morrow, I ſhall wiſh to hear good accounts of my Lord Duke, and all with you, and am, with the utmoſt ſincerity and regard,

Hon. Sir,
Your moſt faithful and
moſt obedient Servant,

JA. SCOT.

Septʳ 29ᵗʰ 1745,
5 horse, 48 minutes at night.

XXXV.

Dᴿ Sir,

I am by his Grace defired to acquaint you that he received your Letter, for which his Grace returns you thanks, and had not yᵉ Letter been mifplaced, would have anfwered it himfelf. His Grace has alfo rec^d your Letter to Mr. Mercer of 27th,[1] only this day, and has given an order as you defire to Mr. Robertfon of Bohefpie, ye Bearer, to receive from Mr. Carmichael all the publick money in his hands, for which Mr. Robertfon is to give his receipt. His Grace defires you'll be fo good as advife Mr. Robertfon in every ftep he is to take in this affair, fo as may be beft for the publick good, to let us know from time to time what you think neceffary to be done in your parts, and it will be taken care of accordingly.

I am, with great Truth and Affe&tion,

DEAR SIR,

Your moft, &c.

30th *Sept^r* 1745.

XXXVI.

SPALDING OF ASHINTULLY TO THE DUKE OF ATHOLL.

MY LORD DUKE,

Had I not been perfuaded by fome people, who I now believe are unfriendlie to me, to delay it untill your Grace were farther advanced in ye Country, I would have gone and meet your Grace upon your arrival. After your Grace came to Atholl, I was afhamed to go without fome men, and therefore went to Perth in order to have got a party; where I had the honour of waiting on my Lord George Murray, your Grace's Brother, who ordered me to wait on your Grace, and that you would fend a party for raifing my men, and affured me of your Grace and his own favour. I went to Dunkeld in order to have gon to Blair, but by mif- fortune I fickened, which obliged me to return home. I no fooner re- covered than I defired all my Vaffals & Tenants to make ready, other- ways I would put ye party on them, as there was one in ye Country from

[1] This Letter, which is inserted above, at p. 35, is dated the 29th.

your Grace at the time my Ouncle Mormount bailed ·to anſwer, under yᵉ pain and penalty of twenty pound for each man that failed, how ſoon I would be ready; but how ſoon yᵉ party was gone, they were all unwilling. Upon hearing your Grace was marched I followed after; but after I went to Edinbourgh I learned your Grace was returned. The day before the Batle I ſpoke to Lord Nairn, who deſired me to go to my Lord George of a new, your Grace being abſent; but finding his Lordſhip was with yᵉ Prince, I could not preſume to demand acces be reaſon of the hurry they were in, therefore went on with a relation of my own who commanded a Company in yᵉ Duke of Perth his Regiment having tranſiently met with him; after yᵉ engagement meeting with my Lord George he deſired me to return to yᵉ Country to wait on and attend your Grace; which order I have accordingly obeyed. I beg your Grace will ſend an order to the Commander of yᵉ party here, or ſend an oyʳ to aſſiſt me in raiſing yᵉ men who have deſerted from Edinʳ, and ſuch as have not gon forward, and unwilling to go. I reckon your Grace has been informed of my miſſortouns, altho my Commiſſion from yᵉ Uſurper is of date yᵉ eight of June laſt, I never received but ten pounds, which I got for recruiting, and is all exhauſted; and my Lord George deſired me to apply to Mʳ· Mercer for ſubſiſtance to myſelf and men. I expeᴕ your Grace will honour me with an anſwer, and am, with yᵉ greateſt reſpeᴕ,

MY LORD DUKE,
Your Grace's moſt faithfull, moſt
obedient, and very humble Servant,
DAN. SPALDING.

ASHIN, *Septʳ.* 30ᵗʰ, 1745.

I beg your Grace will exenſe paper; and believe I have been miſrepreſented to your Grace. I wiſh my accuſers and I were in your Grace's preſeance at yᵉ ſame time, I would think it the beſt opportunity to vindicate myſelf I could have.

XXXVII.

FRASER OF FOYERS TO THE DUKE OF ATHOLL.

My Lord Duke,

I am juſt now honoured with your Grace's exceeding kind letter of the 25th current, being a reſpeƈt put on me more than I challenged, by not giving obedience to his Royal Highneſs' firſt call, which I was ready to do with all my pith, (ill provided as I was,) had I not been ſtopt by my chief, Lovat, who aſſured me he was to raiſe his name with all expedition to join his Royal Highneſs, and that his name ſhould go together he judged more proper.

But now, whither Lord Lovat move or not, I ſhall gather my people with all expedition, and ſett out from here the 5th of Oƈtober next, in order to join your Grace.

If I underſtand that Lord Lovat will be ready againe the eight, or ſome few days thereafter, I ſhall not ſay but it will be convenient for me to wait him, of this I ſhall adviſe your Grace.

There is one thing occurs to me, that is, the want of armes, of which I expeƈt to be ſupplyed how ſoon I come to Atholl.

With the greateſt eſteem, I am,

My Lord Duke,

Your Grace's moſt obedient
and humble Servant,

JAMES FRASER.

Foyers, 30ᵗʰ *Sept*ʳ 1745.

XXXVIII.

Dʀ. COLVILL TO JAMES SCOTT.

Sir,

There are a confiderable number of priſoners under the care of Shian, who are expeƈted at Logiereat to-morrow evening, and are to be put in fafe cuftody fomewhere in this country. Upon receipt of this, his Grace defires you'll immediately get horfes and fend up ten bolls meal to Logiereat, to be delivered to James Robertfon, officer there, who is to give his receipt for it.

The ifland in the Loch of Clunie is thocht to be the propereft place for the abode of the prifoners, and, therefore, his Grace has wrote the inclofed to the Earl of Airly, proprietor of yᵉ ifland, to afk his concurrence in getting them accommodated there. His Grace, therefore, defires you'll forward yᵉ inclofed by exprefs to my Lord Airly; the exprefs will call firft at Auchterhoufe, and, if he mifs my Lord there, he is to go forward to Cortichie.

You are to fend along with the meal half-a-ftone candles, for the ufe of the guard.

You'll defire the exprefs to call firft at Drimmy and deliver Mr. Rattray's letter, it will be little or nothing out of his way.

I am, &c.

To James Scott.
 1st October, 1745.

XXXIX.

Dʀ. COLVILL TO JAMES RATTRAY, YOUNGER OF RANYGULLION.

Sɪʀ,

My Lord Duke expeɛted to have feen you here, as you promifd, and, as his Grace wants to fpeak with you about bufinefs, I am, therefore, defired by his Grace to intreat you will, upon receipt of this, fet out direɛtly for Blair Caftle. I offer my moft humble fervice to your Lady, and am with great Truth, &c.

To James Rattray, *Youʳ of Ranygullion.*
 1ˡᵗ Octʳ 1745.

XL.

DUKE OF ATHOLL TO THE EARL OF AIRLY.

MY LORD,

The Prince has fent a confiderable number of his prifoners from the battle of Gladfmuir into thefe parts. Every body thinks the fafeft and moft convenient place they can be kept in is your Lordfhip's ifland in the Loch of Clunie, not fare from Dunkeld, from whence provifions and neceffary orders may be eafily fent, for taking care of fuch a troublefome and dangerous fett of people as they are; and for the preventing any bad confequences from fuch turbulent difpofitions, all friends to our king and country are fully perfwaded you'l cheerfully incline to contribute whatever is reafonably poffible for that end.

Therefor, I prefume your Lordfhip will not only cheerfully make every thing be carefully prepared for their reception, but alfo contribute what's poffible to prevent any dangerous mutiny or efcape amongft them, being fatiffied that none is more inclined towards contributing what's praЙticable for advancing our king and country's fervice, for which none of us ought to fpare any pains or trouble. Counting on your LoP's affiftance, I fhall, with the outmoft diligence, fend people to prepare fuch quarters as are indifpenfibly neceffary for thefe difloyal tho to be pity'd fellow fubjeЙs of,

MY LORD,

Your LoP's moft humble and

moft obedient Servant,

BLAIR CASTLE, *October* 1ft, 1745.

I beg your Lordfhip will exeufe the not writing with my own hand, having really fo much to do as renders it almoft impoffible.

XLI.

INSTRUCTIONS BY THE DUKE OF ATHOLL REGARDING THE PRISONERS.

By WILLIAM DUKE OF ATHOLL, &c. Commander in Chief of his
Majeſtie's Forces benorth the river of Forth:

THESE are requiring you, James Robertſon of Killichangie, John
Robertſon Your of Eaſtertyre, and John Stewart in Kinnaird, to be aiding ·
and aſſiſting to James Robertſon, officer at Logyreat, to provide barns and
ſuch other out houſes in Logyrate as are fitt for quartering the priſoners
that are comeing from the Prince's army under Mr. Menzies of Shiau's
command, and to the providing beef and mutton for them, which I ſhall
pay for; meall comes from Dunkeld to Logyrate, where they are expected
to-morrow night. Shian will inform you how he uſed them on their march
from the army, and you are to uſe them in the ſame manner, both as to
their neceſſaries of life and their being ſtrictly kept; Shian is to con-
tinne, with your aſſiſtance, to guard them, till others fitt for that piece
of ſervice be got againſt the beginning of next week: All which you are
carefully to perform, as you will be anſwerable.—Given at Blair Caſtle,
the firſt day of Octr. 1745.—You are to acquaint me next day after they
arrive how they are provided for, and their exact number.

XLII.

DUKE OF ATHOLL TO LADY GEORGE MURRAY.

MADAM,

Two days agoe I had the pleaſure of your LaP's moſt agreeable
letter, and delayed returning anſwer till now, hoping to been able to ſend
you a deer at the ſame time that your ſervant returns; but, as in many

other things, I'm much difappointed, for I've but juft found out this morning that feveral deers have been verry lately kill'd in the Foreft and difpofed of without my knowledge. However, if the feafon is not too far advanced, the firft good deer that's kill'd fhall be fent you.

The Letter your La^p fent me from my Brother George, with fome other accounts that I have from him, fays little, but that there's about a thoufand Dutch landed near Berwick; and that a fpeedy return is impatiently expected of the men from this country, who, it feems, in great numbers has unworthily return'd from Edin^br. having unworthily left their Commanders, as well as other true Countrymen there, which gives me, as well as every honeft man here, no fmall trouble, befides the uneafinefs we are in how to difpofe of ane unworthy pack of prifoners that is fent us. Pray remember me in the moft affectionat manner to your Loving children, having nothing further to add but that I fhall ever be found with perfect efteem,

MADAM,
Your meft affec^t Brother,
and moft humble Servt,

BLAIR CASTLE, *October* 1st 1745.

My Lady Dowager of Nairne, and her two youngeft Daughters, who are here, fend your La^p their moft affec^t humble Service.

XLIII.

FRASER OF FOYERS TO THE DUKE OF ATHOLL.

MY LORD DUKE,

After doing myfelf the honour of writing a return to your Grace's kind letter as a Teftimony of my Intention to ferve his Royall Highnefs, and to confirm the fame, I've fome time agoe acquainted the Bearer my people; and feeing that he has obey'd my Commands, and the men comeing fo well prepar'd, I've thought it convenient to order them off from here (as being fo nigh the Garrifon) to join your Grace, and to be difpofed of as you think proper, till fuch time that I come up with the reft of my men to join them, which will be in terms of my laft.

I thought to deprive the Enemys of fo many men in Arms was a good office, and fhall hope that your Grace will take it fo. With the greateft Efteem and Regard,

I am,

MY LORD DUKE,

Your Grace's moft faithfull

humble Servant,

JAMES FRASER.

FOYERS, 1ʳᵗ Octʳ 1745.

XLIV.

LETTER FROM MR. SCOT'S SON TO HIS FATHER.[1]

1745.

Oct. 2ᵈ	24 yds. Broad White Italian Mantua, 7s. 6d.	£9 0 0
	48 yds. Silver Edged Ribbon, 9d.	1 16 0
		£10 16 0
	36 yds. plain, 8d.	1 4 0
		£12 0 ^

EDINᴿ· 2ᵈ Oct. 1745.

DEAR SIR,

I recᵈ your's advifing the Receipt of what was formerly fent:

[1] So quoted upon the back.

receive now 24 yds. more Mantua, and 48 yds. Silver Edged rib., with 36 yds. plain, which was all of the latter could be got in Town. You may ſend the pay[t] of both p. firſt ſure hand, as it will come in good ſtead, and be obliging. I received a letter from Brother yeſterday, he's very well, and anxious to hear about you; he's afraid the confuſions in the North will prevent his ſailing ſo ſoon as he expected, w[h] will throw him a little back; we are here in ſuch confuſion being threatned with Canonading from the Caſtle, that we don't mind news. The Caſtle has been firing upon the upper part of the Town all laſt night. Give my duty to all with you, and am, &[ccc.]

Adieu.

Since writing I have rec[d] the contents of the above Acc[t.] amounting to £12 St. from Mr. Murray, and have given him a receipt on the Back hereof for it.

Edin[r] 2d October 1745.—Received the within Twelve pounds Sterling from Mr. John Murray.

NAPIER & SCOTT.

To Mr. James Scot at Dunkeld, with a bundle.

XLV.

DUKE OF ATHOLL TO SPALDING OF ASHINTULLY.

SIR,

I received yours of the 30th of Sept[r] yeaſterday; I am ſurpriſed you left the Prince who, if neceſſary, would certainly given you a commiſſion according to H. R. H. his declaration: Tho' I have been for ſome time in theſe parts without having the ſatiſſaction of ſeeing you, yet, for your father's fon there's nothing poffible that's proper I wouldn't do; Therfor, muft leave it to Glenkillrie to inform me of what you reafonably expect, which fhall be accordingly performed by,

SIR,

Your moft affect humble Servt,

BLAIR CASTLE, *October* 2nd, 1745.

XLVI.

LORD ROLLO TO THE DUKE OF ATHOLL.

MY LORD DUKE,

I congratulat your Grace in comming to your oun Cuntray, I would ere now weated on your Grace, but am not abell to make fuch a jurnay on horfback. My Wife joins me in our refpectfull Compliments to your Grace, and begs the favor you would alow hir near relation, Mr. Dunbar, prifonar, Enfing in Coll. Lie's Regment, to ftay heear, and I fhall anfuer for him, which will veray much oblidg,

MY DR LORD DUKE,

Your Grace's moft Obediant

hu^l. Ser^t

ROLLO.

DUNCRUB, 2nd *Oct.* 1745.

XLVII.

GEO. STIRLING TO DR. COLVILL.

DEAR SIR,

I was favoured with yours of the 30th aft, by Mr. Robertfon, but was forie I could not be fo ferviceable to him as I inclin'd, being confined to the houfe with Rheumatick pains for fome days; however, I fent for one who put on the method to get what monnie was got in of the Stent fince Glenbucket left this place, for he carried all off he could reafe, eather of Stent or Excife; but I fuppofe after this neather will be got, if a Governor be not appointed over that Countrie, and Parties fent with the proper Officers to collect it. The Excife and Cuftom-houfe Officers are returned, and will infult over the brewers, and make them pay up for a 2nd time their Excife. I mentioned to Mr. Mercer the appointing a Collector for the land taxe, of which there's at leaft half a year due, which [will] come to monnie if reafed all this fide of Forth. Mr. Robertfon has got £50 fterling, for which he's granted Jo. Carmichael of Beglie a receipt on the back of his Grace's order. Pleafe offer my moft humble dewtie to my Lord Duke, and believe wherein I can ferve his Grace, or any employed in fo juft and good a Caufe, none fhall be more readie or willing than I, who am, with all Efteem,

DEAR SIR,
Your meft humble Servant,
GEO. STIRLING.

PERTH, 2nd Octbr 1745.

XLVIII.

LORD GEORGE MURRAY TO THE DUKE OF ATHOLL.

EDR. 2d Octr. 1745.

DEAR BROTHER,

I received your letter of the 29th Septr. by John Murray, yefterday, as we were going to diner. If I do not write fo often as you would incline, I hope you'll exenfe it, as I have had all along more bufinefs and duty to perform than came to the fhare of any one man. I have wrote you two letters which you have not as yet acknoledged, one by Shian, the other by Kynachan; and as they could inform you of every tranſaction here, I thought it needleſs to be more particular, eſpecially as I was hurry'd at the time. Sending off a perſon from the Field of Batle, who could tell you twenty things more fully than could be wrote, I judged better than ſitting down in that confuſion to ſcrall two or three words (which, however, I did to my Wife, having a common letter-bearer only to ſend), but his being ſtopt by Glenbucket was what I could not forſee. I 'm very glad my Wife made ſo good uſe of the few lines I ſent her, ſince by that means you had the firſt news of the Batle.

I ſhow'd your letter to his Royal Highneſs, as well as the coppys of them you wrote to ſeveral of our Friends in the North, and both He, and Sʳ· James Stewart, and the Prince's Secretary, aprove exceedingly of them; and his Royal Highneſs deſires you would write again to Clunie, the Macintoſhes, and Fraſers, and that you, in his Highneſs' name, order them up imediately, and that they are not to wait for others, nor for one another, but each of them come up with all poſſible expedition.

I have been as preſſing about money to be ſent you, both formerly and now, as if my life depended upon it. There is £300 ſent at preſent, moſtly in ſpecie. You are deſired to write to people in the country to advance money, particularly to Lady Methven, which if they do not imediately, their corns and other effects will be ſeized, &c.

There is a Commiſſary or Factor apointed here to remitt to the Priſoners, both the Officers at Perth and the common Soldiers at Lougierat, their pay; ſo that you are to have no trouble that way. The perſon is Mʳ· Thomas Dundaſs, Merchant here, who I ſupoſe will apoint Mʳ· Jo. Anderſon, Merchant at Perth for his Correſpondent.

It is propoſed to get in all the Pleat we can and coin ſhillings, for, beſides the want of Caſh in general, there is great penury of Silver. The Town of Glaſgow have given L.5,500, what in Bank notts, Bills on London, and ſome Merchandiſe, &c.

For God's ſake ſend up what men of your own people you can, and don't let them wait for any body elſe; and His Royal Highneſs deſires, ſo foon as the Frafers, Macintofhes, and M<sup>c</sup>Pherfons come up, that you would alfo yourfelf come in Perfon.

The Caftle of Ed<sup>r.</sup> fired a good deal laft evening upon the out Sentinels and houfes nixt them, as our people were firing to hinder people going in with provifions, but no great harm is done on either fide. The Regular Troops that were at Berwick are gone South, and only left a garifon of four Companys there. We hourly expect to hear from abroad. The money fent you juft now is £100 in Bank notts, £100 in Leuidors, and £100 in Guineas. I would gladly have got £500, but it was not poffible.

There is one Henderfon, who I fend with John Murray; he can be of great ufe to you in erecting Girnells, either at Perth or in the country, and will obey what other orders you give him. He is one who can be very ufefully imploy'd. I ever am,

Your Faithfull Humble Servant,

GEORGE MURRAY.

Widenfday, 10 *in the morning.*

Receive Aldie's Commiffion.

XLIX.

SECRETARY MURRAY TO THE DUKE OF ATHOLL.

MY LORD,

Your Grace will eafily imagine the hurry I have been in from our comeing fouth, and efpecially fince the battel, which was the only reafon of my neglecting my duty in writting you. The Prince is waiting here with the greateft impatience for his friends joining hi proceed into England without a greater force; and, at there is nothing can fo much hurt the Caufe as a

G

advancing very faft, and, fhould we be oblidged to ftay much longer, the people of England will, by degrees, get the better of the confternation they are in; for which reafons the Prince defires your Grace will continue to ufe the fame prudence you have hitherto taken to haften up your neighbours, without letting one waite for the other. Lord George will write fully of every thing, which makes it needlefs for me to trouble your Grace with a long letter. And I am, with great regard,

My Lord,

Your Grace's moft obed^t. and

moft humble Servant,

J°. MURRAY.

Holyroodhouse, *Octr. ye 2^d, 1745.*

L.

LADY GEORGE MURRAY TO THE DUKE OF ATHOLL.

My Lord,

I was honoured with your Grace's letter laft night, and returns you many thanks for your kind intention in defigning to have fent me a deer.

I had a letter from Lord George, dated on Tuefday, wherein he defires me to acquaint your Grace, "that the Governour of the Caftle, &c. fent word that they were to fire upon the town, if they did not get provifions from that as formerly; upon which, the Prince, on Munday forenoon, allow'd a deputation of fix of the moft fubftantial people of Ed^r. to go to the Caftle, to expoftulate about the threatening to cannonade the town, (and, as the town had no command of the military who pof_ feff'd it, they cou'd not conceive how fuch a threat cou'd be put in exe_ cution;) the generals in the Caftle, (Prefton and Gueft,) at laft returned for anfwer that they wou'd allow time to the town to fend an exprefs to London to have thefe orders revok'd, and in the meantime the Caftle wou'd not fire except they were attack'd.

" All the regular troops that were at Berwick, confifting of about 700 Dutch, and the few dragoons that Cope fav'd after the battle are march'd fouthward, fo none remain in Berwick but four companys that formerly were there in Garifon. The London government are colleɕting all their forces, as it is imagin'd, to oppofe any landing, which they feem now afraid of, and have given up this country entirely."

This bearer takes two mules, which were fent to Blair fome months ago, and came here tother day by themfelves, but, as your Grace may have ufe for them, they being very good drudges, I return them agen.

I hope your Grace will forgive this confuf'd ferall, I being in a hurry feting out to Arnhall, where I am to ftay with my mother eight or ten days.

With the greateft regard, I am,

My Lord,

Your Grace's

Moft affeɕtionate fifter

and moft humble Servant,

TULLIBARDIN, 3^d *Oct*^r. 1745. ÆMELIA MURRAY.

I beg to make offer of my moft humble duty to my Lady Nairn, with affeɕtionate fervice to her daughters.

LI.

LORD GEORGE MURRAY TO THE DUKE OF ATHOLL.

Ed^r. 3^d *Oct*^r. 1745.

DEAR BROTHER,

I wrote to you fully yefterday by John Murray, who alfo carried £300 fterling for you, which I hope has come fafe to hand.

I now write you this by the Vifcount of Strathallan and Galk, whom
his Royal Highnefs has appointed Governor and Depute-Governor of
Perth, to take care of the Government, civil and military there, and in
the whole Shire under your directions, as long as you ftay in the Country,
and to command in chief in your abfence, for which you can give his Lop.
a Commiffion when you leave the Country.

It will be proper you meet with Ld Strathallan as foon as you can, to
concert every thing that is proper for the good and advantage of the
Service, and that every thing be conducted with order and regularity in
the Country; for every body agree with his Royal Highnefs that it is
abfolutely neceffary a Perfon of weight, and diftinction, and character,
fhould be left behind after you come away. His Highnefs further defires
you may let my Lord Strathallan have a company compleat of 60 men,
with Captain, Lieutenant, and Enfign, to continue at Perth under his
Lop's immediate orders, and who are to be regularly pay'd. The Duke
of Perth is to apoint another Company in the fame manner, fo that there
will be in all 120 men, befides Officers, which indeed is as few as can
well be.

LII.

LADY OGILVY TO THE DUKE OF ATHOLL.

My Lord Duke,

I read your Grace's letter to my Lord Airly, my Father, in his
abfence; and as for the Houfe of Cluny, within the Loch, it is at his
Royal Highnefs the Prince's Service; I afure your Grace you may com-
mand it. The preacher at Cluny has the Keys of the Houfe, and he con-
fequently muft be taken prifoner or he deliver them.—I am,
My Lord Duke,
Your Grace's moft Humble Servant,
ELIZ. OGILVY.

Auchterhouse, Octr. 3^d 1745.

LIII.

JAMES SCOT TO DR. COLVILL.

Hon. Sir,

The Bearer, James Robertfon, a mafon in this place, who was out with my Lord Duke in the 15, is the man I fent out with Mr. Stewart and Peter M⸰Innes, to infpe& the pool of Cluny; and as there is a hutt to be built on the Loch fide for a guard-houfe, as he is well acquainted in the place, he may be a very proper hand for getting it done, and will alfo be a fit perfon to be trufted, if it be his Grace's pleafure, with fome poft in the Guard.

I obeyed your order in fending the ten bolls meal, and half-ftone candles, to Logyreat, and defired Bohefpick to tell you that yefterday arriv'd here 2 officers and 32 men from Glenfhee, to whom I gave 2 guineas for their fubfiftence, till they received his Grace's orders; they alfo told me, that laft night or this day the party from Strathardle would be here, and yet (11 at night) there is no account of them, and left they alfo might have a demand for money, I took ten pounds from Bohefpick, for which I gave receit.

David Laird has fent in here this evening, 8 guns, (which want very much to be in the hands of the gunfmith,) fome old fwords and piftols, for which I'm to fend for the Smith in the morning.

We have as yet had no colle&ion, but as it is a quarterly one, when all the Compounders fhould pay their quarter's Excife, I wifh my Lord Duke would appoint a day againft which the feveral Officers might be ordered to fummon in all the Compounders in their refpe&ive divifions, if they'll expe& their Salarys; and that every man fhould bring with him their laft receits, qch commonly fhows the arrears, and in cafe the Officer's books cannot be had, the former receit may ferve to regulat their next payments; and becaufe there is no Excife Officer in Ruffle, his Grace's Officer here may Summon fuch as ufes to pay their Excife in this place, where a man of fame authority may be appointed to colle&t; there will be fome arrears for Malt, the Duty of which cannot be taken off without an A&t of Parlia.ᵗ Mr. Crook is here on his way to Blair; I'm glad my Lord Duke has 2 fuch fufficient men about him as Dr. Colvill and Crook, but fmall ufe may his Grace have for either of you; may God long preferve and profper him. I fuppofe you'll mind Lord George's health to-morrow, when he enters into his 52 year, I hear his Lady had an entertainment prepared for 84 captive Officers, but only 16 call'd.

The Exprefs I fent to the E. of Airly is not yet return'd. I have got a fevere cold and exceffive cough, but while I am able to ftir you'll ever find me,

DEAR DOCTOR,

Your much obliged and

very grateful Servant,

JA : SCOTT.

*Oct*ʳ. 3ᵈ.

I long much to hear good news of the Clans.

LIV.

STEWART OF KYNACHAN TO THE DUKE OF ATHOLL.

MY LORD,

I fend your Grace James Darling, Merch.ᵗ to be kept in fafe cuftody, and free from any Correfpondence. I am inform'd that he is a fubtle dangerous fellow, and has been in a conftant courfe of correfponding with fome of his R. Highnefs Enemies, which I fhall acquaint your Grace more fully of when I have the honour to wait of you att Blair Caftle, which, if I am not otherwife ordered, I hope may be Saturday or

Sunday att fartheſt. I have ſent one Alex^{r.} Duff alongs with the party that attends Darling, that he may acquaint your Grace of all thoſe that have either deſerted or ſtay'd att home in the Biſhoprick, that they may inſtantly be raiſed; this ſame Duff will be very uſeful in putting this in Execution. I have the honour to be, with the utmoſt Eſteem and ſin-cerity,

MY LORD,
You Grace's moſt obed^{t.} humble Servt.,
DAVID STEWART.

PERTH, 3^d Octr 1745.

LV.

ROBERTSON OF KILLICHANGY TO Mr. MERCER OF ALDIE.

SIR,

Mr. Menzies of Shian arrived here yeſterday afternoon about ſix, with one hundred and thirteen priſoners. So ſoon as he delivered them, he ſaid, his party was much fatigued, and would take no farther charge of them; upon which I reaſed all the men in the Barrony of Ballnagaird, and mounted Guard upon the Priſoners. But as we have no arms, it's ex-pected His Grace will ſupply us immediately with Arms. Shian gave the priſoners on their march a halfpenny roll, and a chapine ale to each man Morning and Evening, and I have ordered the Brewers in this town to make meat for the priſoners, and have given a lippie of meal and a chapine ale for each man per day; I kill'd neither Beef nor Mutton for them till his Grace's further orders, which I expect by this bearer, with particular orders what men I ſhall raiſe to mount Guard while here. This you'll pleaſe communicate to His Grace, and Diſpatch and pay the Expreſs as ſoon as poſſible. I am,

SIR,

Your moſt humble Servant,

JA: ROBERTSON.

LOGYREAT, 3^{d} *Oct^{r}*. 1745.

The priſoners are kept in the Court houſe, but as all the windows are very large without Grates, it's a very inſecure priſon.

SIR,

It was late laſt night before I came home, but I ſent my Son and all my men to aſſiſt Ballnagaird's men. The above was write before I came here: all I have to add is, to ſend us any Arms you can ſpare. I ever am,

SIR,

Your moſt humble Servant,

JA: ROBERTSON of Killichangy.

LVI.

DUKE OF ATHOLL TO ROBERTSON OF KILLICHANGY.

SIR,

Two hours agoe I ſaw yours to M$^{r.}$ Mercer, and am ſatiſſied with your conduct hitherto. You are to give each of the Priſoners at the rate of two pecks of meal a-week, out of the meal that came from Dunkeld, which James Robertſon, the officer, has, and a penny a-day to each of them, to be diſpoſed by them for drink, or how they will.

The bearer, M$^{r.}$ Fraſer, has twenty-two men fully arm'd; you are to raife 40 more, with fuch arms as can be got for them. Thirty men are fufficient to mount guard at a time, and thefe are to be fully arm'd out of the whole.

Receive ffive pounds to pay the prifoners their penny a-day, and your 40 men at the rate of two fhillings a-week and a peck oatmeal, which you are compt for. Mr. Frazer has money to pay his men, and you are to give them meal, as they fhall demand, on his receipt. If there's any thing els neceffary for the prifoners fubfiftance, furnifh it, and it fhall be allowed by,

SIR,

Your affec! humble Servt.

BLAIR CASTLE, Octr. 3d 1745.

LVII.

LORD GEORGE MURRAY TO NEILL McGLASHAN, SECRETARY TO THE DUKE OF ATHOLL.

EDINa. 4th October, 1745.

SIR,

I wrote to my Brother yefterday by my Lord Strathallan and Gafk, to which I refer. I'm extreamly anxious to have our men here, at leaft as many as would make Lord Nairu's Battalion and mine five hundred each, for at prefent I cou'd get them fupply'd with Guns, Targets, Tents, and, thofe who want them, fhoes alfo; but if they be not here foon, them that come firft will be firft ferved; fo you will reprefent to ye Duke of Atholl of what confequence it is for his men to be here immediatly; how far he will judge it proper for himfelf to come, he knows that beft; But if ye Clans be coming up, it is thought that his ftaying in Atholl will prevail with them to haften their march; but, as I faid before, this muft intirely be determined by himfelf.

H

perfon appoint'd who will have ye charge of ye Country as well as the prifoners there; my only objection is that I am affraid that Glenkildrie, as he's old, has not activity enough for fuch a Command. How far M^r· Mercer of Aldie would incline to take the Government of ye Country of Atholl in ye Duke of Atholl's abfence, muft be left to his Grace and him to determine. I fhall be exceeding impatient till our men come, for I'm perfwaded that Fafcally and Kinichan will be, as Diligent in that fervice as poffible under my Brother's Directions. I have nothing more to add, but that I am,

SIR,

Your moft humble Servt·

GEORGE MURRAY.

P.S.—John Anderfon, Merchant at Perth, has orders for fupporting the Officers at Perth, and ye Soldiers at Logierate in their pay.

LVIII.

GEO. STIRLING TO DR. COLVILL.

DEAR SIR,

In obedience to yours of the 1st Curr^t· I've cawfed cuffer the Chaife with a head that at pleafure will fall back; it's made as tight and light as pofible. The Coachmaker has done nothing fince it cam but fitting it, and it was not pofible to have it fooner done; he's wrought night and day. The horfe Dick is mended, one acc^t of both you have inclofed. The Exprefs I fent Sunday laft to M^r· Mercer got only 3s. St: from M^r· McClafhen; the ordenary is twopence a-mile, I meft make it good, or I will not get any to travell. I wrot you by M[r.] Robertfon of Bonhefpick, what furder I thought neceffary. There's no furvieing the ale, &c., as the only Excife Officer offered to ferve the Prince, and gave in his books when M[r.] Mercer was here, (M[r.] Moncrife), and affifted and dereﬆed how to rafe the Dewties, when Glenbucket was here was negleﬆed, and his 6 weeks fellery refufed him, wherfore he has never aﬆed fince, fo I think my Lord Duke fhould fend him one order to officiat, and payment for his paffed Sellery, with a fmall reward for his readnefs to ferve. There's likways fome thing to be allowed the Muyre Officers who are employed in bringing in Carrige horffes, and many other things; both thefe may be payed out of the Stent of this place that is paying in, w[ch] will not be a great dale more than will doe this and pay the Colleﬆor; but if thofe things be not done the Prince will not be well ferved, for thofe Creaturs have nothing elfe to maintaine them. The Gager Moncrife's name is Thomas, his Sellerie is £35 ⅌ Ann:

The Muyre Officers demands is about thretie fh: Ster: and very litle confidring the pains and trouble they have been at. My Lord Duke fhould wret an order to M[r.] Stewart of Garth, left here with the Prifoners, to clear w[t] Jo: Carmichall of Beglie, the Colleﬆor of the Stent, and to pay all thofe things, with his aun Sellerie, and take upe the remender, we fhall get him affifted in doeing this.

Pleafe offer my moft humble Dewtie to my Lord Duke, and wherin furder I can be ufe or fervifable to his Grace or you, non fhall be readier y[n] he who with much efteem am,

DEAR SIR,

Your very humble obed[t] Serv[t]

GEO. STIRLING.

PERTH, 4th Octb[r] 1745, 11 forenoon.

LIX.

LORD GEORGE MURRAY TO THE DUKE OF ATHOLL.

Eᴅɴ. 4ᵗʰ *Octʳ.* 1745,
Frieday, seven in the morning.

Dᴿ. Bʀᴏᴛʜᴇʀ,

I am defird to let you know that there is one Kimber, an Anababtift, who came from London with a defign to affafinat the Prince; he is about 27 years old, black hair, of a midling ftature, talks fluently and bluntly about his Travels in the Weft Indys. It is wrote that he dined the 20ᵗʰ Sepʳ. with you, and got a pafs from you; he has readily changed his name, and perhaps cutt his hair. Laft night, one was taken up here, by the name of Jeffrys, who poffiblie is the fame perfon. Let us know, as foon as poffible, if any perfon that can anfwer the above defcription dined with you the 20ᵗʰ and gott a pafs, or any other ftranger. For God's fake fend up your men, that at leaft Ld: Nairn's Batalion and mine may be 500 each. If they come foon, I will get evry thing for them. I refer you to what I have wrote farther to Mʳ Neighle McGlafhen. I ever am,

DEAR BROTHER,

Moft affectionatly yours,

GEORGE MURRAY.

LX.

LORD GEORGE MURRAY TO THE DUKE OF ATHOLL.

Eᴅɴ, 4ᵗʰ *Octʳ.* 1745, *four afternoon.*

Dᴿ. Bʀᴏᴛʜᴇʀ,

I wrote to you this morning, & I now fend this exprefs to let you know that it is refolvd in a Councile of Ware to march Southwards Thurfday the 10th. I believe we will not make quick marches for fome days after that; but I conjure you let your Atholl men be with us at or before that time, that I may fee every thing got right for them as far as it is in my power. If you come not yourfelf I intreat you to difpatch Keynachan, Fafcaly, &c. with the men. Adieu.

Yours,
GEORGE MURRAY.

LXI.

LADY GEORGE MURRAY TO THE DUKE OF ATHOLL.

MY LORD,

The enclof'd from your Brother has this moment come to my hands. I received a Letter from him about an hour ago, which is dated this morning, wherein he orders me to fend an Exprefs to your Grace about your men coming up; and his words are: "I entreat for God's fake that the Duke of Atholl fend off the men here immediately, or they will be too late for Arms, Targets, Tents, &c., nay, for our march, which begins on Thurfday."

He alfo fays, "That the Caftle of Ed^r, under the protection of their cannon, made a Lodgement laft night at the recervoir of water. I was there for three hours; and believes, as the Caftle feem refolv'd not to fpare the town, (for they burnt two houfes above the recervoir laft night) they will by degrees make the Highlanders retire from all above the Weigh houfe, except thefe laft wou'd rifk fome of their men, which is thought not expedient to venture them againft common foldiers fupported by Cannon, &c. They have loft none as yet; only fome Voluntiers, day before yefterday, were furpriz'd near the Weft kirk."

Lord Strathallan and Gafk came from Ed^r yefterday, & I hear they are

to ſtay moſtly at Perth.   There is a report in this country of ſix thouſand
Spainards being landed in England, & ſome French in Scotland.   I pray
God this news may prove true; but alas it wants confirmation.   I find
that I'll be oblig'd to return to Tullibardin on Munday; ſo hopes that
when your Grace comes down the Country I ſhall have the happyneſs of
ſeeing you there.   I ever am, with the greateſt regard,

My Lord,

Your Grace's moſt affectionate Siſter,

and moſt humble Servant,

ÆMILIA MURRAY.

ARNHALL, 5th Oct^r,
  Ten at night.

LXII.

SIR PATRICK MURRAY TO DAVID STEWART OF KYNACHIN.

DR. DAVIE,

I received yours this night, a litle after eight of the Cloack at night,
and a letter from Mr. Mercer of Aldie; Gaſk likewiſe received his letter.
I return you moſt hearty thankes, and am quite ſenceable that Davie Stewart is Davie Stewart, let fortune whille about as it pleaſeſs ; neither
Jamie Farquharſon or I have any horſeſs here; but you may be aſſured
that we'll contrive to waite of the Duke Munday or Tueſday at fartheſt,
(if horſeſs can't be got we'll foot it).   Pleaſe make my compliments to
Mr. Mercer, and return him thankes for his kind letter to Jamie & me.
Gaſk, how ſoon Faſkily relives him, will ſet out from this, and obey your
orders with all the expedition poſſible.   I ever am,

D: D:

Yours,

PAT: MURRAY.

PERTH, 5th Octr. 1745.

LXIII.

DUKE OF ATHOLL TO LADY GEORGE MURRAY.

MADAM,

I can't fay how much Satiffaction and Pleafure your Ladyfhip's moft diftinct Letters give me; I received feveral very agreable Letters from my Bro[r.] George, at the fame time I had the laft you fent me from him; by all of them I find the Prince is, with much Reafon, very defirous to have his Troups which are in thefe parts foon with him. I am well inform'd the Northern Clans are now coming up; and after much Pains and Trouble, I hope, in a day or two we fhall march to Perth with a confiderable number of men out of this Country, in our way to join his Royal Highnefs.

There is one of my Bro[r.] James's Favorites call'd Commiffary Biffet, who I was kind to, yet has acted a moft unworthy Part, & is a very dangerous as well as difagreable Perfon to all Honeft People in this Shire, befides being odious to all in the Royal Army: I am told he has been runing about fowing feditious & Rebellious Sentiments every where; at laft 'tis faid he is gone to Stirling, with defign to do mifchief, by the affiftance of that Garifon. As he may be fculking backwards and forwards the better to execute his bafe Defigns, fince your La[p.] fays you will be fome days near that place, if any body about you could be employed to get certain accounts of his motions, fo that he might be apprehended & fafely fecur'd, it would be a fingular fervice done both to our King & Country. I have again detained your Servant a day or two, Fintry having made me every minute expect a Deer, which fhould have been fent your La[p.] fome time ago, tho' hitherto to no purpofe; as foon as it arrives, you may be fure it fhall be directly defpatched with an Exprefs.

I thank you kindly for the two mules you fent me, which will be very

MADAM,
Your Ladyfhip's moft affectionate Brother,
and moft humble Servant,

BLAIR CASTLE, *6th Oct^{r.}* 1745.

To LADY GEORGE MURRAY.

Memorand.—That Mr. D——y was ftill buffied in goeing about the town of Perth propogateing news of landing of Dutch troups to intimidate people from rifeing or continueing in the Pr——'s fervice.

Item, he was, Friday and Saturday the 27 & 28 of Septr. about Strathmiglo, and Abernethy, and Bridge of Earn, in company with Thomas Biffet of Glenalbert, and on Monday the 2^{d.} of Octob^{r.} was at Dunkeld as a fpy & intelligencer, &c.

LXIV.

LORD STRATHALLAN TO THE DUKE OF ATHOLL.

MY LORD,

I have fent by this Exprefs the inclofed from your Brother Lord George Murray, by which your Grace will know his Royall Highnefs pleafure with regard to me, and of your giving a Company of your men to ly at Perth ; this makes me defire to know when and at what place I fhall waite upon your Grace, to receive your commands. I am, with the utmoft efteem and regard,

MY LORD,
Your Grace's moft ffaithful
and obedient humble Servant,
STRATHALLAN.

MACHANY, *Octr. 6th* 1745.

LXV.

DUKE OF ATHOLL TO LORD STRATHALLAN.

My Lord,

Late this night I had the honour of your Loᴾ's. I hope to be againſt Wedneſday or Thurſday at fartheſt in Perth, ſo hopes to have the pleaſure of ſeeing you there. In the mean time I am, with perfeᴄt eſteem and regard,

My Lord,

Your moſt humble and

moſt obedient Servant.

Blair Castle, 7 *Octʳ.* 1745.

Pray, my Lord, give my moſt affeᴄtionate humble ſerᵛice to my cuſin the Viſcounteſs of Strathallan.

LXVI.

DUKE OF ATHOLL TO THE LAIRD OF MACKINTOSH.

Bl. Castle, *Octr.* 7ᵗʰ 1745.

Sir,

It was with the outmoſt Joy I heard you had abandoned the Uſurper, to Joyu in reſtoring the King at the Head of your numerous Clan, that has ever been loyaly inclined. I ſhall be extreamly glad to ſee them make a greater figure than ever under you, to whom I am ſo nearly allyied. I had an expreſs laſt night, telling me the Prince was to leave Edᵍʰ ſoon, by which he orders 'me to march with the utmoſt expedition, and bring all the men I cou'd with me. As Clunie and you are the two who are neareſt me, I earneſtly deſire you will march with the outmoſt expedition to Joyn us before we croaſs the Forth, for which reaſon I leave this to-morow in my way to Perth. I make no doubt but you will be uneafie to think you are ftill behind the Prince, whilft your deuty and ardour for the King and Country's caufe want your Prefence. I expeĉt to fee your brother-in-law, Mr. Farquharfon, this night or to-morow, having wrote for him and Sir Patrick Murray to be with me. Pray make my affeĉtionate compliments to your Lady, who I wifh cou'd come alongeft with you fo far as to fee her Relations in Perthfhire.

I am, with the utmoft efteem,

SIR,

LXVII.

DUKE OF ATHOLL TO CLUNIE MACPHERSON.

B. C. *Octr. 7th* 1745.

SIR,

I had an exprefs laft night by his Highnefs order, telling me he intended to leave Ed^{gh} foon, therefor Orders me to Joyn him with all Ex-pedition, which makes me fend this to acquaint you I am to march hence tomorow with what men I have readie by Dunkeld, that I may be with his Highnefs as foon as poffible; and, as I doubet not you are ready, defire you will march immediatly without waiting of any bodie whatfomever, and if poffible Joyn me at croffing the Forth, or fooner. I hope alfo Mack-entofh will be with us, to whom I have alfo wrote. As to thofe who are not come your length, they muft follow as they beft can. How unluckie fhou'd we think ourfelfes if ftill behind our young Mafter, while he is ex-pofing himfelfe no lefs for our Liberty than his own juft Right. I am, with perfeĉt eftime,

, SIR,

LXVIII.

DUKE OF ATHOLL TO LORD GEORGE MURRAY.

BROTHER GEORGE,

Within thefe few days I have had the fatiffaction to receive feveral very plain and diftinct Letters from you, which are mighty kind and obliging, but being all of them much to the fame purpofe, they may be anfwered in the fewer words. In the firft place, I have received £200 by Shian, and £300 more from John Murray, all which, with what I have formerly received, or whatever elfe comes to my hands, fhall be carefully, and with the utmoft exactitude, laid out for his Royal Highnefs Service. As for the Lady Methven, and others to whom I was addreffed for money, I can't find out any reafonable Methods how to make her or them contribute effectually for the publick Service. You write to me a terrible account of one Kimber, who came from London with a moft horrid defign againft the Prince's perfon. I nor any body with me knows not what he is, nor never heard of any fuch, nor has any unknown perfon dined with me, much lefs got a pafs upon any account whatever. About ten o'Clock laft night, I received your exprefs, dated the 4th, 4 o'clock afternoon, and am very much concerned to find that it is morally impoffible for me, or any of the men in thefe parts, to be up with you againft Thurfday night, the Day you fay It is refolved in a Council of War to March Southward. Did any of us endeavour to make too much hafte to join the Prince, I am afraid we would be too like a good Milk Cow, that gives a great Pail of Milk, and after kicks it down with her foot. Forgive the comparifon. As we are ftated here, fhould any abfolutely endeavour to force a march forward before men can be regularly brought up, we would certainly lofe the fruit of all the pains and trouble has hitherto been taken. Nobody but people on the fpot knows the almoft infurmountable Difficulties we have had to ftruggle with, which muft unavoidably hinder fuch a fudden junction, as you imagine, of the Prince's faithful wellwifhers. Therefore, all that I can fay further for your fatiffaction is, That if his Royal Highnefs Army Marches Southward againft the time you write me, fhould he be pleafed to leave with a fufficient guard on the road, Arms, Ammunition, Tents, Money, &c., I may fafely fay a confiderable body of men are now ready to follow him, not only from thefe parts, but alfo from the North. I hope in a few days they will not be far from his Camp, fince, with the beft inclinations imaginable, they are not able to be with his Army before his Royal Highnefs fets out from Edinburgh, and then I fhall fully demonftrate it was abfolutely impracticable for me to perform any thing more than I have done towards materially advancing our Mafter's Intereft and Service. Which, with my moft humble duty, I beg you'll be fo good as to let his Royal Highnefs know in the moft reafonable manner, Whereby you will infinitely oblige,

DEAR BROTHER,

Your moft affectionate Brother,

and humble Servant.

BLAIR CASTLE, 7th Oct^r.,
3 o'clock in the morning, 1745.

As formerly, I hope you will excufe the not writing with my own hand, for my continual occupation renders it almoft impoffible.

LXIX.

DUKE OF ATHOLL TO LORD GLENORCHY.

MY LORD,

Since his Royal Highnefs, our young Mafter, paffed through this Country, I hardly had the honour to fee him, being ftill employed for the publick Service in thefe parts, therefor knows not in what manner you have paid your duty to him. In which uncertainty hearing you have been conveening your men, as I am perfwaded for no other end than to quickly wait with them on your Prince, according to the dutiful example of your Predeceffors, particularly your Lo^{p's} Grandfather, who told me, when fpeaking to him about his following, that he had no men, for, faid my Confin, the venerable old Earl, I have no men, thefe whom I am particularly concerned with belong to the King, and therefor will always faithfully ferve his Majefty in fo far as I have any intereft among them. I prefume at prefent your Lo^{p.} does not degenerate from his loyal and honeft principles. On fuch a Suppofition, being left by the Prince Commander in chief of his Majeftie's forces benorth the River Forth, this is defiring you'll pleafe let me know if your Lo^{p.} can be ready in a few days to agreeably meet your friends, who will foon pafs the Forth in our way to join the Royal Standard. You fee, by a wonderful chain of fuccefs, God and the nation has declared for his Royal Highnefs ;—be, my Lord, amongft the firft to valuably congratulate him on fuch a bleffed occafion, whereby you will gain the Efteem and affection of thofe who are difinterefted Lovers of Truth and Juftice, which for ever will endear you to,

MY LORD,

Your Lordfhip's moft affectionate Coufin,

and moft humble Servant,

BLAIR CASTLE, 7th Oct^{r.}, 1745.

I beg your Lo^{p.} will forgive the not writing with my own hand, for my continual occupation renders it almoft impoffible.

LXX.

MR. SHERIDAN TO THE DUKE OF ATHOLL.

MY LORD DUKE OF ATHOLE,

Having fortunatly arrived at Monrofs yefterday with a frigate from Dunkirque loaded with armes, amunition, & fome mony for his Royal

Hygnefs, we unloaded all, & has lodged them at Brechin, under the care of Mr. Brown, and two gentilemen we met at Monrofs, who is raifing a company for yᵉ Service; fearing left yᵉ men of war that lyes in yᵉ firth fhud have an account of this Imbarkment, I make bold to addrefs you this, hoping your Grace will fend a ftrong detatchment to efcort faid armes and amunition to yᵉ Camp.   Mr. Brown will remaine at Brechin untill your Grace's detachement arrives there.   This Armement has been fent undre the care of a French gentileman, who has left all in yᵉ care of Mr. Brown.   He fends a lettre inclofed with this, acquainting faid Brown of this Expedition.   I expeᴄted to have yᵉ honnour of delivering this mef- fage myfelf, but this French gentileman is unwell, fo is obliged to fend by an Exprefs, which I would willingly doe myfelf, having yᵉ honnour of being known to your Grace fence before yᵉ Combat of the Elefebath man of war.

I am, with refpeᴄt,
Yr. Grace's moft obedient Servᵗ.
MIC : SHERIDAN.

Coupar, *Octr. yᵉ 8ᵗʰ* 1745.

———

LXXI.

DUKE OF ATHOLL TO LORD LOVAT.

My Lord,

This morning I had the honour to receive a meffage by Mr. Frafer, with your Loᵖ's moft agreeable refolution of quickly fending up your fol- lowing, and the Mr. of Lovat, to join His Royal Highnefs, who will be ex- treamly fatiffied to hear of the care you are taking to gett all your neigh- bours to follow without further lofs of time.   I need add nothing to the inclofed coppy of the Letter from that Gentleman who is juft arriv'd from France, but that all poffible endeavours fhall be uf'd to get whatever can bef́par'd of the Arms, Ammunition, &c. fent to Blair Caftle, which is the neareft and fafeft place they fhall wait, where the men from the north fhall have provifions waiting for them, with what other directions may be further neceffary, which the Vifcount of Strathallan and Gafk will tranfmitt, who are left to take care of the King's intereft in thofe parts. All I can add farther is to beg your Lo^{p.} will ftill continue to recommend defpatch and unanimity amongft your neighbours for advancing fo good a caufe as the fafety of our King and country, which in a great meafure depends on you.

I am, with all poffible efteem,

MY LORD,

Your moft humble and moft obedient

Servt.

MILNEARN, 9th Oct^{br.} 1745.

The Prince will be very fenfible, as well as I am, of your Lo^p's forward-nefs to ferve him, by your having particularly contributed towards Clunie's fpeedy march; who I hear will join us in a day or two. I 'm forry to hear your Lo^p's indifpofition, as well as years, is the only thing can prevent your waiting on the Prince in perfon.

LXXII.

l

DUKE OF ATHOLL TO CLUNIE M^cPHERSON.

MILNEARN, Oct^{br} 9th, 1745.

SIR,

After coming this length, I find ye backwardnefs of the men's rifing is much, if not altogether, owing to the irrefolutenefs of the Gentlemen; wherfor I fee it 's abfolutely neceffary you bring the Gentlemen as well as the commons up with you without diftinction, except fuch as you 'l fee have my power of ftaying at home to take care of the Country. You can verry well affure them you are pofitively required not to part with them.

Juft as this is writing, I got letters with the good news from a gentleman who came in a fhip from France with arms, amunition, and money, which is presently lying as near us as we cou'd defire, fo that we want nothing but men to carry arms; wherefor I intreat you 'l make all poffible heaft up, that we may go together over Forth, and by all means bring the whole people with you without referve, except as above. You 'l get meal as much as you want till you come to Dunkeld, where you 'l get more. Patrick Mackglafhan will give the meal at Blair. I fend off this day a party to efcort the arms, &c.; this you may affure all your friends of.—I need fay no more, but leaves it to your prudent management, only begs dispatch.

I am, &c.

My baggage being gone on to Dunkeld, exenfe my writing on fuch a foul fcrape of paper as I found here on the road.

LXXIII.

DUKE OF ATHOLL TO MR. SHERIDAN.

SIR,

This minut I received your moft agreable and valuable letter of yefterday's date, and have fent orders to a detatchment to efcort the armes. The Prince has in his camp fpare arms, &c., it 's chiefly in thefe parts they are firft wanted, with a full account of your prefent fituation, that we may take the beft meafures can be thought of for the imediat advancing the King's fervice to H. R. H. Therefor intreats to have the pleafur of feeing you at Dunkeld fo foon as poffible after the receipt of this, where the bearer, Mr. Rattrey, will, without lofs of time, conduct you; fo, hoping to quickly meet with you, I fhall add nothing farther here, being, with perfect eftime,

SIR,

Moulinarn, half way on my road
from Blair to Dunkeld,
9th October, 1745.

LXXIV.

SECRETARY MURRAY TO THE DUKE OF ATHOLL.

MY LORD,

Having this opportunity, his Royal Highnefs orders me to acquaint your Grace that he defires you may gett all the men together you can and join the army without delay, being determined to ftay here as fhort time as poffible. There is a furmife that a fhip with arms are landed att Montrofe, which has occafioned his fending Mr. Oliphant with orders that Galk fhall take care to have them fent carefully hither, and give what fhall be found neceffary for your people, and defires your Grace will be aware that they don't leave any behind on account of this fupply.

I am, with great regard,

MY LORD,

Your Grace's moft obed[t]. and
moft humble Serv[t].

J[o]. MURRAY.

HOLYROODHOUSE,
Oct[r]. y[e] 9th, 1745.

K

LXXV.

LORD GEORGE MURRAY TO THE DUKE OF ATHOLL.

EDᴿ. *9ᵗʰ Octʳ.* 1745.

Dᴿ. BROTHER,

I am vaftly impatient for your comming up, at leaft the men and officers.   Once more, for God's fake, caufe make all the heaft in your power, for the fuccefs of our caufe depends upon expedition.   I have no more time but to tell you his R. H. depends much upon your diligence upon this ocafion, and bids me fay he is very fenfible of your having done already more then could be expected, all fircumftances confider'd.

I ever am,
Your faithfull Servant,
GEORGE MURRAY.

LXXVI.

SIR THOMAS SHERIDAN TO THE DUKE OF ATHOLL.

MY LORD,

His Royal Highnefs orders me to acquaint yʳ· Grace that he has thought fit to grant liberty to two of yᵉ Prifoners now in yʳ· Country, vizᵗ⁾ to George Mufchet, Dragoon in Gardiner's Regiment, and William Laxcet Collier, a Soldier in Lafcelles Regiment, upon condition they fwear never more to bear arms againft him; and this, with his beft compliments, he defires you would order to be done.   I take with pleafure this opportunity to affure y^{r.} Grace of the refpe&t and fincerity with which I have the honour to be,

My Lord,

Your Grace's moft humble

and moft obedient Servant,

HOLYROODHOUSE, *Octr. ye 9th.* 1745.   THO. SHERIDAN.

LXXVII.

ROBERTSON OF STROWAN TO THE DUKE OF ATHOLL.

MY EVER HONOURED DUKE,

I have the happynefs to know your Grace thefe many years, therefore am convinced of its nice Integrity; and that you are not capable of forgetting fervices tho' but indeavour'd to be done to you. I am order'd by the Prince to this Country to carry all my Tenants and Followers to the Camp; Sir George Robertfon is one of the latter, whofe Father Fafkeilly was made Knight and Baronet, for his early rifing for the King under my command in the year 15. I am perfuaded if your Grace had known this remarkable Fa&t, you had thought it Juft to have left the raifing that Gentleman and his men to one who you know is entirely at your Service. I alfo hope your Grace will give me fome help of a litle mony in this criticall conjun&ure, for I never was in greater want; and I cannot but let you know, that your Brother and the reft of your Friends at Rome allow'd your Bill many years ago to be protefted, tho' fome of them reaped the benefit of, while the fmal fervice was done to Him whofe faithfull fervant I am,

AL^{R.} ROBERTSON OF STROWAN.

CARIE, *Oc^{r.} 9th.* 1745.

I afk not all at once, but in parcels as can be fpair'd, tho' I never was poorer in any Country.

LXXVIII.

DUKE OF ATHOLL TO LORD ROLLO.

My Lord,

I had not the honour of your LoP's, dated the 2nd inst till yeſterday on my way hither from Blair. Were it poſſible I ſhould wait on you to return my hearty thanks for your kind congratulation on my return to Britain. Pray, my Lord, give my reſpectful complements to my Lady Rollo. Her Ladyſhip may command every thing I can do to oblige her till the Prince orders otherways. I ſhall ſend leave to Mr. Dunbar, priſoner, Enſign in Col. Lee's Regimt, to go and wait on her Ladyſhip at Duncrub, on the ſame footing as he is now at Perth, on his parole of honour, from whence he is not to go above two miles diſtance. If any thing elſe is in my power can be agreable to your LoP, it ſhall be readily performed by,

My Lord,

Your Lordſhip's

Dunkeld, 10 October, 1745.   Moſt obedient humble Servant.

I beg your LoP. will exenſe the not writing with my own hand, continual occupation renders it almoſt impoſſible.

LXXIX.

THE MASTER OF STRATHALLAN TO THE DUKE OF ATHOLL.

Machany, October 10th 1745.

My Lord,

I trouble your Grace with this line to acquaint you that upon our arival here, we were informed that Lady George Murray's Servants were taken prifoners by a Man of War's long boat, as they were crofling the Forth at Alloa; and we were alfo told, that if we went by the foard above Stirling, that there was a great rifque, by reafou of parties that are fent from the Caftle of Stirling all there about. As we have difpatches of confequence for the Prince, the French Gentelman would not run the rifque of pafling the River without a ftronger Detachment, wherefore I fent an Exprefs to the Prince to let him know of it. If it were poflible for your Grace to fend us a Detachment of 100 men to efcort us with our pakets two or three miles other fide of the Forth, it would be of great ufe; and have the honour to be, with profound refpeĉt,

MY LORD,

Your Grace's moft humble and

obedient Servant,

JA : DRUMMOND.

LXXX.

UNTO HIS GRACE THE DUKE OF ATHOLL, THE REPRESENTATION OF JOHN STEWART IN KINNAIRD. 1745.

UNTO ANE HIGH AND MEIGHTY PRINCE WILLIAM DUKE OF ATHOLL, &c., THE REPRESENTATION OF JOHN STEWART IN KINNAIRD, BROTHER-GERMAN TO ALEXANDER STEWART OF KINNAIRD.

HUMBLY SHEWETH,

That I willingly ferved my lawfull Soveraigne the King, in the year 1715, by my going to the Battle of Preftown, where I had the miffortune to be there taken prifoner, ftood tryall for my life, receaved fentence of death, (pardoned) and y'after banifhed to Virginea, in America, and by the affiftance of God efcaped, and came home to my native country; and now, as I am moft willing to ferve my Prince and your Grace in any ftation at home, as your Grace fhall think fitt; as I am now unable to travell by the former hardfhips I underwent, and well gone in yeares, I hope your Grace will be pleafed to take it to confideration.

It's four weeks paft fince I receaved your Grace's orders for raifing the Bifhoprie men, which I did, and went to Crieff with them, and Delivered them to Collonell Mercer, fo that I have nott a fervant man at prefent to take care of my own affaires att home, for which trouble I receaved no reward as yet, altho' I have been putt to fome charges; as alfo in my going twice to fee the Caftle of Cluny putt in repair for the prifoners. Your Grace anfwer to your moft obedient and very Humble Ser.

(Signed)   J^{O.} STEWART.

DUNKELD,
Octr. ye 10th, 1745.

This Petition is to be confidered, and Directions given about it before the Duke leaves Dunkeld.

LXXXI.

DUKE OF ATHOLL TO ROBERTSON OF STROWAN.

The Stile of your Letter, dated the 9th inft. from Carie, is fo lofty, and [I am] in fuch a continual hurry that at prefent I can hardly endeavour the anfwering it to purpofe, therefore am forced to refer you in general to what I have told your difcreet meffenger, Mr. Alexander, on the confiderable points which you hint at. Did you ftick clofe by your near neighbours, true friends, & real wellwifhers, it is not impoffible that you, as well as they, might be more fatiffied with one another than it feems (Great Elector of Ranach) we are at prefent, both as to publick and private concerns.

I am heartily forry for your Situation as to money matters; mine is really little better, Having as yet little or nothing of my own farther than what is abfolutely neceffary for publick affairs; when it's otherways, with joy & pleafure you fhall command every thing is in my power can be ufeful to you. In the meantime, I'll prefume to fhare with you what can be fpared of his Royal Highnefs money which is in my hands. If fifteen or 20 guineas will be acceptable with this Letter, they fhall be put into the hands of your faithful meffenger; befides, if your men can foon appear in any place where I am, their pay as it comes to my hands fhall be regularly given whoever has the care and infpe&ion over them. Pray be perfwaded that, without Ceremony or Compliment, nobody can more effentially wifh you well than he who is, without referve,

DEAR ELECTOR,
Your moft affe&ionate, and
moft Humble Servant,

DUNKELD, 11th *October* 1745.

LXXXII.

SECRETARY MURRAY TO THE DUKE OF ATHOLL.[1]

HOLYROODHOUSE, *Octr. y^e* 11th 1745.

MY LORD,

I had the honour to write your Grace laft night by his Highness orders, which I hope you will receive in due Courfe. His Highnefs now defires your Grace may bring up all the arms along with you, being inform'd that there are only twelve hundred of them. As His Royal Highnefs writes himfelf, it is needlefs for me to fay any thing farther than that it is the opinion of every body we have already been too long here. I had a letter from Cluny, dated the firft of the month, telling me he intended to march next day, but I have heard no more of him, which fur-

My Lord,
Your Grace's moſt obedt.,
and moſt humble Servant,
Jo. MURRAY.

LXXXIII.

LORD GEORGE MURRAY TO THE DUKE OF ATHOLL.

EDINBURGH, 11*th* *Octr*. 1745.

DEAR BROTHER,

I write once more by His Royall Hignefs ſpecial commands, who defires you to come in perſon, and all the men poſſible, with the utmoſt expedition, and join him. Any that are comming from the north you muſt leave orders about their folowing you, and wait for non but ſuch as have join'd you before this comes to your hands.

It is certain that all depends upon expedition, and the moment you join us his Royall Hignefs will march for England, if he do not march foonner. Every thing is in great confuſion in England, particularly in London, where credite is at a ſtand; the greateſt Banquiers have ſtopt payment; all would go to our wiſh if we could but march imediatly. Setle every thing with Lord Strathallen about the police of the Country, civle and military. Adieu. I hope to fee you before I write again. I ever am,

Your moſt affect. Brother,
and faithfull humble Servant,
GEORGE MURRAY.

The King of Pruſia has given a totall defeat to the Auſtrians.

LXXXIV.

JAMES FARQUHARSON OF BALMORALL TO THE DUKE OF ATHOLL.

MAY IT PLEASE YOUR GRACE, MY LORD DUKE,

I have the Honour of the Prince Regent's orders to raife this Countrey for His Majefty's fervice, and am forry to tell your Grace that I meet with fuch Difficultys from Invercald's Backwardnefs, and the bad Exemple given to the Neighbourhood, that wee can hardly gett our own men to obey, let alone Invercald's, without military execution. According to my orders from his Royall Highnefs att Holyroodhoufe, (which place I left on Saturday laft, and all verry weele,) leaft the King's Caufe may fuffer by fuch backwardnefs, I muft begg your Grace will direct a full Company of Men here with a proper Officer to affift us in the execution of His Royall Highnefs' orders; your Grace will fee the thing can admitt of no delay, becaufe wee are already too long from our Duty to our King and Countrey. It gives me great Joy that your Grace is fafe in your own Countrey—I had the Honour to be known to your Grace when I was Aid-de-Camp to my Lord Mar in the fifeteen; your Lordfhip may direct the pairty to Captain James Shaw of Dalldouny, one of our Officers, leaft I fhould be abfent when they come. I wifh all Health and good fuccefs to the King's ffriends under your Grace's Command; God blefs yow, and fend us all a happy meeting.—I have the honour to be, with all poffible Duty,

MY LORD DUKE,
Your Grace's moft ffaithfull and
obedient h'ble Servt.,
JAMES FARQ^RSON.

BALLMORALL, 11th *Oct^r.* 1745.

LXXXV.

THE DUKE OF ATHOLL TO SECRETARY MURRAY.

SIR,

This day I had the honour of your's dated the ninth, with two of my brother George's letters, which on the main were anſwered ſome days ago. I allways intended, according to H: Royall H: orders, that all of us who could ſoon be got ready ſhould march with the utmoſt expedition imaginable, and ſhall concert every thing neſſeſary in theſe parts with my Lord Strathallan and Gaſk, in ſuch a regular manner as may ſhow the Prince I have negle&ted nothing could be reaſonably performed for his ſatisfa&tion and the King's ſervice. It's probable before this comes to hand you'll know, by the Gentleman who is come from France, that the arms, ammunition, &c., which he brought, falls much ſhort of what you imagined. In ſhort, I hope whatever can be brought up of theſe effe&ts, with the men I've been endeavouring to get ready, ſhall ere long be brought ſo near you as to be immediately diſpoſed of according as his Royal Highneſs ſhall think fit. I am, with perfe&t eſteem and regard,

SIR,

Your moſt obedient and moſt
Humble Servant,

DUNKELD, 12 *October* 1745.

I beg you'll communicate this to my brother George, ſince it contains all I can ſay at preſent in anſwer to his no leſs kind than preſſing Letters. Having not a minute's time to loſe, I entreat you'll forgive the not writing with my own hand.

LXXXVI.

THE DUKE OF ATHOLL TO FARQUHARSON OF BALMORALL.

Sir,

This morning I hade the pleafure of your agreeable Letter, dated 11th inftant, and am glade to find by it that you are ftill hearty and in good health.

According to your defire, I've fent to Strowan Robertfon, by one of his Gentlemen, ane order to march a hundred of his men to aid and affift you in raifing the Braemar men with the outmoft expedition; Therefor hopes they'l march without delay to join you as foon as poffible, and that you will immediatly after bring all down with you to Perth, in our way to join the Prince without lofs of time. So hoping foon to have the fatiffaction of feeing you with a fufficient body of good men, I fhall add no more, being, with all poffible efteem,

Sir,

Your moft obedient humble Serv[t.]

Dunkeld, *Oct[r.]* 12th, 1745.

LXXXVII.

DUKE OF ATHOLL TO THE LAIRD OF GASK.

Sir,

I have the honour of your's dated this day, with the three inclof'd letters, and that to you from Secretary Murray, which, as defired, is here inclof'd; it's needlefs to fay any thing now as to the armes, &c., mentioned by you and him, having write all is at prefent neffefary to the latter, and hopes perſonally ſoon to let you know what's proper on that ſubjeƈt, being intirly,

Sɪʀ,

Your moſt obedient

Humble Servant,

Dᴜɴᴋᴇʟᴅ, 12th *Octob^{r.}* 1745.

Having not a minute's time to loſe, I entreat you'll forgive the not writing with my own hand.

LXXXVIII.

DUKE OF ATHOLL TO SIR THOˢ· SHERIDAN.

Sɪʀ,

This day I had the honour of your's with his R. H. Commands, I beg you'll give my moſt humble duty to the Prince our young maſter. It ſeems the Soldier called Coallier in Laſcelle's Regim^{t.} never came here, for none of the priſoners know any thing about him; but you have here incloſed George Muſchat's depoſition, who has ſworn never to carry arms ag^{t.} the Royal family, nor any having Commiſſion from our Sovereign, which is all required of me by yours. With the utmoſt ſatiſfaƈtion I ſhall lay hold of every occaſion to convince you that I am with perfeƈt reſpeƈt,

Sɪʀ,

Your moſt humble,

& moſt obedient Servt.

Dᴜɴᴋᴇʟᴅ, 12th *Octob^{r.}* 1745.

Dear Sir Thos. I beg you'll forgive the not writing with my own hand, for really continual occupation puts it almoſt out of my power to ſhow all the regard I ought to have for you.

LXXXIX.

LAURENCE OLIPHANT OF GASK TO THE DUKE OF ATHOLL.

My Lord,

My Son brought from Edin^{r.} the three inclofed Letters directed for your Grace. I had one at the fame time from Mr. Murray, Secretary to His Royal Highnefs, which I have likeways fent, as your Grace will be better fatiffied of its contents than from my writeing. If your Grace fend the Arms, &c. to this place, it will be abfolutely needfule to fend a ftrong party to guard them. I am,

> My Lord,
> Your Grace's
> Moft obedient humble Servant,
> LAU^E OLIPHANT.

Perth, *Octr 12th,* 1745.

Your Grace will pleafe return the Letter directed to me from Mr. Murray.

XC.

THE MASTER OF STRATHALLAN TO THE DUKE OF ATHOLL.

Doun, *October* 12th.

My Lord,

I ariv'd here juft now with the French Gentelman, upon hearing that James Drummond was here with two hundred men, and are to crofs the Forth to morrow morning with them, fo we wont be oblidged to trouble your Grace for an efcort, which makes me trouble you with this line ; it was very lucky we met with the men here, for there is no paffing above one or two perfons at the foard, becaufe the Garifon of the Caftele, we are told here, make patroules all about to hinder people from paffing; and have the honour to be,

My Lord,

Your Grace's moft humble

and obedient Servant,

JA : DRUMMOND.

XCI.

DAVID STEWART OF KYNACHAN TO Mr. MERCER OF ALDIE.

12th Oct^{r.}, 1745.

D^R. Sir,

I haue the pleafure to tell you that I now believe we fhall haue all the men of Glenlyon, Rannoch, and this country raifed in a few days, but there is an abfolute neceffity for a ftrong party of ftrangers to put this in execution, which is my reafon for fending you this exprefs att this unfeafonable hour.

Now, we are informed that Cluny is juft now with his men att Dunkeld, and, as he is the propereft in the world, fo I beg you'll, on receipt of this, get on order from his Grace to fend Cluny, with his whole party, (for the more the better,) here to-morrow night, that they may affift Shian att once to raife the men in the different places he is to be concerned with. I intreat you'll not delay this, for it will be of great confequence to us to have Shian and his 2 or 300 good men ready to march along with us to the Prince. Let Cluny haue the proper orders to be directed by Shian: If he is not yet come it muft be delayed till he comes, for I find this muft be done by ftrangers. I fancy you'll take notice that it will be haftning the matter to fend Cluny his orders to march ftraight here from Blair or Dalnacardoch, if he is not yet come your length. I haue ordered a full company for Strathbrawn to-morrow morning, and moſt of the reſt are to be ordered on other parties, which I ſhall acquaint you of att meeting, who am,

D. SIR,

Your moſt humble Servt

CASTLE MENZIES,
Saturday, 12 *o'clock att night.*

DAVID STEWART.

XCII.

SIR PATRICK MURRAY TO MR. MERCER OF ALDIE.

D^R. SIR,

Yeſterday's afternoon, at four of the cloack, my Lord Strathallan and Gaſke convined all the officers priſoners here, and my Lord Duke's letter was reade in preſence of us all; every body was very ſenceable of the kind uſage meant towards us by my Lord Duke's letter, and, in conſequence thereof, every body very naturally thought of applying my Lord Duke to have his leave and intereſt to go to the different pleacefs where their buſſineſs and circumſtanceſs call them moſt. As I told you at Dunkeld ſeverals of my fellow priſoners here, being Engliſhmen, would willing choiſe to go to the different pleacefs of England where their conections laẏ; but at the ſame time I can ſay, in name of all my fellow priſoners, that none of us would aſke any thing of my Lord Duke that ſhould be thought ane unreaſonable demand, ſo I beg you'll let me know by the bearer what libertys we haue reaſou to expe&t or look for, and believe me ever to be,

D. SIR,

Your affe&tionate Couſin,

and humble Servant.

PERTH, 13th *Oct^r.,* 1745.

PAT. MURRAY.

Pos.—If my Lord Duke is not to be here to-morrow, I beg you'll be fo good as obtaine my Lord Duke's liberty for Colonel Bleaton, Colonel Hacket and me, to write of my Lord Duke, when we will let my Lord Duke know the libertys the officer prifoners wifh for.

XCIII.

LORD STRATHALLAN TO THE DUKE OF ATHOLL.

My Lord,

You was fo good as fend for Sir Patrick Murray to Dunkeld, when I hapned to be there; I fear it was unlucky, as my fon and thefe gentlemen from France came at the fame time to waite upon your Grace; I faw Sir Patrick ftill with that gentileman who could fpeake nothing but French. I had, this evening, advice of fome new odd behaviour of the Knight, and fhall foon have the particulars, and this is to give your Grace my hearty wifhes not to liften any thing comes from him. I have inclofed a letter I had from Mr. Murray, the Prince's Secretary, about fending to Ed^r. Captn. Scot, in which your Grace will fee that the Prince defigns to give no enlargement to the gentilemen prifoners there. Gafk omitted to write your Grace, that it was the Prince's defire that you would fend a party to try the raifin the Braedalben men; and there feems the more reafon for it, that a good many of them, it's faid, will be raifed againft us, how foon your Grace leaves this fide of the Forth. With the utmoft efteem and fincerity, I am,

My Lord,

Your Grace's moft faithfull and

obedient humble Servant,

STRATHALLAN.

Perth, Oct^r· 13th, 1745.

XCIV.

COL. WRIGHT TO THE DUKE OF ATHOLL.

PERTH, *Oct^r* 13*th*, 1745.

MY LORD,

I have the honour of your Grace's moſt oblidgeing letter, which I communicated to the Officers who are priſoners here. I am defired by them to return your Grace their fincere thanks, for the offer of your good offices towards our farther enlargement. Tho' they are as happy in the pre-fent quarters as their fituation will admit of, yet the bad ſtate of health of fome, and the circumſtances of others, make them wiſh to be removed to other places, which I ſhall lay before you when I have the Honour to wait on your Grace here.

We have all of us the moſt gratefull fenfe of our generous treatment, which we ſhall on all occafions readily acknowledge.

I write in the name of the Officers, as well as my own ; and have the Honour to affure your Grace that we are, with the greateſt refpeƈt,

MY LORD,

Your Grace's moſt obedient,

& moſt Humble Servants,

J. WRIGHT.

XCV.

MR. MERCER TO SIR PATRICK MURRAY.

DUNKELD, *Oct^r* 13*th*, 1745.

SIR,

I juſt now received your's, which I immediately ſhowed the Duke of Atholl, who intends to be at Perth Tuefday or Wednefday next at far-

M

theft, he will then be glad to fee the Gentlemen Prifoners.   However, if Collonell Bliton, Colonell Halket, & you, has any thing to fay that's pref-fing, which cannot admitt of fuch a delay, you'll be very welcome here, provided my Lord Strathallan is fatisfied with your journey ; if the Gentile-men acquaints him of their reafonable defire, I'm perfwaded you'll find him ready to oblidge them in every thing lyes in his poure ; therefor it's plain you are free to do as thought proper on this occafion, as I wifh you ever may, being without referve,

SIR,

If any of your Gentlemen comes here, they are defired to bring Mr. Farquharfon alongft with them.

———————

XCVI.

THE DUKE OF ATHOLL TO LORD STRATHALLAN.

MY LORD,

Juft before leaving Blair, your Lo^P's Brother-in-law, and my valuable Coufin German called Mr. Mercer of Aldie imagin'd that if Sir Pat. Murray of Ochtertyre was allowed to come here, he might be induced to abandon Hanoverian principles, and to take the benefit of the Indemnity offered by the King & our Gracious Prince's Declaration ; which really I thought he was not in the wrong to hope would been readily embraced by his father's fon.

I fhall be forry to abfolutely find both of us were much miftaken, which cou'd not be well difcovered by the fhort time he ftaid with us ; therefore at his requeft I did not abfolutely refufe to fee him again in this place, provided your Lo^{P.} though it proper, which was the condition which made me hearken to his new propofal he made Mr. Mercer of coming again to

this place. I am glad to know you find not his behaviour altogether or-
thodox, which makes me far from inclining to hearken to him, or any
other of your prifoners, otherwife than as your Lo^{p.} fhall think proper. I
fhall fay nothing about raifing the Broadalbin men, till I have the honour
of feeing you, being told that my Lord Glenorchy received the Letter I
writ him from Blair in the moft obligeing manner. I am, with perfect
efteem & affection,

My Lord,
Your Lordfhip's
Moft obed^{t.} & moft humble Servant.

Dunkeld, 14 Octr. 1745.

I beg your Lo^{p.} will forgive the not writing with my own hand, Continual occupation renders it almoft impoffible: Secretary Murray's Letter
is returned inclofed.

XCVII.

LORD GEORGE MURRAY TO THE DUKE OF ATHOLL.

Ed^{r.} 14th Octr. 1745.

Dear Brother,
The Prince Regent is in the utmoft concern for the prefious time
which is loft by your not comming up. I have wrote to you fo often, by
his orders, upon that fubject, that I can add nothing to what I have
already faid, only that it feems the oppinion of every body if you delay any
longer it will be the uter ruine of the Caufe. You fhould wait for no
body but your own men, and if you bring them you will never be blamed

for the fault of others.   Mr. Strathallen and his Company are arived fafe.
I ever am,

DR. BROTHER,
Your moft Affe^{ct.} Brother,
and Faithfull humble Servant,
GEORGE MURRAY.

XCVIII.

ROBERTSON OF STROWAN TO THE DUKE OF ATHOLL.

MY HONOURED LORD DUKE,

I had the pleafure of your Grace's of the 12th of Oa^{r.} 1745, wherein you order a hundred of my Regiment, with a proper Officer at their Head, on fight to march to Breamar, and there execute fuch orders as fhall be given them by Mr. Ferquharfon of Balmorall, or Mr. Shaw of Dalldownie, in raifing the Breamar men for the King's fervice, for which this fhall be to all concerned a fufficient warrand, figned Atholl.

But I beg leave to informe your Grace, that the Prince, previous to this order, has commanded me under his fign manuell, dock'd by his Secretary, and feal'd by his Royal H^{s.}, expreffly ordered me to raife all my Vaffells, Tenants, and Followers, and foon as I have raifed them hurry them to his Army, wherever the fame fhall happen to be for the time. Thus, my Lord, it feems a difficult point for me to put both orders in execution, unlefs, as the man faid, I can be in two places at once like a bird. Befides, a tafk of this nature is ufually given to a Detatchment raither then put intirely upon one individuall Corpe, for it feems better to divide a difobligation then roll it over upon one fingle perfon. However, if I was affured the Prince's orders and yours did not elafh,—however, my men fhall be ready on your Grace's return to this; tho' I hope, on fecond thoughts, you will think what I hinted not altogether unreaſonable, when you are told that my Camerons in Ranoch want to be threatened to riſe like ſome of our neighbours.

I have taken from M^r· Chas. Alexander the 20 pieces, your Grace's intention at this time; I know he'll be accountable for the reſt, as an honeſt man ought.

I wiſh your Grace had let me into the particulars of our Foreign Succours, it had done great ſatisfaction to

Your ever faithful Servant,

AL^R· ROBERTSON of Strowan.

CARIE, *Oct^r·* 14^*th*, 1745.

XCIX.

LORD STRATHALLAN TO THE DUKE OF ATHOLL.

My Lord,

The incloſed Letter for your Grace had been ſeiſed by one W^m· Whytt at Kinroſs, and was recovered at Aloa, as your Grace will ſee by Sir Harry Stirling's Letter to me, incloſed with the note of ſeiſing the carryer of it, who is alſo ſent on to your Grace, that he may account for his behaviour.—I am,

My Lord,

Your Grace's

Moſt obedient humble Servant,

STRATHALLAN.

PERTH, *Oct^r* 15^*th*, 1745.

It is Sir Harie Stirling's Servant who is ſent forward to your Grace with this.

C.

MR. MURRAY OF TAYMOUNT TO THE DUKE OF ATHOLL.

My Dear Lord,

The bearer of this is Mr. Lockheart younger of Carnwath, who has defired me to write this to introduce him to your Grace, which I prefume you will be fo good as to exenfe from, my Dr. Lord,

Your Grace's Afe&ionate Coufin

and moft humble Servant,

W. MURRAY.

Ed^{br.} *Oct^{br}* 15th, 1745.

I hope to have the honour and pleafure of feeing you foon here. This young Gentleman is one of the Prince's Aiducamps.

CI.

BOYËR MARQUIS D'EGUILLES TO THE DUKE OF ATHOLL.

Milord Duc,

Je ne puis affes vous temoigner combien je fuis fenfible aux bontés dont il vous a plû de m'honorer, me voicy enfin arrivé a Edimbourg ou je compte voir inceffamment vôtre adorable Prince, qui fait les delices de fes peuples, et qui fera bientot l'admiration de l'Europe.

Je fuis avec refpe&,

Milord Duc,

Vôtre tres humble

et tres obeis. ferviteur,

BOYËR.

[Ed^{r.}, 15th *Oct^{r.}* 1745.]

CH.

Dr. COLVILL TO THE DUKE OF ATHOLL.

My Lord,

I have the honour and pleaſure to acquaint your Grace that the Crowned Herring arrived ſafe laſt night in this Harbour, Captⁿ· Barlemont Commander, loaded with Arms, Amunition, &c., on board of which are Colonel Richard Warren, his two brothers, Captains, and two other friends. They are very buſie unloading, and as it is very dificult to get carts here, we cannot ſet out hence till to-morrow morning early for Brichin, where we will wait what guard your Grace is pleaſ'd to ſend, which we beg may be as ſoon as poſſible. This cargo is ſomewhat greater than that landed lately at Montroſe. I beg your Grace will pardon the coarſe paper, as the place afords no better.

I have the honour to be, with the outmoſt Eſteem
and Reſpeᴄt,
My Lord,
Your Grace's moſt obedient and
moſt faithfull humble Servant,
GEORGE COLVILL.

Stonhavin, 16ᵗʰ Octoʳ· 1745.

CIII.

LADY MᶜINTOSH TO THE DUKE OF ATHOLL.

My Lord Douke,

The Beraer of this is a veray Pretay fellew, Brother to Mᶜenzie of Killooway. He had a Compannay Refed for the Prince's fervace, but was handred by Lord Siforth to keray them of, which meks me geve this trobal to beg of your Grace to geve hem en ordar for rafing hes men & thene he can wous a lettel forfe. My God preaferf your Grace, and all that will fearve ther Prince and contray, which is the ernaft woufh of

Your Grace Moft
Affnett. & obd. Sarvant,
A: M^cINTOSH.

MOYHALL, *Oct^r* 16^{th,} 1745.

CIV

Dr. COLVILL TO THE DUKE OF ATHOLL.

MY LORD,

I have the honour to acquaint your Grace that there is juft come into this Harbour another Ship, with Arms, Money, and Ammunition; befides fmall Arms, fhe has fix Swedifh Cannon, four-pounders, which can be fired nine times in a minute, and 1800 ball for them. This laft Ship was chaced by a Man-of-war, of Twenty-two Guns, and as the wind fell towards evening would have been taken, had it not been for fome fifhing-boats we fent out, who towed her along 4 miles, and brought her fafe into the Harbour. We faw the Man-of-war plainly, but night coming on, we know not what is become of her; however we are making the heft provifion we can, ordering a Guard, with fome to patrole round the Town all night. There are eight Officers of the Irifh Brigade come in this laft fhip, and twelve Gunners with an Officer. The loading of the firft fhip fet out hence this morning for Lowran-Kirk, confifting of 118 Carts. Col. Warren and I luckily ftaid behind, having fome difpatches to give the Capt. of the firft fhip, and we are to ftay till we fee every thing fafely ordered about this laft loading. As this Country is much drained of Carts by this morning's Convoy, it will be Saturday at fooneft before we can get Carts for the other, and I wifh we may have them ready then. The Gentlemen tell me that the forces defigned to affift our King are all ready at Dunkirk, Oftend, &c., and that Lord Marfhal is to come to Scotland with fix thoufand. As your Grace knows our fituation, I need add no more but that I have the honour to be, with the utmoft efteem and refpe&,

My Dear Lord,

Your Grace's moft faithful and moft

obedient humble Servant,

(Signed)   GEORGE COLVILL.

Stonehaven, 17 *October* 1745.

Pleafe turn over.

After writing the foregoing letter, Col. Warren and I agreed to delay fending off the Exprefs till this morning, when we might know further about this Man-of-War, which we now fee plainly about fix miles off; and as there is water enough for any fuch into this Harbour, we are pre-paring againft the worft, as we are pretty certain fhe has g t information concerning our fhip by means of the Cuftom-houfe boat of Aberdeen.

18 *October*.

As we can find no fit Exprefs here for fending to Edinr. Col. Warren begs leave to afk your Grace will be pleafed to order the letters for the Prince and Sir Thomas Sheridan to be fent off with all Expedition. I am juft now informed that Mr. Blake, fupercargo of laft fhip, is refolved to keep the fhip here till a return to thefe difpatches comes from the Secretary, which may meet Mr. Blake on the road as he goes along with the Convoy of this laft Cargo. As all the difpatches from Colonel War-ren, &c. were fealed up before Mr. Blake came to this Refolution, and as time preffes for difpatching the Exprefs, I am therefore obliged to intreat your Grace will pardon this freedom, as it proceeds from a fincere inclin-ation to ferve the good Caufe.

CV.

DAVID STEWART OF KYNACHAN TO GEORGE ROBERTSON OF FASKALIE.

D. GEORGE,

When I received yours I was with Lord John Drummond, getting a Carriage for a Large Boat to carry alongs to facilitate our paſſage. I was juſt ſending for other two when John Murray came from Aloa, aſſuring me that we may have boats in plenty there; wherefor I am ordering 200 men or ſo back with John Murray, ſo as to be att Aloa to-morrow morning, in order to ſecure the Boats and be maſters of the Paſſage. If this ſucceeds it will make every thing eaſy, if it fail, we muſt carry on the boats we can get from this water. Incloſed you have my receipt for 50£, & John McEwan's for 34£. 6 ſhill. I intreat you'll always let me know by Expreſs my Lord Duke's Rout, that I may know from time to time how we ſhall move. It has been a very rainy day, & ſtill rains hard; the poor ffellows are very wet, ſo you may gueſs it to be no eaſy matter to get them to march to Ardoch this night, as I propoſe they ſhall. It is now paſt 3 o'Clock, & am in great hurry getting our men together, who am ſincerely yours, &c. &c.

DAVID STEWART.

CRIEFF, 18ᵗʰ Octʳ· 1745.

CVI.

GEO. LOCKHART OF CARNWATH TO COL: MERCER OF ALDIE.

ALOWAY, *friday night*, 18ᵗʰ Octʳ· 1745.

SIR,

We are juſt now arrived ſafe at this Place, after having had a very good journey; we immediately fent for y⁰ Mafter of y⁰ Boat, who carries our friends over y⁰ water; & he tells me, that their are Boats in y⁰ Place that will carry over 100 men; he likewife adds, that if there were 2 or 300 men here, he could feize feveral large Veffels, which would carry over 4 or 500 men at once. Thefe Veffels are now lying in y⁰ Harbour here; by what I can learn from our wellwifhers here, they think it proper that his Grace of Athol ought to take poffeffion of this Place very foon, with a force able to refift y⁰ Garrifon of Sterling, fhould they make a Sally to diflodge us. I beg you'l pay y⁰ remainder of y⁰ hiring, which we fhall pay at meeting, I have given him 5 fh:. Captain Brown, and I, prefent our humble Duty to my Lᵈ· Duke.

> I ever am,
>
> Sʳ.
>
> Your moft obed. Servᵗ·
>
> GEO: LOCKHART.

The long boat of y⁰ man-of-War is more to be fear'd than y⁰ Caftle of Stirling.

CVII.

Mʀ. MIC: BROWN TO THE DUKE OF ATHOLL.

My Lord,

We this inftant are arrived the fouth fide of y⁰ Forth, and have converfed with one William Virtue, Shipmafter of Aloa, who is a very zealous fubject and an underftanding man. He affured me yᵗ with four fmall pieces of Canon, whereof two of one pound, y⁰ other two a pound and half, yᵗ he will engage to keep off any long boat that might be dif-patched from the man-of-war to interrupt your Grace's embarquation of men and convoy:—thefe four pieces of Canon are in a Brigg in this harbour which waits a loading. If your Grace thinks proper to fend a number of men to take poffeffion of this port, they can be here time enough to make a little redoubte, and garnifh it with this little Artillery, which I believe may fuffice to hinder yᵉ approach of yᵉ long boat, till your Grace arrives with yᵉ Convoy.

I thought it proper alfo to agree on fignals with fame man, if any body fhould be fent by his Highnefs; I thought it incumbent on me, my Lord, to acquaint you of this man's fentiments, the more fo that they feem reafonable I think, that fhan't hinder, but I fhall punctually execute your Grace's orders in reprefenting to His Royal Highnefs that fome field pieces would vaftly facilitate your fafe paffage.

I hope your Grace will excufe this undigefted fcroul, by yᵉ impoffibility I'm in to write here otherwife.

I am with refpect,

Your Grace's

moft humble

and obedient Servant,

MIC: BROWN.

No more arriv'd at Aloa.

CARSIE, *four o'Clock.*

(*Endorsed.*)—" Received Perth, 18 *Octr.* 1745."

CVIII.

ROBERTSON OF STROWAN TO THE DUKE OF ATHOLL.

MY DEAR DUKE,

I need not prompt a man to be honeft who makes nice Confcience of wronging the King; few people fcruple in that point. I have been curfedly uf'd by your Grace's Relations, tho' I am fure they were not properly related to your Grace. My ever honour'd Duke, you take me ; if you don't, I refer you to Neil Macglaſhan for half a pair of Speɛtacles, for he can tell what he fees as well and better than

My Lord,

Your ever faithfull humble Servant,

AL^R ROBERTSON of Strowan.

Carie, *Oct^{r.}* 18^{th,} 1745.

God direɛt you & your good natur'd Frailty.

(*Endorsed.*)—" Letter from Strowan Robertson, which the Vis. of Strathallan, Mr. Mercer of Aldie, and other gentlemen, present at the receiving of it, could make nothing of ; dated Carie, 18th Oct^{r.}, Received at Perth the 20th."

———————

CIX.

ROBERTSON OF KILICHANZIE TO THE DUKE OF ATHOLL.

Carrie, *Oct^{r.}* 18^{th,} 1745.

May it Please your Grace,

At my coming here I found Strowan refolved to joyn the Prince's Army with all fpeed, which I fee is His Royal Highnefs Exprefs orders to him, and he feems to incline more to follow that Intention than goe or fend his men to Braymar. He recommended fome ɛhings by word of mouth to his laft Exprefs fent to your Grace, but fince he was not admitted to an audiance they are ftill to be a fecret.

In the main I find and fee that Strowan is proud of obeying your Grace, but as he is order'd to Joyu the Prince he'll be proud to know your Grace's orders in executing the Royall Intention. I am glad to find

Strowan a nice Servant to the Prince, as I am to the Duke of Atholl.
With all Dutifullnefs I am,

May it pleafe your Grace,
Your Grace's moft faithfull
and moft obedient Servant,
J^{o.} ROBERTSON.

I find Strowan is timirous to call for money, altho' he'll want to pay
his men as others are, alfo he wants to have fome Arms for a good many
of his men; a good many of them wants Guns, and moft of them Swords
and Piftells.

CX.

Mr. C. ALEXANDER TO Mr. NEILL MACKGLASHAN.

Dear Sir,
Killichangie has wrote my Lord Duke Strowan's anfwer to him
about fending men to Braymar, fo he intends as foon as poffible to march
for the Camp; I was very fond of the Mar Expedition, had it gon on.
Killichangie has dropt to his Grace that Strowan will want money to
cary on his men to Ed^r, alfo he wants fome of the Arms that's come—a
word from you will be feafonable. Strowan was not well pleafed the
Pink was not admitted to his Grace, it feems he had fomething to fay by
word of mouth; however, I wonder the pink did not let you know he had
fomething to fay, being fure you would gott him admitted. I make bold to
trouble you once more about a ffuzie, if there be any fuch, or elfe a hand-
fome light gun of the fort there is; the Bearer expeêts you'll help him to
a fword. With all refpeêt I am,

Dear Sir,
Your moft humble & ob^t Servt
CHA^{s.} ALEXANDER.

Carrie, *Oct^{r.}* 18th. 1745.

CXI.

DUKE OF ATHOLL TO SECRETARY MURRAY.

SIR,

I can add nothing to what I writt inclof'd to his R. H., but to affure, without lofs of time, the outmoft diligence and expedition fhall be uf'd, not only in going perfonally to receive His Royal Highnefs Commands, but alfo to bring up in the fafeft manner the Arms, Amunition, Money, &c. which is arriv'd at Stonehaven, with all the men I have been able to get together through all fort of difficultys and conftant labour; befides, by the Copy of a Letter, here inclofed, from the Lady McIntofh, I am well affur'd that name, the Frazers, and feveral other of the Northern Clans, will quickly join the Prince. The news I fend him of this laft Ship's Landing, with the hopes of their being fupply'd with what they want, will certainly contribute not a litle towards quickening their March. As M^r· Lockhart of Carnwath and Captn· Brown will inform you more fully; as alfo every thing els can be faid by me: So fhall trouble you no further, having the honour to be,

SIR,

Your moft obedient
and moft humble Servt·

PERTH, 18th Octo^{br} 1745.

Having not a minut's time to loofe as formerly, I entreat you'l exenfe the not writing with my own hand.

CXII.

MUNGO MURRAY, SECRETARY TO THE DUKE OF ATHOLL, TO JOHN MURRAY AT ALLOA.

This night my Lord had yours of this day's date from Crieff, and bids me tell you he is much pleafed with your diligence, care, and active capacity in every thing he has employed you, particularly this new inftance in having, without lofs of time, fecured a paffage over the Forth; but fince the Accounts of a new Convoy of Arms, Ammunition, &c. that is juft coming up to join the Prince, we can't be with you for thefe two or three days to come, Therefore hopes you will continue your affiftance to Kynachan, who he has ordered to go and take poffeffion of that poft, which 'tis poffible the Prince may have likeways fent to have kept open. Continue to behave with prudence and conduct, and you may be fure of My Lord Duke's particular efteem, as well as all honeft men's that hear of your valuable actions.—I am, with truth, entirely

Your moft obedient Humble Servant.

Perth, 18ᵗʰ October 1745.

CXIII.

WILLIAM DUKE OF ATHOLL, &c.
UNDER THE PRINCE REGENT,
COMMANDER-IN-CHIEF OF HIS MAJESTIE'S FORCES.

Thefe are Ordering and Requiring you, David Stewart of Kynachan, Major to the Earl of Nairu's Regimᵗ to go according to the fure Intelligence you receive, and take poffeffion of Aloa; to force, if poffible, a paffage over the Forth there, or any where near it, provided it can be kept open by you on this fide, and affift any men on the other fide, in cafe the Prince thinks fit to give orders for that purpofe; but you, nor any of the different bodies of men with or near you, are not without pofitive orders to pafs the River, only fuch as may be found neceffary for fecuring your communication, and to get all Intelligence poffible of what the Enemy is doing up or down the River, befides fending Us particular Accounts of that and your own Situation, fince 'tis like I may be ftopt by the new landing at Stonehive of a new Convoy of arms, ammunition, &c. which is now coming up to join the Prince. Therefore fend directly to Mr. Mackewan with the Grantully men, and Shian with the Laird of Weem's followers, as alfo Cluny McPherfon with his men, to let them know they are not to pafs the Forth, no more than you, till further orders. In all events, if poffible, take along with you or fend for the boats and carriages were offered you at Crief,—All which you are carefully to perform and do, as you will be anfwerable, for which this fhall be to you and all concerned a fufficient warrand.

CXIV.

SECRETARY MURRAY TO THE DUKE OF ATHOLL.

Be fure to bring up all the money.

My Lord,

Information is now arrived from Couper of Fife that a fhip is arrived att Stonehayve with arms, amunition, and money, and that the arms, &c. were brought the lenth of Brechin. It is fuppofed they are advancing as faft as poffible, and have by this time paft Perth; fo that by

o

halting one day att Down your Grace will give them time to come up; or if the main body come the lenth of S^t· Ninians, and a fmall party left att Down, by waiting a day they may equally join you. It is left to your Grace to leave what number of arms you fhall judge neceffary for thofe who are comeing up. A thoufand ftand Swords efpecialy are neceffary to be brought here, and the reft to be depofite att Dunkell, or Blair of Atholl, as you fhall judge moft proper. As there are ftill two fhips a-comeing, the other Clans mult be more than compleatly arm'd with thofe that are left behind, fo bring as many as poffible. I am,

M$_Y$ L$_{ORD}$,

Your Grace's moft obed^t· and

moft humble Servt·

J^O· MURRAY.

E$_{D^a}$ *Octr ye* 18th· 1745.

CXV.

SECRETARY MURRAY TO THE DUKE OF ATHOLL.

M$_Y$ L$_{ORD}$,

I had the honour to write your Grace this day by His Royal Highnefs's orders, to ftop a day att Doun, or leave a body there and advance the lenth of St. Ninians with the reft, fo as to bring up the arms, money, and ammunition, landed att Stonehayve; but in cafe that fhould retard your march, the Prince defires you may leave 500 men att Doun till fuch time as they come up, and march here with the main body without the leaft delay. Your Grace will give orders that none of the arms be left behind, and that the 500 men left may follow with the outmoft expedition, his Highnefs having this night received intelligence from the

South which renders it abfolutely neceffary for the Army to march from this as foon as poffible. I am, with great regard,

MY LORD,

Your Grace's moft obed^{t.} and

˙moft humble Servant,

J^{O.} MURRAY.

Upon receipt of this, you will fend Mr. Lockhart with Intelligence fo as to have quarters provided.

HOLYROODHOUSE, Octr. ye 18th. 1745.

CXVI.

ARCH^D MENZIES OF SHIAN TO THE DUKE OF ATHOLL.

MY LORD DUKE,

The difficulties arifes in Conveening the men committed to my care gives me a good deal of uneafinefs, as it difappoints my joining your Grace fo as to pafs the Forth Munday.

It will be Munday at fooneft befor I can expect the party or the Glenlyon men back here, and Tuefday or Wednefday befor I can march from hence. In this tardy way I woud know your Grace's orders as one who has ado with different Gentlemen's people & fuch as does not incline to appear in a light to facilitate my march. This goes by ane Exprefs from Strowan to notifie to your Grace exprefs orders from his Royal Highnefs to join the Camp w^t all Expedition, by whom your Grace will pleafe to let me know what I am to do; and if your Grace has abfolutely promif'd to fend a party to Breamarr & thinks it for the bene- fitt of the fervice, I'll do in that what your Grace thinks proper. I have return'd a letter addreffed to Mr. Ferquarfon of Monaltry which fhoud have been deliver'd by Mr. Alexander, I prefume was to command the if a party of my men be sent to Breamarr, more money will be necessary, if not, I'll do my best ere I join your Grace, which I'll endeavour to do as soon as possible.   I am, w: the outmost respect,

My Lord Duke,

Your Grace's most obedient

& most humble Servant,

ARCH.^D MENZIES.

FARLEYEAR,
19th Octr. 1745.

CXVII.

FARQUHARSON OF MONALTRIE TO THE DUKE OF ATHOLL.

MAY IT PLEASE YOUR GRACE,

Altho' I have not the honour to be acquainted with your Grace, I have presumed to give you the trouble of this line, to show that I have got a warrand from the Prince to raise as many men as I can in this Countrie for his Service, but I find it cannot be done to any purpose without a pairty of men out of some other Countrie.   I understand Balmorall apply'd your Grace to the same purpose, and I desired Mr. Stewart of Cainachan (whom I saw att Perth) to put your Grace in mind of it.   I am of opinion 40 or 50 men would be sufficient, and I intreat your Grace would do us the favour as to send about that number, with a Gentleman to command them, and Balmorall and I shall take cair of them.   I hope your Grace will excuse this trouble, and I sincerely remain,

May it please your Grace,

Your Grace's most obedt: and

most faithfull humble Servt.

FRAN: FARQ^RSON.

MONALTRIE,
Octr. the 19^{th,} 1745.

CXVIII.

COL: WRIGHT TO THE DUKE OF ATHOLL.

PERTH, *Oct^r.* 19th. 1745.

MY LORD,

Encourag'd by your Grace's goodnefs, the Officers Prifoners at Perth, take this oppurtunity to entreat the continuance of it, and that you would be pleaf'd to ufe your good offices to have us endulg'd with leave to go to the particular places of our abodes, or that we may be allow'd to name fuch other places, as my Lord Strathallen may have inftru&ions to permit us to refide at. Your Grace's compliance with the above requeft will add to the favours already conferr'd on us. I have the Honour to be, in the names of the Officers,

MY LORD,
Your Grace's moft obedient,
and moft Humble Servant,
J : WRIGHT.

CXIX.

COL: WRIGHT TO THE DUKE OF ATHOLL.

PERTH, *Oct^r.* 19th. 1745.

MY LORD,

It is no fmall addition to my prefent affli&ion, the mortification of being depriv'd of the honour of waiting on your Grace perfonally, and of delivering the demand I have the honour to fend your Grace enclof'd

I am fully convinced that the fame motives that prompted your Grace to offer your good offices, will pufh you on to perform them, which makes me with relu&ance afk any thing of one of your Grace's difpofition, who is fo ready to oblidge ; but I muft mention to your Grace, that the bad ſtate of health of ſome, and the preſſing buſineſs of others, make them wiſh how ſoon your Grace's good intentions towards them might be put in execution, as the advanc'd ſeaſon of the year, and the badneſs of the roads, will make it the more inconvenient for them, which I am perſwaded would give your Grace pain, as you ſeem to feel the ſufferings of others. The timeing a favour greatly raiſes the value of it, and the reflection of doing good natur'd and human actions, gives to a generous mind the greateſt joy.

I ſhall ever retain the higheſt ſenſe of your Grace's goodneſs, and have the honour to be, with the greateſt reſpect,

My Lord,

Your Grace's moſt obedient

& moſt humble Servant,

J : WRIGHT.

CXX.

LORD GEORGE MURRAY TO THE DUKE OF ATHOLL.

Holyroodhous, 19ᵗʰ Octʳ. 1745.
six at night.

Dʳ. Brother,

Yours by Captⁿ: Brown, his R : H : has received juſt now, & deſires me to write to you (as Sʳ Thoˢ Ker does by another expreſs) that he inſiſts you ſhould come up with all your Force with the utmoſt expedition, for all depends upon our marching into England, & nothing will hinder a moment after you join. You are to bring the whole that came in the laſt ſhip with you, & as many of the Armes of the firſt as you think can be ſpard after arming thoſe with you, & leaving a few for the men you are ſure are to come up very ſoon. It is thought by all here, that Low Country men can be gott in Angus & Perthſhire, who for pay, will ſerve & anſwer all intentions in Perth, & the other towns in the north;

& his R : H : has fent directions & orders to the moft of thefe Towns. As to your paffing the Forth it is left to your judgment and thofe whom you confult when you come the lenth of Dumblane. There fhall be Canon fent to guard this fide on Tcufday. Adieu.

Yours,

GEORGE MURRAY.

CXXI.

NEIL MACKGLASHAN TO MUNGO MURRAY, SECRETARY TO THE DUKE OF ATHOLL.

SIR,

There has been no accounts of the Mackintofhes or Frazers being on this fide Drumachter, but we expect to hear of them this night by the return of the exprefs that was fent to Foyers with His Grace's Letter. I have order'd up 20 bolls meal to Dalnacardoch, with a proper perfon to give it to them upon Receipt. As foon as I hear of their march over the hill, I'll goe on to meet them, fo that they'l meet with no hinder for want of meal or money. I realy believe that the bad weather yefterday & the day before, fwell'd the waters fo high that there was no paffing of them.

If his Grace leaves Perth to-morrow, it's not poffible for me to be with him there, otherwayes I muft return without doing that I came for; but if my Lord Duke wants I fhould wait on him at any rate, I'll go off directly for any place I'll be ordered to, to receive His Grace's laft commands for this Country.

I fhou'd think, with fubmiffion, that if His Grace wou'd pleafe fend his commands by this bearer, or any other he pleafes, I fhou'd ftay to deliver that £100 to the Frazers, fince they're not come already, fo as I might have time eneugh to overtake His Grace at Perth.

If my Lord Duke pleafes to order any thing he thinks proper for me out of the £100 I got for the Service of the Country, or out of any other happinefs and profperity, and am,

SIR,
Your moft humble and Obedient Servt.
N. MACKGLASHAN.

BLAIR, 20th Octr. 1745.

CXXII.

JOHN MURRAY TO MUNGO MURRAY.

S^R.

Yours by the Bearer I received, and am glad to hear of the fafe Arrivall of the new Convoy. Every thing here is in a much better way than could have been expected; and I am,

S^R.
Your moft humble Servt.
JOHN MURRAY.

ALLOA, *Sunday, 11 o'Clock forenoon.*

CXXIII.

MR. JA: SCOT TO MR. WILLIAM FLEMING, ATTENDING HIS GRACE THE DUKE OF ATHOLL AT PERTH.

DUNKELD, 20th Octr. 1745.

DEAR SIR,

I'll be glad to hear by your return to this that my Lord Duke is well, and that he has got quit of his Rheumatifm. You may tell his Grace that, conform to his order, I fent 40 Bolls meal to Blair, & that there is only about a firlot remaining. Pray acquaint me when his Grace leaves Perth, & if you have got any good news.

After I had befpoke Thurfday laft 6 horfes for Captn. Brown and his Attendants, it feems fome Officers had made free with fome of them; & on M^r. Ochterlony & one of the French men's being left at Iuwar wi^tout horfes, I fent along wi^t them 2 of my own, & all the thanks I had was, that when my fervant afkt wherew^t to maintain his horfes all night, M^r. Ochterlonie threw him a fixpence, and bid him go hang himfelf; & the 2 horfes ftood me a fhill^s for hay, befides corn and the lad's expence. I think he has requit me ill, q^ch I beg you'll tell him. I am,

DEAR SIR,

Your moft aff^t. humble Servt.

JA: SCOT.

Afk M^rs. Hickfon if fhe received the £1: 11: 9 for the cherry Brandy & porter q^ch I fent by John Stewart, Ochtertyre's fervant, for q^ch he fhould have got me a receit.

CXXIV

DUKE OF ATHOLL TO COL: WRIGHT.

SIR,

With pleafure I had yefterday, under a double cover from Col. Halket, both your polite Letters, with the two lifts of your Officers and their demands. I am forry to know from all hands that you are in a bad ftate of health. Did it depend on me, your ficknefs and affliction fhould

P

be equally fhort with the uneafy fituation of your Gentlemen, who I
heartily wifh well.   All I can do for the fatiffaction of both is to reprefent to the Prince Regent your immediate melancholy condition in the
moft moving manner; [which] may foon produce fuch worthy as well as
agreeable effects as is earneftly defired by them or thofe, whofe dutiful
fentiments, befides humanity, makes wifh well to true Britons.   With what
is materially due on that account, a particular regard for your perfonal
merit will alwife oblige to be in the moft fignificant manner poffible,

Sir,

Your moft humble

and moft obedient Servant,

Perth, 20 October, 1745.

I hope you'll excufe the not writing with my own hand, continual
occupation renders it almoft impoffible.

CXXV.

NOTE ENCLOSED IN THE PRECEDING LETTER.

Oct. 20, 1745.

The Duke of Atholl was told that the Gentlemen prifoners here
in Perth, afked to know, If he would have morning levees, becaufe they
intended accordingly to wait of him.   His anfwer is, That He thanks
them kindly for the polite Compliment they defigned him.   His Grace is
not fond of ceremonious vifits, tho' he will be always glad to cultivate an
acquaintance with Gentlemen, whofe actions fhow they are true Britons,
by ftanding up for fupporting the ancient Conftitution and liberties of
well-born Subjects, whofe honour is engaged to fhake off the Slavery of
a foreign yoke.

CXXVI.

DUKE OF ATHOLL TO KILICHANGY, AT CARIE.

Sir,

This afternoon I had your obliging Letter, with one from Strowan Robertfon, which neither my Lord Strathallan, the Laird of Aldie, nor any body here could make any thing of. Pray, with my Compliments, let him know that it is now no more time to be talking of fending out parties, Therefore He'll be pleafed to obey his Royal Highnefs Commands in the manner that appears moft expeditious and convenient for his Service. Had Neill McGlafhan been here, I know not if that Gentleman, as he fays, would have underftood or explained his meaning better than other people. In his abfence I opened the Letter Mr. Alexander writ him, but never heard of one called Pink's having any particular meffage to me; for in that cafe, if fent by a very fmall Subject I fhould have feen him, how much lefs then would I have failed in fpeaking with one lent to inform me of any thing from a perfon of fuch merit and confequence as is my former friend Strowan Robertfon, for whom I fhall ever have all poffible efteem and regard, which I hope you'll let him know in the moft agreeable manner: However little confidence it feems Strowan puts in me, yet fure he might freely call for due fubfiftence to any of the King's troops who are under his command, without your having fent a known perfon for that end; yet by Drumachine's advice, I truft the bearer of yours, and one of Strowan's Tenents, who is going to him, with £25 fter. for that end, for which I hope our dear Elector will be accountable in the exacteft manner. I am, with Efteem,

Sir,
Your moft affectionate
Humble Servant,

Perth, 20th October 1745.

CXXVII.

DUKE OF ATHOLL TO MENZIES OF SHIAN.

SIR,

All I can fay in return to your long letter dated the 19ᵗʰ, which I received about 2 o'clock this afternoon, is, That two fhips having arrived at Stonehive with frefh fupplies of arms, money, &cª. to the Prince, the Convoy of which, confifting of about 250 cart loads, not being able to arrive here before to-morrow or next day at furtheft, has retarded our march till then from hence. His Royal Highnefs having fent repeated and exprefs orders to me that all His Troops in thefe parts fhou'd march forthwith without lofs of time, therefore this is requiring you to do the fame, with Cluny Macpherfon, to whom pleafe communicate this, that you may both directly, without ftopping longer, proceed immediately forward in your way to the Army, and quarter yourfelves at Crieff, Muthil, or any where elfe you can find moft convenient thereabouts, till I come up, or till further orders; but if we are paffed before you come that length, you are to follow with the utmoft diligence and Expedition. So hoping foon to have the pleafure of feeing you, I am, with perfect Efteem,

SIR,

Your moft obedient

PERTH, 20 October 1745.   Humble Servant,

CXXVIII.

DUKE OF ATHOLL TO LADY GEORGE MURRAY.

DEAR SISTER,

Some days ago I was mightily concerned on hearing you were in danger on paffing the Forth at Aloa, your Chaife horfe being fhot, and wearing apparel taken, which, except the fright, I am glad is all the hurt has happened you. This day, before receiving the pleafure of yours dated the 19th inft. from Arnhall, I have one of the fame date, 6 at night, from my Brother George, with the Prince's laft orders, and fhall do all is poffible to get yet further inftru&ions, as two Ships, one after the other, are arrived from France at Stonehive. I know not, as yet, if I fhall march for a' day or two more from home, nor can I tell if we may'nt pafs the River at Aloa; whatever happens I fhall be fure to endeavour meeting with your Ladyfhip in the way. In the meantime, pray take care of your health, and give my Kind Service to Lady Strowan, being, with perfe& efteem and regard,

MADAM,
Your moft affe&ionate Brother,
and moft humble Servant,

PERTH, 20th October 1745.

As formerly, I entreat you'll forgive the not writing with my own hand, having now far lefs time than ever.

CXXIX.

LADY GEORGE MURRAY TO THE DUKE OF ATHOLL.

MY LORD,

I give your Grace this trouble, being juft inform'd that the people of Stirling are intending to make an attack on your Grace in your march, and, the better to deceive, I'm told that they have put on white cokades, and many of them in Highland drefs. Their number, what with fo many out of the Caftle, the foldiers in the town, and the militia, will, it's given out, amount to fix or feven hundred men, fo that it will be neceffary to have a ftrong body along with yourfelf.   I wifh that thefe things wh^ch came in the laft fhip may be foon with your Grace, for, by the refolution that was taken, Friday evening, at the Abbey, they wanted much that your Grace and men might be foon up.—If your Grace comes to Dumblain, pray let me know before, that I be there, for it is improper for your Grace to be here, but in cafe you don't come that road, (as I hear a report to-day that the paffage is open'd at Alloa,) pleafe fend a fure hand here by whom I fhall write what I was defir'd to tell your Grace.—I am, with great regard,

MY LORD,
Your Grace's moft affectionate fifter,
and moft humble Servant,
ÆMILIA MURRAY.

ARNHALL 21*t* *Oct^r.*,
four afternoon, 1745.

I fent a letter to your Grace yefterday morning, wh^ch I hope you have rec^d

---

CXXX.

DUKE OF ATHOLL TO LADY M'INTOSH.

MADAM,

A minute before leaving Dunkeld, I had the pleafure of your moft agreeable letter dated from Moyhall the 12th inft. and am very glad to find by it that the Laird of M'Intofh is the loyal fucceffor of his anceftors. Having no time to write the inftant I received yours, made me then only fend £100, which might be neceffary for the fubfifting of his men, which was all feemed abfolutely neceffary at that time for them who, I hoped, would foon after been up with us. This day I had the fatiffaction of a letter of recommendation from you in behalf of Mr. William M'Kenzie, brother to Kilcoy, to whofe fatiffaction every thing is done I thought could contribute to the King's fervice. He affured me that your people will be quickly up to join the Prince, which gives no fmall fatiffaction to all friends who have heard it, as well as to one who is, with perfect efteem, entirely,

MADAM,

Your moft aff. coufin,

and moft humble Servant,

PERTH, 21 October, 1745.

I beg you'll excufe the not writing w^t my own hand, continual oc_cupation renders it almoft impoffible.

———

CXXXI.

DUKE OF ATHOLL TO MONALTRIE.

SIR,

With pleafure this day I received your's of the 19th, and in anfwer, as preffed by the Prince's commands to join him without delay, I am forry to tell you how unable I am at prefent to be ufeful to you in raifing the Braemar-men. You'll fee by what I writ to Balmarall, as well by the two enclofed Letters, the one from Mr Steuart of Keinachan, & the other from Meinzies of Shian, that I have done all I could for being effectually ufeful to you. Since nothing has as yet fucceeded, I fpoke laft night to Lord Lewis Gordon, who was here in his way to raife the Duke of Gordon's people, to be affifting in getting out your men, which he frankly promifed to do, fo foon as he could be on his march Southward. This is

all remained further practicable to do for the King's Service towards effectually raiſing your people.   I heartily wiſh more were in my power.   It
ſhould be ſoon performed by,

SIR,

Your moſt obedient
humble Servant.

PERTH, 21 Oct^r, 1745.

CXXXII.

DUKE OF ATHOLL'S SECRETARY TO NEILL MACGLASHAN.

SIR,

Three o'clock this afternoon I received your's of yeſterday's date,
which I immediately ſhowed to my Lord Duke, who was much ſurpriſed
that inſtead of ſeeing you before this time, as he poſitively required at
your parting, to find, inſtead thereof, you have ſent by an expreſs a Letter
which ſignifies little or nothing; which he ſays is not only loſing of time,
but alſo gently giving him the ſlip the ſecond time, as you did firſt at Creif.
In ſhort, he hopes you will now leave the ſmall Commiſſions you were
charged with, as formerly deſired, in the hands of your Nephew, Patrick
Mackglaſhan, who ought, and may eaſily diſcharge that truſt, and come
directly here without loſing any more time; where perhaps you may be
ſtill uſefully employed in helping to ſend off neceſſary Diſpatches, inſtead
of precious time being loſt in writing to you, as you may very well imagine,
ſince knowing how few my Lord has about him fit for being employed in
putting pen to paper.   As for me, I am not alone able to anſwer innumerable demands and Letters, which arrive every minute from all hands.
Conſider, then, if you have judged well in leaving my Lord deſtitute of your
aſſiſtance on ſo preſſing and critical a juncture.   The day after you parted,

another Ship arrived at Stonehive with more Arms, Cannon, Money, Officers, &cᵃ·, which helps to multiply the care of many affairs which lie on our hands. Think then what you have to do quickly, as you wiſh well to a good cauſe; which is all at preſent from,

SIR,

Your moſt humble & obedient Servant.

PERTH, 21 *Octʳ·*, 1745.

I ſend you encloſed from my Lord ſix of the Prince's laſt Declaration, which he deſirés may be left in the hands of honeſt people about Blair.

I forgot to tell you, that if bare words can do any Service, He wiſhes, as you do him, all happineſs & proſperity may attend you. ·

CXXXIII.

MONSᴿ· BOYER D'EGUILLES TO THE DUKE OF ATHOLL.

MILORD DUC,

Etant arrivés a.Macani, nous avons appris que les gens de miledi Georges Murray avoient eté enlevés hier, au paſſage de la riviere d'Edimbourg, par le canot d'un vaiſſeau Anglois; et qu'il ſortoit des partis du chateau de Sterling qui venoient faire des incurſions a plus de 12 milles, au nombre quelquefois de 150 hommes. Nous avons crû qu'il ſeroit trop imprudent de nous expoſer a être pris; ce qui le ſeroit d'autant plus que nos depêches ſeroient ouvertes, et nous mis hors d'etat dêtre d'aucune utilité au Prince; nous avons donc pris le parti de nous arrêter icy juſqu'a nouvel ordre, et nous avons ecrit au Camp nos raiſons et nos craintes. J'ay crû que vous me permettriés de vous en rendre compte; les bontés

Q

dont *Votre Grace* m'a honoré, et le rang quelle tient dans ce pais ici me font un devoir de cette attention,

Je fuis avec refpeɛt,

Milord Duc,

Vôtre tres humble,

et tres obeifs : Serviteur,

BOŸER D'EGUILLES.

A Machani, ce 21. 8ᵇʳᵉ· 1745.

CXXXIV.

THE DUKE OF ATHOLL TO MONSIEUR BOYER D'EGUILLES.

Monsieur,

Vers les quatre heures apres midy, J'ay eu l'honneur de recevoir votre Lettre de Machany avec cette de Monfieur Drummond, fils de Monfieur le Vicomte de Strathallan, qui mes les envoit par un Expreft. Je fuis bien mortifié de fçavoir que Monfieur eft obligé de f'areté en chemin faifant vers le Prince, par le foin que l'on na pas eû d'empecher les Ennemis a couper la communication que doit etre avec l'armée de fon Alteffe Royale et ce pays icy, par les Endroits les plus comode fous la Riviere du Forth. J'auroit eû le plefir d'envoyer a Monfieur fur le champ une efcorte de cent hommes fi il y avoit icy affés d'armes pour le meftre en Etat de fes Defendre devant l'arrivés des votres, qui doivent etre icy Dimanche au plus tard. Mais j'efpert que vous ne feré pas obligé d'atendre jufqu'au tems quils puiffent vous joindre, parceque fur la bruit a Edimbourg que des Troupes, des armes, eft munition etoient arrivez de France fous les coftes de ce pays icy.

Le Secretaire du Prince a Envoyé un Expreft avec les ordres ne-ceffaires a ceft egard, par une perfonne q'hier au foir a heureufmᵗ· paffé la

Riviere; eſt il ma dit qu'il Eſperoit pouvoir vous faire paſſer de meme avec votre Compagnie : Ainſſy il doit informer Monſieur particulierem^t. ſi cela ce puit être fait en ſureté demain, peut être devant cecy puit vous être rendu ; Etant ſur le champ partir d'icy, pour parler a Perth a M^r. Le Vicomte De Strathallan en chemin faiſant.

En tous cas auſſy tot que vos armes feront arrivez j'envoyerez les cent hommes que l'on a Demandés pour votre Eſcorte a Machany, ſi on ne me fait pas a ſçavoir quils ne vous ſont plus util.

Je ſuis infiniment ſenſible Monſieur de vos Politeſſes a mon Egard, et feroit charmé de pouvoir être util en vous rendant le moindre ſervice qui êt deub a une perſonne de votre merite, Etant avec Reſpeſte,

MONSIEUR,
votre tres humble et tres
obeiſſant ſerviteur.

A DUNKELD,
ce 22. 8bre 1745.

De Grace Monſieur ayé la bonté d'excuſer ſi je vous Eſcriſt par une autre main que la mienne, parceque des occupations continuels fait quil eſt preſque impoſible de faire autrem^t.

CXXXV.

MR. JA : SCOT TO MR. WILLIAM FLEMYNG.

Octr. 22.

SIR,

I wiſh the Duke could think of removing theſe Gentlemen we have here priſoners on their parole to Perth, or ſome oy^r more convenient place, for I'm convinced they'll do no good here; the encloſed was writ laſt night, & was returned this morning by the man propoſed going to Perth.

CXXXVI.

LADY MONCRIEFF TO GLENLYON.

Dear Sir,

Since the Duke of Athole has ufe for my horfes, I have fent fuch as I have to his Grace; my three beft went before with the Prince, and as you know I have a prety lerge labouring, I muft be oblidged to provide others the beft way I can, or let my ground lie, fo it will be a great favour done me to procure his Grace's protection for fuch as I muft either buy or borrow. I am glade to hear my fifter is well and makeing up for your abfence. If it be convenient, I fhould be glade to fee Captain Archebald. My duty to my fifter, and, wifhing you good health and a bapie return, I ever am,

Dear Sir,

Your affectionat Sifter,

MARGARET SMYTH.

Moncrieffe, October 22ᵈ, 1745.

P.S.—If I had had fadles, I would have have fent them, but all I had was taken when my firft and beft horfes was taken. Pleas keep the berrar till you get the protection.—Adew, my Dear Sir.

CXXXVII.

WILLIAM DUKE OF ATHOLL, &c.
UNDER THE PRINCE REGENT,
COMMANDER-IN-CHIEF OF HIS MAJESTIE'S FORCES,
TO ALL OFFICERS, CIVIL OR MILITARY.

As fome of Lady Moncreif's horfes were formerly taken up for the Prince's fervice, and that her Ladyfhip has now fent here, for the fame end, two more, Thefe are requiring all parties who are in fearch for arms, &c.ᵃ not to difturb her any more on account of what horfes fhe may have for her perfonal ufe and labouring, as they will be anfwerable; for which this fhall be a fufficient warrand.—Given at Perth, 22ⁿᵈ October, 1745.

CXXXVIII.

PATRICK ROBERTSON TO COL. MERCER.

DALNACARDOCH, 22ⁿᵈ Octʳ 1745.

SIR,

Haveing the agreable informatione from the bearer yᵗ Sir Alexʳ. McDonald, McLowd are on theire march, the fervant wanted much my advice which road to hold; I thought proper to direct him to his Grace the Duke of Atholl and you, that ye may get all his news.—I am,

SIR,

Your moft obliged
moft humble Servant,
PAT: ROBERTSON.

CXXXIX.

LORD KINNAIRD TO THE DUKE OF ATHOLL.

MAY IT PLEASE YOUR GRACE,

Our friend Capt. Crichton has been here, agreeable to your Grace's orders, which we have feen, and has feized my horfes; but, as I have none other but what goes in my ploughs, it will be extremly hard upon

me if they are kept, confidering it is juft now our time of wheat feed;—
May I therefore beg the favour of your Grace, as I am no enemy to the
Caufe, to return me my horfes, or part of them, efpecially my wife's chaife
mare, becaufe fhe is tender, and is oblidged to ride out for her health:—
It will be doeing me a fingular favour, and a favour I fhall allways have a
gratefull remembrance of.—I hope your Grace will pardon this trouble
from,

Your Grace's moft obedient humble Servant,

KINNAIRD.

Drimmie, 22d Octr. 1745.

CXL.

MR. FRASER OF FOYERS TO THE DUKE OF ATHOLL.

My Lord Duke,

I am honour'd with your Grace's favours of the 15th curt. and the
reafon of my not doing myfelf the honour of makeing ane anfwer fooner
was owing to the Mafter of Lovate's comeing to this country the fame
day I purpofed to have fet out from here wt my people, who rende-
vouzed his men, and at the fame time he begg'd that I and my few ffol-
lowers fhould wait for a few days, when he and all that were to join him,
wt his own two battalions, would be clear to march, which defire I
thought proper to obey only for few days; I hope will give fome fatiffaction when wee appear.—Begging pardon for this and former freedom,
wt the greateft efteem and regard, I ever am,

My Lord Duke,

Your Grace's moft affect.

and faithful Servant,

JAMES FRASER.

Foyrs, 22nd Octr. 1745.

CXLI.

LORD NAIRNE TO THE DUKE OF ATHOLL.

My Lord,

The bearer, adjutant to Lord George's regiment infifts much to go home upon fome preffing buffinefs, and promifes to return in fix or feven days att moft;—I have only allowed him to wait of your Grace wherever he can find you, and then allow him to go home or not, as may be thought propereft.—I am,

Your Grace's moft obedient Servt.
NAIRNE.

Holyroodhouse, Octr 23^d, 1745.

CXLII.

SPALDING OF ASHINTILLY TO THE DUKE OF ATHOLL.

My Lord Duke,

I referred to Glenkilrie to inform your Grace of what I reafonably expect conform to your Grace's defire; but as he has proved delatory, I beg live to inform your Grace myfelf. I am, my Lord, a poor dependant, altho' young, and am therefore willing to obey directions; and I likewife hope your Grace will make me equall with fome of my Inferiors, at any rate, if I am as deferving, and I do believe I have a Claim: In the firft place, I was an Officer in the oy^r Army, where I had full pay; fecondlie, in going to Gladfmuir a Volinteer; and, fourtly, I have fome men along with me; and I alfo believe there is non of the Gentlemen with whom I have been upon Command fince I came here can reflect much upon me. May it therefore pleafe your Grace to preferr me to an Company, and to give me fuch pay as I can live upon, without beeing too much fcrimped, efpecially when I go on party. I have now the experiance of traveling; and am, with the greateft Refpect,

MY LORD DUKE,

Your Grace's moft faithfull and

moft obliged humble Sert,

DAN: SPALDING.

PERTH, *Oct'* 23^d, 1745.

CXLIII.

PATRICK ROBERTSON TO MR. MERCER.

DALNACARDOCH, 23^d Octr. 1745.

SIR,

Kinloch Mudart, and M^{r.} McKenzie, who were heir this morning, told me that ye told them that money and meall, and everie thing fit for the Armie, was to be hade from me heir; ther's onlie twentie bols meall fent heir from Blair; no money; wherefore I thought proper to acquent you of the fame. My Lord Duke huried me away when laft at Dunkeld, foe that I hade no time to fpeike of any thing. I have not been two nights on end at home fince the Prince and his Grace came to Atholl, foe that I have been a good deall of money out of pocket for the fervice; wherefor I hope His Grace the Duke of Atholl will order fome money for me, if it were but twelve pounds Sterling, for to help my charges in goeing about the fervice. I have given fome money to Expreffes already. I can be as ufefull at home as if I had gone with the Armie; and I am,

SIR,

Your moft obliged moft humble Servt,

PAT: ROBERTSON.

CXLIV.

LORD GEORGE MURRAY TO THE DUKE OF ATHOLL.

FOORD OF FORTEVIOT, 23^d Oct^r, 1745.

DR BROTHER,

We have ride the water, and if this wether had [hold], I hope it will be very paffable at Kinkell, both for horfes and Carriages to morrow.

Collonel Warran, and the Gentlemen with me, recomend two Officers who are advanced in age, and who will not be able to endure much fatigue, the one to ftay clofe at the Caftle of Blair, and the other can be with my Lord Strathallan at Perth. Thofe Gentlemen's names are, Mr Oudaniel and Collogan. I am,

DR BROY^R,

Your moft affe^{ct} Brother,

& Faithfull Humble Servt,

GEORGE MURRAY.

CXLV.

LORD GEORGE MURRAY TO THE DUKE OF ATHOLL.

ALLOA, 23^d Oct^r, 1745.

DR BROTHER,

We came very well here this evening, and found our partys much upon their guard, and alarm'd. I have feen Gentlemen who can be depended upon, who obferv'd the Happy Janet, with two Kinghorn boats they had man'd, come up the lenth of Boroftunefs, with an intent to difturb this paffage. I have left all the Officers (being 4) who came with me, to give the neceffary orders & advice in any imergency; but, for God's fake, fend up the Swedifh Cannon & Guners with an Efcort & amunition, for otherways our Friends may be afronted here. I fhall give all

R

the directions I can to-morow morning, but depend much on Coll: Waren, &c.

There are two hundred Cartes to be ready at two hours warning, and the fame is order'd from Dumblean; fo if you write Keynachan, and tell your horfe to be mett at Ardoch, it will be done. I am very weary, fo hope you will excufe my concluding with affuring you, I ever am,

DR. BROTHER,

Yours, &c.

GEORGE MURRAY.

Glengyle, who is at Doun, and Kynachan here, will be apointed pofts when the Canon pafs, viz. at Bridge of Alen & the Abby Crage.

CXLVI.

MR. JA: SCOT TO [THE DUKE OF ATHOLL'S SECRETARY?]

DEAR SIR,

I'll be glad to hear, by your return to this, that my Lord Duke is in good health, and quite free of his Rheumatifm, May God blefs and profper him. Pleafe acquaint his Grace that, conform to his orders, I fent the 40 Bolls meal to Blair, for which I want, at 16 pence ℔ Boll, 32£. Scots, or 53 fhi: 4^{d.}, q^{ch} I paid the men. Be fo good, if time will allow you, to fend us fome of your news, and when the Duke leaves Perth.

Laft night there was a man here who came from Kynachan, who told he left at Kynachan's houfe, yefterday morning, Sr. Alex^{r.} McDonald, whofe men were lodged in the neighbourhood, but could not tell their number. Pleafe let me know if it be true, as reported here, that the E. Marfhall came in the laft Fr. fhip.—I am,

DEAR SIR,

Yours moft faithfully,

JA: SCOT.

Octr. 23^d, 1745.

I wrote Monday to Mr. Flemyng, but got no return.

CXLVII.

LADY DOWAGER OF OCHTERTYRE TO THE DUKE OF ATHOLL.

My Lord,

I hope your Grace will pardon my giveing you this trouble, and believe that notwithſtanding your long abſance, ther's ſtill manny off your Grace's friends that does moſt ſincearly congratulat your happy return, amongſt whom I ſhall be ever proud to be reckened one. Being infformed your Grace is ſoon goeing South, I woud take it as a very ſingular favour iff your Grace woud be ſo good as make this your way ; I woud gladly flatter myſelff, iff it's not inconvenient, a meetting with ane old friend woud not be diſſagreeable to the Duke of Atholl, at the ſame time lay an unſpeakable obligation upon Hir who has the honour to ſubcrive myſelff,

My Lord,

Your Grace's Affect˙ Couſen, and

moſt obedient humble Servent,

CA: MURRAY.

OCHTERTYER, *Octtober* yᵉ 23ᵈ, 1745.

CXLVIII.

DUKE OF ATHOLL TO LADY METHVEN.

Madam,

When the Prince left this Town, I was ordered to call for £200 Sterl. which you had ready for his Royal Highneſs' Service. I delayed ſending to aſk for it, thinking to have had the pleaſure of waiting on you myſelf, which I now find impoſſible. Therefore hopes you will be ſo good as to excuſe this, and at the ſame time be pleaſed to give Mr. Oliphant, younger of Gafk, that money, who takes the trouble to go with a receit for it. Did not the King's Service require immediate difpatch, you fhould not have fuch a preffing demand from a near neighbour, who will always be glad to fhow how much he is,

MADAM,

Your moft humble

& moft obedient Servant.

PERTH, 24 *October*, 1745.

I beg, Madam, you'll excufe the not writing with my own hand, con-ftant occupation renders it almoft impoffible.

PERTH, 24*th* *Octr*, 1745.

Received for the King's Service, and in the Prince Regent's name, from Lady Methven, the fum of £200 Sterl: for which I am accountable to his Royal Highnefs.

CXLIX.

CHARLES STEWART TO THE DUKE OF ATHOLL.

MY LORD,

After coming here, I inquired for Clunie Macferfon and the reft of the officers your Grace expe&ed to have been here, but there is non cum up this length, but Captn. Fraifer and M^r. Stewart of Clunes, who have with them about forty-feven men, and only twenty of them airmed. There is an exprefs difpatched to Captain Menzies of Shian, and Clunie Macferfon, but whether they are att Amulrie or Taybridge I am uncertain. M^r. Brice afhures me that the water of Earn is not foordable; I am to wait here for your Grace's return, becaufe there may be fome danger in martching fo few men up to Dumblain, it being fo near the Caftle of Stirling.—I am, with great refpeᗊ,

Your Grace's moft obedient Servᵗ·

CHARLES STEWART.

CRIEFF, *Octʳ·* 24ᵗʰ, 1745.
    9 at night.

CL.

CLUNY MᶜPHERSON TO THE DUKE OF ATHOLL.

MAY IT PLEASE YOUR GRACE,

My men have been imployed in raifing the people of this Country, Glenlyon and Rannoch, all the while fince I com from Dunkeld; I was befides neceffitate to return to Badenoch wᵗ· a partie to carry on fome of my people yᵗ· ftayed behind: all thefe Jantings have much fatigued my men, however, the throng of them will be this night at Crief; the partie that went to Rannoch have not return'd yet. I am fo drain'd of Cafh that I was oblidg'd to borrow thirty pd: and fome od fhill: Sterg. from Shian to fubfift my men, and Shian tells me he is now quite ex-aufted, which oblidges me fend the bearer, Mʳ· MᶜPherfon of Breakachie to raife money from your Grace for our fubfiftance :—I had the honor to receive your Grace's orders this day, appointing Shian and me to march to Crief, which fhall be carefully obeyed by us both, tho' at the fame time we are oblidged to leave a few men to carry all before them.   I am, wᵗ· all due attachment and refpeᗊ,

MAY IT PLEASE YOUR GRACE,

Your Grace's most Affectionate and

most ob: faithfull fervᵗ·

KIRKTOWN OF WEEM,
    25ᵗʰ *Octʳ·* 1745.

E : MᶜPHERSON.

Pleafe excufe bad paper, bad write, &c., being in great hurrie.

CLI.

COLONEL KERR TO THE DUKE OF ATHOLL.

My Lord,

    As Lord George is not to return to this place, his Royal Highnefs fent me here in order to fecure the paffage here for your Grace's paffing, which fhall be done fo far as the fituation and the conveniences here will admite off.   His Highnefs recommends to your Grace to make all poffible haft, as it's inform'd that troops are affembling from all parts, in order to difpute the paffages betwixt Edin^{r.} and Newcaftle, fo that your Grace's marching (even faft marches) with the utmoft expedition is of the greateft importance, as it will conduce much to his Royal Highnefs's fervice ; and if the Cannon could be forwards, in order to place on the battaries, prepaird for fecureing the paffage which is of the utmoft importance, wou'd be of great fervice.   I am,

My Lord,

Your Grace's moft obed^{t.} humble Servt.

KEN : KERR.

Alloway, ye 26th Oct^{r.,} 1745.

    P : S :   It's hop'd that your Grace will let me know from time to time your Grace's motions, that Carriages may be ready on the other fide of the water, who waits for nothing but the hour of your Grace's arivel.

    Your Grace will pleafe direct to Coll : Kerr, at Elphifton.

CLII.

THE DUKE OF ATHOLL TO [COLONEL KERR.]

Sir,

    Your's, dated this day, I received at the Bridge of Ardoch in my way hither; my anfwer to his Royal Highnefs' preffing orders which you mention for my marching is, were it to gain the Univerfe, it is impoffible to make more difpatch than I do, as is evident to all the Gentlemen with em. I hope to be up time enough to morrow at Aloa, fo that the convoy may be able to pafs the river before night; therefore, according to promife, be fo good as to have boats, carriages, and every thing ready for marching forward; to which I can add nothing further here, but that I am.

<hr>

CLIII.

D. ROBERTSON OF DRUMACHINE TO THE DUKE OF ATHOLL.

MY LORD DUKE,

I rejoice to hear that your Grace is arrived in Scotland, in good health, which I wifh may long continue, for the benefit of your Prince and your Country.

I propofed to have fent Gourdy to wait of your Grace, as he cou'd have given more particular information with regard to the fituation of affairs in this Country, than can be contained in a Letter, but as he is not at hand, and that things feem to admit of no delay, I thought it neceffary to difpatch this Exprefs.

Before I had a dozen of men to command in this country, I found Strathardle, Strabrawn, and fome parts of Atholl, fo crowded w^t. deferters, that I found it impracticable for me either to confine them or fend them to the Army, as I had no prifons, much lefs troops either to guard or efcorte them. As foon as poffible, I indeavour'd to fecure the paffes upon Tay and Tumble, to cut off Intelligence between Invernefs and Stirling, and prevent defertion from the troops that came fouth after the

Prince march'd to England; but the deserters have some time ago found a passage acrofs Loch Tay, where our authority is not as yet establish'd. Upon making this discovery, I got 24 Ranoch men that undertook to do duty in the braes of their own Country, the Route taken by those deserters, and these Ranoch men have already given some proof of their fidelity, but they complain that the command is too weak, as deserters come often in such bodies as they cannot pretend to stop, nor do I know where to find Funds sufficient for the Expenses of preventing this fatal evil. It wou'd take a hundred men for the Braes of Ranoch, and between 3 and 400 more betwixt that and Perth, to guard the Passes, guard the Hanoverian Prisoners, and send deserters to the Army, and perhaps, it wou'd be found by experience that such a Battallion wou'd be usefully employed, provided it were commanded by tolerable Officers; but the missortune is that there are few well affected Gentlemen remaining in this Country, and I can stir very little, as my health has been dayly impairing since I had the mortification to part with your Grace.

Deserters come now to Atholl in such crowds as I am asham'd of; nor can I take any notice of them, my small posse being wholly employed in seenring those that propose to go farther north, who cannot be brought again to the Army without great loss of time and money, besides that the Arms they carry with them seldom return. As for our people I believe a few active Officers of each Battallion wou'd soon get them together and carry them to their colours; and then a proper command establish'd in Perthshire might go a great way to keep the Army entire, but, for that purpose I am afraid your Grace's presence wou'd be necessary.

As to private affairs, Kincairney says, he begg'd your Grace wou'd excuse him from accepting of the Factory, and when I asked Neil McGlashan why he did not begin to levy the rents at the proper time, he told me, he cou'd not act by himself, as he was only join'd in Commission with Kincairney; and I know nobody else in Atholl or the neighbourhood that is capable and wou'd be willing to execute the thing.

I have had no assistance from such Gentlemen of influence as I apply'd; Glenkilry offered me his for raising men, but I had no funds for them.

I hope your Grace will excufe fo long a letter, & believe that I am, w[t.] all Refpe&t,

MY LORD DUKE,

Your G.'s moft humble & obed[t.] Serv[t.]

BLAIR CASTLE, *Jan.* 11th 1746.

D. ROBERTSON.

CLIV.

LORD GEORGE MURRAY TO THE DUKE OF ATHOLL.

FALKIRK, 11th *Jan[r.]* 1746.

DEAR BROTHER,

I have juft now a line from Blarfeety, telling me of a great defer-tion amongft your people; I would gladly hope it is not fo bad as he calls it, but I think if the Officers were in their Duty it could not have hapned. I know of but one remedy that can be efe&tuall, and that is your immediat prefence at home; and, in the firft place, to fend off to us all the good men that are already gather'd. Thofe who have gone home without a fpecial licence or Furloff muft be exemplarly punifh'd, either in their Perfons or Effe&ts, or in both, for when our all depends, lenity would be folly. If we can always keep two Batalions of 500 each of the beft men it will be very well, & if you will leave it to me, tho' we may have more officers than the number, I will get them named fupernumer-ary, and they fhall have pay. A garifon of fifty men will be enough at Blair Caftle, & a hundred or 150 about your perfon will be enough till you find it proper to rejoin the Armie, but not to regiment them, only as Independent Companys always to be in the Country; good old men would ferve very well for this. I would have you take as few of the Officers as pofible alongft with you. Keynachan nor Blairfeety can not poffibly be fpar'd, but advife with them before you go; and for God's fake, fend the men off, if it were by dozens, as quick as you can after you get

S

to the country. If Rewards and Punifhments do not do, I know not
what will. By the laws of God and man you have both in your power &
in your Perfon. Docter Colvile, who is a man of Honour, can be of great
ufe to you, & will never advife but what is right. The above is my
Humble oppinion, & if you aprove of it put it in execution immediately.
I ever am,

Dᴿ· Brother,

Your moft Affect· Brother &
faithfull Humble Servant,
GEORGE MURRAY.

I fupofe you will take care to caufe lift your Rents in Falkland, &c.

CLV.

D. ROBERTSON TO JAMES ROBERTSON OF BLAIRFETTY, ESQ., MAJOR OF
LORD GEORGE MURRAY'S REGIMENT.

Dear Sir,
        I am difpatching this Exprefs in a great hurray for the Duke of
Atholl, elfe I had fent to your houfe to afk the goodwife's commands;
your family is all very well, only that fome of the children have the
Chinkcough. Many of your men are come home, and I am told the reft
are to follow foon. I was ordered by the Duke of Atholl to take up and
imprifon all deferters, but I might as well attempt to remove a mountain,
being left here without money, or men capable of being made Officers, I
myfelf being for the moft part confined to the houfe.
        I wifh to God the Duke of Atholl's beft Battallion, as foon as raifed,
had been left to form a Barrier from beyond the Braes of Ranoch to
Perth; it wou'd have faved the exorbitant charge of bringing back the

north country deferters, and the Prince might have marched much fooner and a third ftronger into England, which wou'd have had a good effect. Every man that knows the Highlanders might lay his accounts w^t their marching home after a fcuffle, and therefore I am furprized that none of you ever infifted upon taking all manner of precautions for keeping the Army together, without which, making an appearance may be compar'd to a flafh of powder, that vanifhes in an inftant, and fcarce leaves a veftige behind it.

I am far from mending in my health fince you left the country; I rode about as long as I cou'd, but fince Chriftmafs I have been but twice over this door. I am glad to hear that his R: H: and all his gentlemen are in good health and fpirits,—long may it continue fo. There is but little theft committed in this Country. The Laird of Strowan fwears he'll allow none of my men to quarter at Kenloch. There were 4 deferters of Lord Cromarty's men entertain'd by him at Cary fometime ago, and I was told yefterday that he fent a token to the Boatman at Kenloch to ferry them over; but the fellows were afterwards apprehended by the little command at Dalnacardich and fent to Perth. My complements to Kynachan and the reft of our friends. The Ladies and children at Kynachan are all very well, and fo are the reft of our friends in ye Country. I pray God to blefs both Prince & people, and am ever,

D^a. SIR,

Your affec^t Nephew & moſt humble Servt

D. ROBERTSON.

BLAIR CASTLE, *Jan:* 12th 1746.

I ofer my complements to Fafcaly: I fent for one of his men that return'd home, and ordered him to warn all his brethren in iniquity to make ready to march at a call; he told me they fhou'd be all ready. I expect fome of you home foon to carry your men back to your colours; had I a fufficient poffe and cafh, I might have faved you fome part of the trouble; perhaps, you'll hear more of this from the Duke of Atholl. Pray let me have your frefheft news; meantime, Adieu.

CLVI.

DUKE OF ATHOLL TO LORD GEORGE MURRAY.

DEAR BROTHER,

I received your's of yefterday's date from Falkirk, without a cover, from the Laird of Fafkeily, which I fent by valuable Dr. Collvill to the Prince, defiring he would let me know his intentions about the contents. His R. H: on the main approves of what you propofe ; Therefore, God willing, I fhall fet out accordingly for Perthfhire to-morrow, and will omitt nothing can be expected from fuch an Invalid as I am, who has hitherto fpared nothing could poffibly advance our Countries intereft, as well as the known rights and good of mankind in general. Pray, take care of our young Mafter's glory, as well as your own and the King's Service, which ought to be dear to all honeft men who are above felfifh views. I rejoice to fee you behave in fuch a manner as renders brave men dear to people of virtue and honour, which muft make you for ever efteemed by,

DEAR BROTHER,
Your moft affectionate Brother
and Humble Servant.

POLMAISE, 12 *January* 1746.

Till meeting, pray let me hear from time to time how all goes with you, particularly on every extraordinary occafion. Be affured I am no lefs concerned abfent than prefent, about the valuable fafety of all worthy friends and acquaintances.

Excufe me, Brother George, if not writing with my own hand; fince feeing you exceffive Rheumatick pains has rendered it almoft impoffible.

This is to be tranfmitted to you by Major Robertfon of Blairphety, who, with you and Kynachan, muft be anfwerable for the pay of Mr. Crooks and other officers, who have been too much neglected, which may be of bad confequence.

CLVII.

THE DUKE OF ATHOLL TO THE LAIRD OF MONZIE.

SIR,

As I can't conveniently have the pleafure of feeing you at your own houfe, fince it is neceffary that we fhould meet, Pray be fo kind as to come in a friendly manner to-morrow morning to Lord John Drum_ mond's houfe of Farntoun, which is in my way to Blair, where you may have the fatiffaction of meeting feveral wellwifhers and countrymen, who are no lefs yours than,

SIR,

Your moft obedient

Humble Servant,

CREIF, 14 *January,* 1746.

CLVIII.

LORD GEORGE MURRAY TO THE DUKE OF ATHOLL.

BANOCKBURN, 16th Jany. 1746.

DR. BROTHER,

I fhall be carefull of what you recommend to me by Dr. Colvile, to whom pleafe make my Compliments. We are quite afronted with the fcandalus difertion of your men; it was the takeing money inftead of the beft men, which is the occafion of all the evle; for good men once coming out would have been piqued in Honour, and not deferted us on the point of fighting the Enemy. I dar fay, I need not fay any thing to haften up the men; you know the vaft fervice it will be to the Caufe in gineral, and I wifh you would fend them off if it were but in twentys. We hear the Van of the Enemy came towards Falkirk this day, if they come a little farther forwards, we fhall certainly have a Batle. In the mean time, we have bad quarters, litle provifions, and flow advances made towards the Sege of Stirling Caftle.

I find the Officers of [your]¹ Batalion will not ferve under Col: Mercer, and his being in that command is given as one reafon of their defertion. If you give me leave I fhall fee to regulat that affair the beft way I can. I ever am,

DEAR BROTHER,
Your moft affecte· Brother,
and moft humble Servant,
GEORGE MURRAY.

CLIX.

COPY OF A LETTER FROM [OLIPHANT OF] GASK YOUNGER,
TO HIS MOTHER.

The Army march't from a field eaft of Banackburn, about twelve this day, for Falkirk, where the enemy lay encampt; after we had crofs'd the water Carron, and march't up the Hill fouthweft from Falkirk, we perceived the Enemy marching from their Camp to attack us, we march't up the Hill, and drew up in order of Battle, South and North; the Dragoons, to the number of three or four hunder, were oppofite to our right, where Lord George commanded, and was with him Mr. of Strathallan and Capⁿ· Harie. We are all perfectly well. We advanced, and the Dragouns advance likeways. The enemy keept up their fire till we were very near them, and we both fired, and immediatly they run for it; there was not above twenty or thirty killed and wounded, and not one of ours killed. They fay there was not above a thoufand foot of the enemy en-

¹ A word torn off with the seal.

as there is no force to hinder L^d. Lowdon from coming to relieve the prifoners, and feizing the canon, amunition, &c. at Perth, where, as I am told, there are but 50 men left.

From the above you'll eafily conceive the Duke cannot fend over his own men fo foon as was propof'd by 20 or 30 at a time, as they muft be firft employed in raifing the Brodalbaine men.

My L^d. Duke bids me offer his moft humble and affectionate fervice to you and your Dear Half, to whom I beg leave to offer my moft refpectful compliments. May Almighty God protect and defend our Dear Prince and his brave loyal army : may it always be victorious!

I have the honour to be, with great efteem and refpect,

WORTHY SIR,

Your, &c.

BLAIR CASTLE,
19th Jan^y· 1746.

CLXIV.

LORD STRATHALLAN TO THE DUKE OF ATHOLL:

MY LORD,

Tho' I doubt not but your Grace has got accounts of the victory his Royall Highnefs has got over the enemy near Falkirk, I fend you enclof'd a copy of a letter from Mr. Oliphant Gafk's fon,[1] which is the only fure nottice I have yet had of the action, if your Grace has had any later accts. with more particulars, I beg you will be fo good as let me know them. The letter is but juft come.—I beg your Grace will believe I am, with the utmoft efteem and regaird,

MY LORD,

Your Grace's moft ffaithfull and moft obedient

humble Servant,

STRATHALLAN.

[1] See No. CLIX.

P.S.—I would have fent the originall letter, being wrote in a hurry, is not very legiball to thofe that don't know the hand. I fhall be glad to hear of your Grace's being in good health.

CLXV.

LORD STRATHALLAN TO Dr. COLVILL.

Sir,

As there have been pay'd here betwixt two and three thoufand men for about ten weeks paft, befides a pair fhoes to each of them, charges of ropes to cannon fent weft, and the makeing intrenchments about the mouth of Perth, with other vaft charges, it is not to be fuppofed there is any money here. I doubted not but the Duke of Atholl would have brought money with him for raifeing and paying his men, and, if it fhould be otherways, I fee no other way for fupplying his Grace but by leveing the land tax, without lofs of time, in Atholl, &c. which, the collector fays, amounts to feven hunder pounds fterling. The collector was to fend a party this week for quartering for it, which fhall be done if his Grace is fatiffied it fhould be fo; and the only regular way is, that the cefs fhould be fent doun to the collector, who only can give rĕpts, and, immediatly after, the money will be remitted to his Grace, who will give rĕpts from time to time, as his Grace has neceffary occafion, and the money can be gote collected. I offer my moft humble compliments to the Duke of Atholl, and Gafk begs his may alfo be accepted.—I am,

Sir,

Your moft humb: Servt.

STRATHALLAN.

CLXVI.

SECRETARY MURRAY TO THE DUKE OF ATHOLL.

BANNOCKBURN, *Jan^r· y^e* 21st, 1746.

My Lord,

I had a letter laſt night from Mr. Colville, defireing £500 pound to enable your Grace to bring ſome people from Broadalbain, together with your own recruits. But, as it is thought abſolutely neceſſary to have up all the men poſſible in a few days, his Highneſs does not judge it proper to meddle with the Campbells att this time; but has, neverthe-leſs, ſent 300 pound, of which he defires you may be as ſpareing as poſſible, the caſh being very low, and no proſpe &c of getting more for ſome time.

It is impoſſible for me, by reaſon of the hurry I am in; to write ſo fully [as] I incline, but have mentioned ſeveral things to Mr. Warren; ſo ſhall only beg your Gr. may ſend up men as faſt as poſſible, and believe me to be, with the outmoſt refpe &c,

Your G^{rs}. moſt ob^t. and moſt hum^{ble}. Servt.

J^o. MURRAY.

CLXVII.

LORD GEORGE MURRAY TO THE DUKE OF ATHOLL

FALKIRK, 21st *Jan^y·* 1746.

Dear Brother,

You may think me to blame for not writeing more fully and fre-quently, but indeed I am much hurry'd. I again beg & intreat you may fend your men up to us as foon as poffible, were it but a hundred or two, for indeed we are quite afronted there being fo few left. I have the plea- fure to tell you that thefe few beheav'd admirably well, and the defifion of the batle was much owing to them; for, as they were juft behind the Macdonalds, where I was, after we had routed the dragouns, & that the Macdonalds went in fword in hand (which was not in my power to pre- vent) to deftroy them & fome Militia, the Atholl men with Shian's kept their line of Batle, always advancing in good order: I then put myfelf at their head, & advanced forwards & down the Hill, at the fame time Locheel's, Clunie's, & the Steuarts of Appine, who had gone down fword in hand amongft the Enemy's Infantry, upon finding themfelves outflankt by them, began to retreat, to join thofe who were at the top of the Hill; I had fent Col: Carr to that fide, who bringing up the Pikets that were in the referve to the left, Locheell and feveral others gathring together, ap- pear'd again above the Enemy, juft as I was advancing with the Atholl men, it was then the Enemy made off with fo much prefipitation and confufion.

You fhould let every Taxman in Atholl know that if they do not come out at your order, their Tacts are brok, befides diftroying all they have.

The Enemy have loft many Officers of diftinction: My Compliments to the Doctor, tell him that I have gott fuch a Cheft of Inftruments and two of Drugs, that he has not feen the like; they belonged to the Surgone Major.   Our people have got abundance of bagage.

I ever am,

DEAR B:

Your moft Faithfull Humble

Servant, & affec^{te.} Brother,

GEORGE MURRAY.

I fend you fuch account of the Batle as has occurr'd to me.

CLXVIII.

MERCER OF ALDIE TO THE DUKE OF ATHOLL.

MY LORD DUKE,

As your Grace defired me, I defired all your Grace's Fewers to meet me here to day, & intimat to them to come to your Grace and pay in their few Deutys; and alfo tolde them, that they who were able were to attend you to Hofting, Hunting and Warding, if able, and if not, to finde fuffitient willing able bodied men to ferve in their ftead at their charges: You'll fee few of them have mett me; however, I believe they will pay their few deutys, but I believe want refolution to do what they ought to do. Your Grace will be the only judge how to ufe them, and I am, moft affectionately,

Your Grace's obedient
humble Servant,

CROOK OF DEVAN, *Jan^y.* 22*^nd*, 1746.   RO. MERCER.

CLXIX.

SPALDING OF ASHINTILLY TO THE DUKE OF ATHOLL.

MY LORD DUKE,

I beg your Grace will be pleafed to receive a complent, &c. Ever fince I went to England I could not have a billet once in ten days, altho' unwell, as I informed your Grace while in Glafco, and I demanded a foreloof,[1] which, as Major Ratfon told me, I would have how foon we advanced the length of Stirling; when I came there I fent to the Major to know if I could have one, but received no anfwer untill Rob. Stewart the agitant[2] robed me of my pay, as I refufed to deliver it out of my hand. I

---

[1] Viz. a Furlough.   [2] Adjutant.

know [no] reafon for this, feeing I attended and did my duty while I had
a man under my command of my own; I may fay I had non after ther was
an oyʳ joined with me, for at any time I could not have a fervant altho'
oyⁿˢ had two who did no duty and were moftly my men.   My Lord
George defired me to march before yᵉ fmall number of my own remaining; Fafcalie defired me to march with Solrie, and Solrie defired me to
march in the rier with his Lieutenant: this difobliged me, but this your
Grace knew nowght of; my men was and is willing to follow me, and I
am willing to ferve the Prince; I am now, (as I got neither Liewtenant or
Enfient to affift me, which, with the advices they got, as yᵉ men tells me,
had [been] yᵉ occafion of their deferting, together with double duty,) refolved to place all officers myfelf, as I have relations of my own who will be
as obedient as any your Grace has; but I hope your Grace will fend me yᵉ
money that was taken out of my pocket, and an oyʳ weeks pay, feeing I
ftay'd and borrowed untill I got my expences in loan from fuch as came
along with me: It is conterary to yᵉ Prince's manifefto to refufe me a
commiffion, as I had one from yᵉ Ufurper, befides yᵉ men I brought along,
and is a thing your Grace would never have confented too, altho' I had
not got a letter, by his Highnefes orders from yᵉ Secretary, affureing me
of his favour.   I expeᴄt your Grace will honour me with an anfwer, and
am, with the greateft refpeᴄt,

My Lord Duke,
Your Grace's moft obedient and
obliged Ser.

Ashen. *Janʸ* 22, 1746.   DAN. SPALDING.

———————

CLXX.

LORD GEORGE MURRAY'S DAUGHTER TO THE DUKE OF ATHOLL.

My Lord,
    The inclof'd came here to-day from Papa, and at Mama's defire,

I give your Grace the trouble of a few lines, to enquire about your Grace's health. She has not been well for fome days, fo hopes to be excuf'd for not writing herfelf, and makes offer of her moft affect^e. compliments to your Grace, as I beg to do of my moft humble duty, and am, with the greateft refpe&,

MY LORD,

Your Grace's moft dutiful

and moft obedient Niece,

TULLIBARDIN, 22nd Jan^ry, 1746.   AMELIE MURRAY.

Mama has juft now received Do&er Colvill's letter; fhe defires her compliments to him, as I do.

CLXXI.

OLIPHANT OF GASK TO LORD NAIRNE.

MY LORD,

I expe&ed the badnefs of this day would have ftop'd your journey, and did not get out in time to wait of your Lo^P. I have a letter juft now from my wife, telling, L^d. Monzie was carryed up prifoner to Blair, and begging you would write to the Duke of Atholl in his favours, that he might not be detained long, as he has been in a very indifferent ftate of health for fome years paft. You'l alfo take the trouble to his Grace, defireing he would fend down a fure hand for one hunder and fifty pounds, which is all can be affoorded from this till the £700 land tax that's due in the Hylands can be made good. There was a lift of the debitors left with Coll. Robertfon or Glafcloon, and whatever is brought in here, by his Grace's fending a party to quarter on deficients, fhall be fent back to his Grace.—I am,

MY LORD,

Your Lop's moft affe&. humble Servant,

PERTH, Jany 23^d, 1746   LAU : OLIPHANT.

CLXXII.

ROBERTSON OF BLEATON TO ROBERTSON OF DRUMACHINE.

BLEATON, 23 *Janʳ·* 1746.

Honᴿᴰ. Sɪʀ,

I have intimate my Lord Duke's orders throw all the corners of this country, but, notwithſtanding of my endeavors to raiſe the men in ane amicable way, yet I find it will be impoſible to accompliſh it without a party, and the name of a party of the Boun Rannach men would do much to bring them to meaſhures; I have, therefore, ſent this bearer exprefs, defireing you will immediatly, without lofs of time, ſend eaſt to Kirkmichell 25 or 30 men and ane officer, ſuch as you ſhall think moſt proper, where I ſhall waite of and employ them agᵗ. the refractory, and for gathering up the whole arms can be found in the country.   I find it will be impoffible to raiſe a man out of every mark-land, becauſe there are ſeverall ten mark lands in this country that there are not 5 men living upon the ground, and ſome of theſe not ſufficient for carying arms, and where they are not they cannot be raiſed; however, I ſhall doe my uter-moſt to raiſe every ſufficient man for arms upon the grounds, but I am affraid it cannot be accompliſhed before the latter end of next week, even tho' the party were here already.

I understand that there is 3 qʳˢ Excife due in the pariſh of Kirkmichell, fo if ye pleaſe to ſend me a commiſion for uplifting the ſame, I ſhall doe it and make compt to you, to be applayed to his Royall Highneſs ufe as you think proper.   If ye have got any further particulars of the Batle, pray be fo good as let me heare them.—I am,

H. Sᴿ,

Your moſt obedient humble Servant,

DAVID ROBERTSON.

CLXXIII.

DUKE OF ATHOLL TO LORD GEORGE MURRAY'S DAUGHTER.

DEAR NIECE,

With extreme pleafure & fatiffaction I received a mighty well wrote letter from you, which could not but charm me with your endearing merit. I rejoice at being able to congratulate your Mother and you on the glorious fhare my Brother George has again had in the frefh victory which Providence has given the Prince Regent over his proud Hanoverian enemies. I am forry to find by your's that your Mother has been out of order fome days; but at the fame time glad to know from your meffenger that her indifpofition ended in being fafely delivered of a Daughter, on whofe birth I wifh all of you much joy. Pray give my Sifter my moft affectionate Service; and be affured you fhall ever find me with the utmoft regard & valuable efteem,

MY DEAR NIECE,
Your moft affectionate Uncle,
& humble Servant.

BLAIR CASTLE, 24 *January,* 1746.

Dear Child, I thank you kindly for enquiring about my health. Since comeing here I have been extremely troubled with my long Rheumatick pains, tho' cannot fay they are now greater than I have found them of late. Wherefore hopes you'll excufe the not writing with my own hand, fince fuch an uneafy fituation renders it hardly poffible, as the Bearer, Robert Stuart, who I fend to inquire further about my Lady George's health, can more fully inform you.

CLXXIV.

ROBERT STEUART OF BALLECHIN TO COL. ROBERTSON OF DRUMACHINE.

LAU . . . . CLUNEY, 24th *Janry.*, 1746.

DR. SIR,

I received your's this evening, and yefterday morning I came from Blair in order to meet with the Duke's property, as they appointed the day before, and none of them compeared, and I fee there's no doing with them without a party. I came this morning to Killichaffie; he promifed to come with his men to morrow morning; and I defign to carrie clean before me down Strathtay, and to go with the Strathtay-men down to Tullimet and the Bifhopry, and fo on thro' the reft of my diftrict. No body knows what it is to raife men but he that trys it; not fo much as one of the Gentlemen brought their men, but oblidged me to go myfelf to raife them; and I am, with my Compliments to your Lady and family,

SR.

Your moft humble Servant,

ROBERT STEUART.

CLXXV

THE DUKE OF ATHOLL TO GLENGARY.

SIR,

The great friendfhip was between your family and mine, with the long particular efteem and regard I had for your perfon, makes me lay hold of this occafion by Patrick Maclachen, who goes a purpofe, to let you know how forry I am for the lofs of your valuable fon, who was lately moſt unfortunately killed at Falkirk. The ſecond glorious victory which Providence has given His R. H. over the King's proud Hanoverian Enemies, being in a great meaſure owing to his and the undaunted bravery of your people, which now wants to be ſuſtained, for their honour as well as the good of our Country, by your preſence or one of your Children, makes me hope and intreat, ſince it's neceſſary for advancing the common cauſe, you would ſoon think of perſonally appearing to head and hearten them in vigorouſly aſſerting the rights and liberties of our King and Country.

Therefore, pray, on ſuch a critical juncture, let nothing poſſible depends on you be omitted can valuably contribute towards rendering all of us happy, which is earneſtly deſired and expected you will comply with, by an ever perfect well-wiſher, who muſt be glad of ſuch a worthy opportunity of ſhowing with what unalterable zeal he is,

SIR,
Your moſt affectionate
and moſt humble Servant.

BLAIR CASTLE, 25 *January,* 1746.

Pray give my moſt affectionate kind ſervice to your Lady, by whom I was moſt agreably received when the Prince was at your houſe. I hope you will excuſe the not writing with my own hand, as the bearer can tell you no leſs ſevere than continual Rheumatick pains render it almoſt impoſſible.

———————

CLXXVI.

WILLIAM D: OF ATHOLL, &c.
TO ROBERT GRAHAM OF FINTRY, ESQ^{R.}

PLEASE be ſo good as to deliver to the Bearer, John Murray, my Maſter of Horſe, the minute-book containing a regular Act: of ye Rent of my whole Eſtate, and your Intromiſſions therewith; as alſo, a Rental of my Eſtate, and a Liſt of the Rents due by my Tenants, and likewiſe any other papers in your Cuſtody, which you think may be of any uſe to me in uplifting my Rents.

This you'll pleaſe perform, as you would oblige.

Pray make my kind Compliments to your Lady, and when conveniently poſſible, let me ſee you.

Indorsed " Copy Letter to Fintry at Fowllis,
dated BLAIR, *25 January,* 1746."

CLXXVII.

LORD GEORGE MURRAY'S DAUGHTER TO THE DUKE OF ATHOLL.

MY LORD,

I have the honour of your Grace's Letter, and Mama and I are extreamly ſorry that your Grace is ſtill ſo much indiſpoſ'd with Rheumatick pains; we moſt ardently wiſh your Grace may ſoon get the better of that troubleſom diſtemper, and your health be quickly reiſtabliſh'd again.

Mama returns your Grace many thanks for your enquiring in ſo kind a manner about her health; ſhe has hitherto gone on very well in her recovery, as I hope ſhe will continue to do.

My little ſiſter is a fine lively child, and ſhe is to be named Katherine, after your Grace's mother. I would been ſure to have writ to your Grace on Thurſday morning, to [have] acquainted you of Mama's ſafe delivery,* but I was in a hurry, and did not incline to keep yᵉ bearer, with Papa's Letter, till I cou'd get time to do it, ſo begs you'll be ſo good as to forgive that omiſſion.

I had a Letter from Papa yeſterday, dated the 24ᵗʰ, and he was very well at Falkirk; Mama makes offer of her moſt affecᵗᵉ· compliments to

·your Grace, and pleafe accept of my moft humble duty, which, with our beft wifhes for health and happinefs to your Grace, is all from her who is, with the greateft regard and refpeſt,

MY LORD,

Your Grace's moft obedient
Dutiful Niece, and moft
humble Servant,
AMELIE MURRAY.

TULLIBARDIN, 26th *Jan^{ry}*, 1746.

CLXXVIII.

DONALD McLAREN, BALQUHIDDER, TO CAPT^{N.} JAMES STEWART
OF CLUNES.

D^{R.} SIR,

I was laft night in company with Captn. Allan Stewart, of Collonell John Roy Stewart's Regiment, by whom I underftand that he goes by the order of His Royal Highnefs, to raife the Earle of Murray's tennants in a day or two, which would be a proper tyme for you to fee us, as the one would be affifting to the other; fhall wifh you lofe as little tyme as poffible. How foon you come to the Kirktown of Balquidder I fhall expeſt to fee you. Meantyme I am fincerely,

D^{R.} SIR,

Your moft humble Servt.
DO:.M^cLAREN.

TOUCH, *Janr^{y.}* 26th, 1746.

P. S. After perufall of the above, deftroy fame.—Adiew.

CLXXIX.

LORD STRATHALLAN TO THE DUKE OF ATHOLL.

My [Lord]

I had the honour of a letter from His Royal Highnefs the Prince of Wales, dated the 24th curt., in which His Highnefs defires that the Garrifon here of Lord Lewes Gordon's men fhould be fent up, and that it fhould be replaced by Atholl men from your Grace. This is therefore defiring, that a hunder and fifty men may be fent as foon as maybe, with proper Officers. The reaffon I defire this number, tho' the Prince only alowed 100 to be in garifon, is, that they cannot be fupported with pay if we get not men to goe in partys thro' this fhire, and that of Fyfe, for leavieing both land tax and excife. It's certain 100 is to fmal a garifon for this place, in which is 16 piece of cannon, a great magazine, powder and ball, and about eighty prifoners, and a moft difaffected fet of villans, both in Town and Country. I hope your Grace will fend us of the heft meat, with arms and fufficient Officers, which will much oblige. I am with great truth and efteem,

My Lord,
Your Grace's moft faithfull
and moft obedient humble Servant,
Perth, *Jan*[y.] 27, 1746.   STRATHALLAN.

P. S. Gregor Murray is here with thirty men.

CLXXX.

LORD GEORGE MURRAY TO THE DUKE OF ATHOLL.

Falkirk, 27th *Jan*[r], 1746.

D[R.] Brother,

I am quite difpireted by your men's goeing off and deferting their coullers; for God fake make examples or we fhall be undone. This goes by Fincaftle, whoes men are all off; I hope he will be as expeditious as poffible.

We had a revew here this day and made a fine appearance; it was only thofe of our firft line that were at the laft batle.

The enemy fay they will be foon with us again. I ever am,

DEAR BROTHER,

Your moft affec[t.] Brother,

and ffaithfull Humble Servant,

GEORGE MURRAY.

P. S. Thefe are defiring Capitan Stewart to goe in all heaft to bring up his men.

GEORGE MURRAY.

CLXXXI.

THE DUKE OF ATHOLL TO LORD GEORGE MURRAY.

DEAR BRO[r.]

With extraordinary joy & pleafure I received yours of the 18[th,] giving a fhort Account of the frefh Victory which Providence has given the Prince over his proud Hanoverian Enemies, who have long fet themfelves up as violent inftruments to root out the known principles & Friends of true Honour, Honefty, & right reafon in the Brittifh Dominions. I congratulate his R. Highnefs & You, with all the brave Commanders & Souldiers of the Victorious Army on fuch a happy event; may the generous virtue of our young Mafter, with the unbiaf'd conduct of his well-meaning Followers, always deferve fuch fingular marks of Heaven's protection as we have hitherto experienced fince fuch ane indefatigable Regent landed in the enfient [ancient] patrimony of his Royal Familie.

Whilft writing what is above, I had from your pretty Daughter, (with accounts of her Mother's being fafely delivered of a Daughter, of which I

x

wifh you much joy,) your laft Letter, with a full account of the fecond glorious Victory his R: H: has obtained over the King's obftinately rehellions fubjects. I am likeways glad to hear from all hands the very confiderable part you have had in fuch a happy event, which I hope will be attended with many confequential bleffings; for promoting whereoff, you may be affured, I omitt nothing lies in my power can contribute towards advancing the publick Service. God knows what dilatory and impofing evafions one has to ftruggle with amongft a multitude of refractory people in thefe parts, but now hopes, tho' with unfpeakable difficulty, Fafkeily & Ballechin will at laft be able to bring up a confiderable recruit of men who have not as yet appeared, with the Deferters, who could not hitherto be fent feparately in fmall numbers. I beg you will prefent my moft dutifull refpects to his R: H: who I cannot wait on as I wifhed, having more than ever been terribly tormented with Rheumatick pains fince coming from Bannockburn, infomuch, that I have not been able to go out of my room, & hardly in a condition to rife off the chair I fit on. Pray communicate this to Mr· Secretary Murray, with my affectionate humble Service to him and his heroic young Lady. Let him know that I had the honour of his with £300 for the Prince's Service, for which I fend him here inclofed a Receipt; he may be affured it fhall be carefully employed in anfwering the end for which it was fent me, as every thing elfe here & elfewhere [that] belongs to me has, and fhall be employed, as far as poffible, for advancing our King and Country's Service; tho' I gave a factory to Gentlemen here for uplifting my fmall Rents in thefe parts before our march into England, yet they did not take any ftep or pains towards rendering me the leaft Service, but other people who have now undertaken the fame tafk, I hope, ere long, will fulfill what I expect from them to much better purpofe. I can add nothing further here, but God fend us foon a happy meeting, being for ever, with perfect Efteem & regard,

DEAR BROTHER,

Your moft affectionate

BLAIR CASTLE, 27 *January*, 1746.   & moft humble Servant.

This goes by our good friend Faſkeily,—Ballechin has got a handſome Gun for the Prince which was found with ſome others [that] our unnatural Brother James was at the pains to get hid in a Coal-house at Dunkeld. I almoſt forgot to tell you that our good friend D^r. Colvill thanks you for your remembrance of him and what regards the Cheſt of Inſtruments & medicines, for which he returns you his hearty Service.

CLXXXII.

DUKE OF ATHOLL TO SECRETARY MURRAY.

Sir,

As I am prodigiouſly diſtreſſed with long Rheumatick pains, which renders me almoſt unfitt for applying to any buſineſs, I hope you will be ſo good as to excuſe my not writing a particular return to yours. You have here encloſed a Receit for the £300 ſent by Colonel Warren, to which I can add no more than what my Brother George will communicate to you, except my moſt dutiful refpeƈts to his R. H: and affeƈtionate kind ſervice to your Dear Lady, being with true refpeƈt intirely,

Sir,

Your moſt humble

& moſt obedient Servant.

Blair Castle, 27 *January* 1746.

Received from the Right Honourable M^r. Secretary Murray the ſum of £300 Sterling, for ſubſiſting Recruits and others of his R. H.'s Troops in theſe parts, for which I am to be accountable.

CLXXXIII.

DUKE OF ATHOLL TO THE VISCOUNT OF STRATHALLAN.

My Lord,

I had the honour of your Lop's. of yefterday's date, demanding from hence 100 men or more to be in Garrifon with you, inftead of thofe you have from Lord Lewis Gordon's Battalion, who are called up to the army; which was likewife the Prince's orders to me before I came from Bannockburn. There is great difficulty in raifing men here. It has not been hitherto poffible to fend you any number as intended, but hopes in a few days to fend your Lop. 100 effective men till more can be got ready, which fhall be done with the utmoft expedition. My thirty years abfence has in a great meafure occafioned the lofs of former principles of honour and loyalty which formerly rendered the people of this country eftimable. Col: Warren went yefterday from hence to wait of your Lop. Pray let him know what you think proper to inform me of relating to publick affairs, that we may in concert do all lies in our power for advancing the King's Service by keeping the Country in fafe and peaceable order. The torment of long Rheumatick pains difables me fetting vigoroufly about any thing, fince hardly able to ftir out of my chair, Therefore begs you'll forgive the not writing with my own hand, no body being with more per-fect Efteem,

My Lord,
Your Lordfhip's
moft Humble &
moft Obedient Servant.

Blair Castle, 28 *January* 1746.

Pray, my Lord, give my affectionate Service to my Confin the good Vifcountefs of Strathallan, not forgetting our worthy friends the Laird of Gafk and his Lady, who is alfo much to be honoured for her motherly virtues. I hope the two Ladies' Sons, Caſtor and Pollux, were well when their Fathers heard laſt from the army.

CLXXXIV.

ROBERTSON OF STROWAN TO Mr. THOs. BLAIR IN ATHOLL.

SIR,

I had the honour of a Letter from God knows who, and the Lord knows how, but it pretends to have authority to take up the feſs due upon my Lands ; however, for anſwer, I tell the Gentleman that my purſs has ever been open at the King's command, and ever will be, but at pre-ſent I am difficulted for mony to ſupport the King's affairs, recommended to me by the beſt authority. I am alſo in great trouble for the murder commited on the perſon of my nephew, Coll. Macdonell, at Falkirk. His Enemys are too plain to doubt of the authors of the murder, which will ſurely be taken notice of by the Higheſt and Loweſt of the Nation. The Gentleman's growing worth made him envyd by Beggers and hated by Traytors, which I never was, but ſtill am in the nicety of my duty to the King and all his ſubjeᛑts,

while

ALᴿ ROBERTSON of Strowan.

Jan. 28*ᵗʰ*, 1746.

His Grace the Duke of Atholl can tell you how I am affeᛑed to mony ; and pray tell his Grace, of all his Family I ſuſpeᛑ him moſt of worth.

I hope his Grace will pity my condition.

(*Endorsed.*)—Letter with unworthy insinuations from the Laird of Strowan Robertson to Mr. Blair of Glasclune, dated Carie 28, Recᵈ Blair 29 Janʳʸ 1746.

CLXXXV.

SIR,

I Received yours Saturday laſt, and as for anſwer pleaſe know that it was Impoſible for me to anſuer yᵉ contents in ſuch a ſuden, conſidering one will not draw Equallie with one another. You may believe they are conſealing yᵉ armes, which will be found after a ſearch. Some of yᵉ deſertors would have a ſecond fie, altho' not a one fourtnight from home. Laſt, I do think there may be two companys raiſed within yᵉ Barronys of Aſhintilly and Balmachruchie, without hurting yᵉ Laboring much when joined with ſuch as are in yᵉ Prince his ſervice already; and by haveing yᵉ aſſiſtance of a partie I will double yᵉ number I can poſiblie have willingly, and it is impoſſible for me to preveal with one of them to quarter on one an ayʳ, altho' they have yᵉ Inclination. I would, therefore, The Duke of Atholl would be pleaſed to order a partie for this Country, which with yᵉ greateſt ſubmiſſion I humblie beg would be rouled by me, which I think will find armes, men, and money. I compted for all the money I received laſt, and acknowledged yᵉ ſame to my Colonell; but I am afrighted every one did not ſo. The Miniſter poſſeſſes a fourt of Donnie. I think it a pitie he ſhould be Exeemed, conſidering yᵉ great oppoſition he makes, and yᵉ corſes he pronounces. Your anſuer is expeⱷed, and am,

SIR,

Your obedient and very faithfull ſer.

DAN. SPALDING.

ASHINTILLIE, 28ᵗʰ, 1746.

P.S.—Excuſe paper.

CLXXXVI.

ROBERTSON OF BLEATON TO Dr. COLVILLE.

SIR,

I had a letter from Drumachine, fabath laft, Defireing me to march the firft and readyeft of the men of this country this Day, and that he had fent for a party of the Brae of Rannoch men to bring up the reft, upon which I conveened betwixt 40 and 50 of them, and was come this length this day on purpofe to be at Blair w^t them to-morrow morning.

But Major Rattray has juft now brought me a verball commiffion from the Duke not to come forward with a fmall part of them, but to ftay and bring up the whole, altho' it fhould take three or four days longer. I thought fitt to obey the Major's orders, as I would wifh to bring up the heall in a body, but have run this Exprefs to tell you that it is Impoffible for me, or any perfon elfe, to near do the thing without a party. Therefore I hope ye will fhow this to his Grace, that he may Immediatly order a partie here, and I fhall give a very good account of the country in a few days. I would certainly come forward with what I had ready, had I not got the above new commiffion by Major Rattray; and if ye think it amifs that I have ftayed, I fhall, upon receipt of your anfuer, march up what is ready.

There is one thing ye will mind in your anfwer, which is Defireing I fhould bring up the late Afhintylie men w^t the reft, for if they be referred to his worthlefs baftard fon, his mother and he will fpoill the whole afair by pretending to have the only power of them by which they are takeing bribes or compliments to pafs fome of them, which I do not like. I wait your anfwer and the party, and am,

SIR, w^t Efteem,

Your moft humble Servt,

DAVID ROBERTSON.

KIRKMICHAILL, 28th Jany 1746.

P.S.—If there be not a party of Rannoch men at hand, you may advife to fend a few of the country men, for I am hopful that the name of a party may do the thing.

CLXXXVII.

MERCER OF ALDIE TO THE DUKE OF ATHOLL.

MEIKLEOUR, *Jan^{ry}* 29th, 1746.

MY LORD DUKE,

I arrived here laft night, when I found my family all very well, and have fent this to know if your Grace has any command for me, and when you intend your men fhould march fouth. I expected to have heard from my Lord George when at Aldie, in cafe there was likely to have been any other engagement; but I reackon the Hanoverians have got enough for fome time, at leaft till they are reinforfed. · My wife and family offer their moft humble fervice to your Grace; and I am, moft affectionatly,

Your Grace's
Moft obedient and
moft humble Servant,
RO. MERCER.

CLXXXVIII.

DUKE OF ATHOLL TO CAPT THOMAS FERGUSON OF BALEYEUKAN, AND CAPT^N JAMES ROBERTSON OF KILICHANGIE.

January 31st, 1746.

GENTLEMEN,

I have feen fome of your Letters to Colonel Robertfon, and am extremely furprifed any of you fhould be the leaft refractory or dilatory in going to join our Prince, from whom I had the honour of a Letter this day, ordering me, without lofs of time, to fend up all the men ought to go out from this Country. In obedience to his Royal Highnefs' commands, I have fent off all the men that were ready; and laft night I defired Colonel Robertfon to order you, after delivering the prifoners at Dunkeld, to march dire&ly to the Army with your men, tho' you fhould have but thirty of them. I here again repeat thefe my orders, which, if readily obeyed as neceffarily required, you may eafily overtake Fafkeily & Ballechin, and go with them to the Camp of our brave Countrymen. I therefore expe&t your immediate compliance as you are friends to honour and honefty, and as you expe&t to be efteemed or regarded by [&c.]

CLXXXIX.

SPALDING OF GLENKILRIE TO DR. GEORGE COLVILLE.

GLENKILRIE, 31st Jan^r, 1746.

D^{R.} SIR,

I hade the pleafhure of 2 or 3 letters from you lately by the Duke of Atholl's orders about the raifing of the Strathardle men to go to Perth. Bleaton would have been at Blair Caftle fome days ago w^{t.} a part of the men, hade not the firft orders been Contermanded by a Mefage from his Grace, p^{r.} Major Rattray of Corb :—Your laft letter onley came to my hands this day about 11 o'Clock, where Bleaton & fome oy^{r.} Gentlemen and I was convining the men to be fent forward to Perth ; & I hope we fhall fend forward this night the number his Grace appoints, & the reft as foon as poffible, either voluntarly or by party [as] they can be raifed ; and I hope the moft part will be got raifed voluntarly, fo that a fmall party, with what we fhall joine to them, will ferve to raife the Refra&tory.

fo at this Juncture nothing in my pour fhall be awanting to ferve 'his Grace, and the good Caufe he is engadged in. As to what you mentioned in one of your former letters w^t. refpect to my affifting Daniell Spalding, a fon of Afhintillies, & John Spalding, a fon of Whitfield's, in raifing the men, I have given affiftance, and fhall continue to do; but as to Daniell Spalding, and his accomplice's behaviour and conduct in reafing the men, reather retards than forwards the matter, of which his Grace will foon be informed. There are feveral cuntry gentlemen that have agreed to go along with the men, which I think would be heft for keeping the men out, but if any of them does not incline to go, his Grace fhall be acquanted, that he may appoint oy^r. Officers in there place.

As to my going to Perth, I never beared a word of till this day: I muft confult both my health and capacity to manage fuch ane affaire, being ane old man; but fo foon as I fee all the men here out, I fhall waite of his Grace at Blair Caftle. I have thoughts to fend my fon to Perth after the men, tho' he be but young, yet his prefence there may be of ufe to keep the men I am moft concerned with together. Pleafe fhow this to his Grace, untill I have the honoure of feeing him.—I am,

D^R. S^R.

Your moft faithful and affectionat
humble Servant,
AN: SPALDING.

———

CXC.

ROBERTSON OF BLEATON TO THE DUKE OF ATHOLL.

My Lord Duke,

The bearer, Robert Stewart, came to me yefterday w^t. your Grace's orders about marching the men of this Country direɛtly for Perth. I likeways received a Letter from Doɛtor Colvill w^t the fame direɛtions, and that I would fett out w^t them this day; but as (upon your Grace's verball commifion by Major Rattray, not to come up w^t any part of the men till the whole were ready) I had difperced thofe I had ready, till there would be a party fent to bring up the whole; it will be impoffible for me to geather them fo as to march this day, but, God willing, I fhall fett out to-morrow. But I wifh there had been a party fent before I left the country; however, I fhall make ufe of what I have already rifen, by way of partie, on the reft of the country, till I make out 100; and fo foon as I fett out, fhall fend an exaɛt lift of thofe that marches w^t me, that your Grace may know how to fend up the difficients when the partie comes. There is three or four Gentilemen in this country that are ready to joyu us by my perfuafion; and I wifh that any vaccancie among their own countrymen were keept for them, rather than beftowed on ftrangers like George Scott, as your Grace has ordered, as it would be the beft way to keep out the men to have their own country Gentilemen w^t them.

I hinted in my letters to Drumachine and the Doɛtor, that Afhintullie's naturall fon, if he had any power given him, would fpoill the raifeing of his father's men, for his mother and he takes compliments from fome, and others are not willing to follow him, as I moft really fay he is but a worthlefs drunken fellow; and as far as his advife will go, will not allow any to march w^t me untill he be ready, which will not be on heaft; he is the only man gives me difturbance, and had it not been for him, I had had a 100 ready ere now; your Grace may do in this as ye fee proper, I take the freedome to fubfcribe, w^t veneration and efteem,

Your Grace's moft humble and moft
obedient Servant,
DAVID ROBERTSON.

BLEATOWN, 31st Jan^y, 1746.

CXCI.

Hon^{D.} Sir,

I had yours of the 30 laſt this afternoon; I went to Strathardle on Wedneſday, and came to Blairgowrie laſt night, w^{t.} the men who went for Perth this day, before I left that place: you have the liſt incloſed. You'll cauſe the partie that goes for that country make diligent ſearch for arms, I am informed there is upwards of a hundred ſtand of arms in that place; there was not above three muſkets and ſix ſwords amongſt thoſe that went for Perth. Let them be ſpared no further than the liſt agrees w^{t.} the merk-lands; they are a ſtubborn pack and deſerves no mercy; there's plenty of men in the country, but will not draw without a party of ſtrangers, which I belive will do. I cannot ſay any thing concerning our Dunkeld company, as haveing only come to town this afternoon, but will ſee you, God willing, on Wedneſday. I hear Captain M'Kewan is to beat up on Tueſday, and as he has got the Straithbran men out of Capt· Stewart's company, I ſuppoſe he will be alowed to keep none of the Dunkeld men in his:—I intend to be buſie amongſt them to-morrow.

My Father and all here offer their humble duty to you.

I am,

Hon^{D.} Sir,

Your faithfull and obedient Ser^{rt.}

GEO. SCOTT.

Dunkeld, 1 *Feby*. 1746.

We hear there are a great number of carts comes this day to Perth Arms, Amunition, Money, &c.

CXCII.

C. STEUART OF BALLECHIN TO Dr. COLVILLE.

BALLECHIN, 1ᵐᵒ *Feb.* 1746.

SIR,

    This evening, after my Sone's goeing off with what men he gott, I'm informed that he came but litle fpeed in his Grace's Barony of Tullimet, and I'm fory I did not know fo much of the ftory before he went off, who I'm confedent was faithfull and true in fo far as he cou'd be informed about them; but I'm affraid fuch as were recommended to inform him (he being an intire ftranger to them) has been very unfair in not letting him know a fair ftate of what men were poffeffors there. My informer tells me he was not acquainted, nor ever brought in his fight the beft men, and made him believe there were few or no men fit for the fervice in all Tullimet, which made my Son very uneafie; and I'm informed there are a parcell of pretty fellows there, &c. which is a fhame, and Mr Low, &c. were much to blame. I'm much vexed about this, it being entrufted to my fon, who I'm perfwaded, tho' he gott but few men, yet took no finiftruous or unfair ways. This brings me on to what he told of a great many of them, their producing Receipts for money paid for men they fhoud have fent out. This, indeed, is a hard cafe; but I think it my duty to offer to his Grace my humble opinion as to this point, which is, in fhort, to allow fuch of the Tennants as paid money what his Grace thinks fitt; for, if things goe right, as I hope by God's affiftance they will, his Grace, or any other from whom thefe Receipts are, will never mifs it, and if otherways, as God forbid, no matter of the allowance. So if his Grace thinks this propofal right, as I'm informed, there might be raifed feverall pretty fellows, which 'tis a pity to keep att home, providing proper perfons be employed that knows the men: they were fo cunning, that I'm certainly informed of fome old men they brought to my Son, who had young fturdie fellows to their fones; but let my Son know nothing of it, I hope you'll not make ufe of my name to none but his Grace, whofe, as ever formerly,

I am, and
Your moft humble and obed^{t.} Servt.
CHARLES STEUART.

CXCIII.

MR. JA: SCOT TO DR. COLVILLE.

DUNKELD, 1st *Feb^{ry}* 1746.

HON: SIR,

This ferves to acquaint you that the Prifoners that were at Logyreat came here yefterday, and are all lodg'd in our Caftle, and the Gentlemen, Sergeants, and Corporals, are fent there this day; they went off at Coll: Warren's fight a little after mid-day.   My Son is not yet return'd; but a Strathardle man, now here, tells me Bleaton and his men were to be this night at Blair-Gowrie, and Geordie along with them, but could not tell what number he had got.   I'm forry to hear from Captain Buchanan, that my Lord Duke continues ill of his Rheumatifm, and pray God fend him a fpeedy recovery.   The Captn. offers his Complements to you, as all here do.—I am, with all fincerity and regard,

DEAR DOCTOR,
Your moft faithful Servant,
JA: SCOT.

Feb. 1st, 1746.

2^d about 10.

Before this comes to your hand, I hope you'll have a real return to yours I was honoured with about 3 this morning; Captn. M'Ewan was here juft now, and propofes to be a piece on his road this night, with 120

Grantully and Strathbran men, and expects a good many more this week; we have yet had no acot^{s:} of George. This comes by Fintry's fervant.

CXCIV.

ROBERTSON OF BLEATON TO Dr. COLVILL.

SIR,

I fend you inclofed, by Mr. Scott, a lift of all the men that has marched w^{t.} me from our country to Perth; and altho' there is not the number defired, viz. a houndred, yet I believe I may fay there are more than any of your Atholl Gentrie raifed without any fort of a partie. I tryed to make the men I firft raifed ferve for a party to raife as many as would compleate the number ye defired, but it would not do. It moft be ftrangers that will make out the thing, fo I hope ye will fend a partie to bring up the reft effeireing to the merk-lands in each ground; for altho' I was oblidged, to pleafe them, (or I had gote none at all) to give a kind of avideamus, (which they took as a protection,) that fo many of them had fent out a man out of fuch a ground, ye are to give orders to the officer of the partie not to notice my lines further than they agree to my inclofed lift, and to the merk-lands in each Gentilman's ground. I have likeways fent you a lift of all thofe that have men in the Campe, fo far as I can remember, when I left them. I wait the Duke of Atholl's further orders at Perth, by the bearer, as ye defired, and am, w^{t.} efteem,

SIR,

Your moft humble Servt.
DAVID ROBERTSON.

BLAIRGOWRIE, 1^{ft} *February,* 1746.

P.S.—The protections I left in the country will only conftruct *pro tanto.* I expect fome to overtake me this day, that will make out 50, being only 41 men w^{t.} me juft now.

2. John Mckenzie and Alexʳ· Ayſone, for Glenbeg.
4. John Grant and Alexʳ· Mckenzie, from Dallhangan.
6. Lachlan McIntoſh and John Ferguſone, from the ground of Dalmungie.
7. William Robertſon, from the Cams.
8. William McIntoſh, from ground of Runavey.
9. John Lyon, from the ground of Bruchdarg.
10. William Lyon, from the ground of Cray.
11. Archbald Grant, from Binzian beg.
12. Thomas Douglaſs, from Kerrow.
14. Thomas Rattray & Peeter Ferguſon, from eaſtr Bleatown; the Difficients in that ground lys upon Da: & Thomas Fleemings.
13. Thomas Scott, from Dirnanain.
14. Andrew Small, from Dalreach.
16. Duncan Scott and Charles Frazer, from Inverchroſkie.
17. Ja McDougall, from the ground of Cullalonie.
19. John Pettrie and John Doulich, from Stronamuck.
20. Alexʳ· Doulich, from Lair.
22. John Campbell and John Ferguſone, from Blackcraig.
24. Patrick Stewart and Alexʳ· Fleeming, from Dalrilzian.
25. Malcomb Reid, from the ground of Straloch.
26. Da: Pantons, from the ground of Weſter Callie.
27. Walter Kinnaſon, from the ſix merk Land in Minnach.
28. John McLauchlan, from the Barron's ground.
30. John Ferguſon & William Leſley, from the ground of Whitefeild.
31. Finlay McDougall, from Eaſter Downie.
33. James Falconer & Thomas Melvill, from Weſter Bleatown.
34. Angus McDonald, from Thomas Rattray there.
35. Robert Ferguſone, from the ground of Aſhintully.

37. Alex^r· McNab & Alex^r· Robertſon, from Soilrzies ground.
39. James Rattray & John Spalding, from Ennoch.
40. Duncan McGrigor, from Ja: Robertſon in Ballachragan.
41. William Robſone, from Jo: Small in Kirkmichaell.

CXCV.

COLONEL WARREN TO THE DUKE OF ATHOLL.

PERTH, 1st *Feb^y*. 1746.

MY LORD DUKE,

I am greatly concerned to tell you that I find, by a friend of mine juſt come from the Quarters, that his Royal Highneſs intends a retreat, and that things are ordered to carry of all our implem^ts to the Hills. The ennemy is greatly increaſed, and the young man[1] come from London; our battery was diſmounted, and a ſixteen and 2 twelve braſs pounders demoliſhed. I ſhall tell your Grace all ye particulars at meeting, wch ſhall be, pleaſe God, in 2 or 3 days.

I am in vaſt hurry, ſeeing, on my arrival here, orders iſſued for 200 horſes to be ready to-morrow. I ſhall part this night for Drummond Caſtle, to confer wth the Duke of Perth, who's come there to order what may be neceſſary.

I ſhall proceed to-morrow to ye Quarters, and thence back to your Grace; Heaven grant I may bring you an account of a complete victory! tho' I doubt our ſtanding the chance of one!

This goes by an expreſs Mr. Blair and Gourdy ſend you. They have not been able to raiſe a farthing; and, as the Glenammon men are come back, I have left this moment a written order with Coll. Creighton to march to-morrow for the Quarters wth his eighty men; wch Lord Strathallan has agreed to, tho' he apprehends Captn. Anderſon's 40 men, and

[1] The Duke of Cumberland.

z

yᵉ Glenammon 30 men are an infufficient garrifon, but I have affured him there will be 50 Strath Earl[1] men here to-morrow night.

I hope your Grace will excufe the hurry I am in, having fo many things to mind, nor paper or time to write your Grace as I would wifh.

I entreat what I here mention may ever be kept fecret, as the affair was in that manner difclofed to me ; fo pray cancell this when read, and let no foul know the contents ; I could almoft even except my worthy friend Docʳ. Colvill, mais il eft prudᵗ. & fage, but it muft not appear even on his countenance.

It is needlefs, I hope, to tell your Grace how much and how gratefully

I am Yours.

P.S.—I faw the Serjeants leave Dunkeld under a guard before I came away.

CXCVI.

DUKE OF ATHOLL TO BORLUM & BALNESPIG.

[BLAIR, 1st *February, 1746.*]

GENTLEMEN,

Having had the Honour to accompany his R. Highnefs the Prince Regent in his Marches thro' Scotland & England, fince his arrival at Stirling, I came here to raife our Mafter's Men in thefe parts, for the fervice of our King & Countrey, where violent Rumatick pains has long detained me. I had the pleafure to meet at Down 250 fine Fellows of your loyal Clan in their way to join the Prince : fhurly there muft be near double that number ftill at home, for I think there were 600 of your name affembled in the year 1715.

I hope, Gentilmen, there's no need of arguments to animate you to

---
[1] Strathardle.

join heartily in a Caufe where the Rights of our Prince, and all that's dear to men of honour, are at ftake: You know the late Borlum commanded your Clan, Anno 1715, and it would give much pleafeur to every honeft Scotfman, & me, to fee his Son & Heir active in the juft Caufe for which he was a fufferer. You know that Strou's company was always reckoned the Grave Vrattich, or ftouteft company of the McIntofhes; fince Stron himfelf is out of the Kingdom, you may be fhure it would give great fatiffaction to men of true honour in feeing Balnefpig bravely afferting our King & Country's Caufe at the head of that Company.

I had yeafterday the honour of a Letter from his Royal Highnefs ordering me, without lofs of time, to fend up all the men I could poffibly rife, for his Highnefs expects foon another vifit from the Enemy; you may believe I will ufe the utmoft Diligence in obeying fuch a meffage; and from the character I have of you both, I perfwade myfelf you will likewife ufe the utmoft expedition in haftning up with all the affiftance you can, for enabling the Prince not only effectually, but alfo with eafe, to give the finifhing ftrock to his juft and glorious Undertaking.

I herewith fend you a printed account of the late Victory with which kind Providence has favoured our young Mafter; having nothing further to add, but you fhall allway find me, with perfect efteme & regaird,

GENTILMEN,

CXCVII.

DUKE OF ATHOLL TO[1] [COLONEL MERCER.]

SIR,

Since our parting at Bannockburn, yours of the 29th is the third Letter which I had the pleafure to receive from you. The two former, as I imagined you were every day to pafs the Forth, were not anfwer'd,

[1] This letter has no address, but it seems to be an answer to No. CLXXXVII.

not knowing well where you was to be found.   After giving me an agreable account of our young Mafter's late victory at Falkirk, where it feems
you luckily happened to be prefent, on which happy event I heartily congratulate you, with all the brave Gentlemen who had a fhare in gaining
that battel, I am very glad you found your Lady & family well at meeting; pray give my affectionate fervice to her & all the pretty Children.
I hope Mr. Laurence is now grown ftrong, & able for a lefs fatigueing
Campaign than our laft.   I am forry to tell you, that, inftead of Three or
four Regiments which this Country fhould have fet out, there is now
hardly men enough togither to make up one.   As for me, did my health
permit, I would quit the Country intirely, and leave it to the Prince to
fend who he pleafes to ufe them with the utmoft rigour fuch fingularly
refractory & chicaneing people deferve; which I find good ufage cannot
do effectually, to the fhame & difgrace of fuch mean fpirited fucceffors, as
the former brave people in Atholl have now fhown themfelves in a moft
pitiful manner, to their own difhonour, befides the fcandalous detriment
which the neceffary Service of their King & Country fuffers, by having
no valuable regard for pofterity, or their own lafting happinefs; from
which you may eafily fee of how inconfiderable ufe you, or any of us can
be at prefent amongft them, when expecting effectually to raife men as
formerly, they having loft the ancient unanimous Sentiments of our brave
honeft Countrymen.

Imagine, then, if I am not forry fince difabled from laying any thing
more to the purpofe about many of fuch men of all ranks as ought to
be a confiderable fupport & honour to me, as well as to our long diftreffed & much abufed nation.   Therefore 'am forced thus to conclude,
being, with perfect Efteem,

DEAR SIR,

Your moft affectionate Cufin,

And moft Humble Servant.

BLAIR CASTLE, 1 *February*, 1746.

Your Meffenger has not been long detained, and is paid his Journey.
I am very glad to hear that my Lord Nairn's hand is much better than it

was, which ere long may enable him to take the field again. Some days ago Major Rattray told me that you and he might be able to make up together near a Regiment in the parts where you live, fince he was fure of getting at leaft 100, if not more than 200 men for his fhare, which, if foon done, might do much honour to both of you.

———

CXCVIII.

THOMAS BLAIR OF GLASCLUNE AND CHARLES STEWART OF GOURDIE TO THE DUKE OF ATHOLL.

My Lord,

Agreeable to your Grace's inftru&ions we fet out for Blairangon, with 30 Glenamond men very indifferently arm'd, but inftead of meeting with any of your Grace's Vaffals or Tenants, we found the country quite deferted, and except Solfgraith not one appeared; we underftood by him and fuch others as we cou'd confide in, that feverals had withdrawn them-felves on purpofe to raife the country, and bring what troops they cou'd find on the coaft upon us, which made us retreat after fix at night as prudently as we cou'd. We brought off twelve oxen belonging to one of the greateft offenders, which wait your Grace's orders here, and about four pound in money. Since we came here it's thought proper to employ the party as part of the garrifon of this place, which your Grace will underftand by Mr. Warren's Letter, who is juft now going for Crieff; and though that were not the cafe, we begg leave to think, we cannot effe&ually promote your Grace's intreft at Falkland, or any where elfe, under a party of 150 men, which will require fome time to fpare that number from this place; meantime we wait your Grace's further inftru&ions here, and are, with the profoundeft refpe&,

My Lord,

Your Grace's moft obedient humble Serv^{ts},

THO. BLAIR.

CHARLES STEWART.

Perth, 1ſt Febrʸ 1746.

CXCIX.

ALEXANDER McGILVRAY, COLONEL OF THE McINTOSHES,
TO CO^L ROBERTSON OF DRUMACHINE.

DEAR SIR,

I'm juft now come here from Stirling in purfuit of feveral deferters from our Corps, who I'm affured have made their efcape by the bridge of Kynachan, which might be very well prevented had there been a proper guard apointed there.   The defertion is now become fo general, that all endeavours muft be ufed to prevent it, oy'wife it muft be of fatall confequence, fo that if many of them are not brought back and made Examples of, I'm afraid our army will in a fhort time be too thin.   I hope you'l reprefent this to the Duke of Atholl, that a ftop in fome meafure be put to this growing Evil.   Delnakairdach and the bridge of Kynachan fhoud at any rate be taken care of.   I doubt not but you'l ferioufly con-fider of this, & believe me to be,

D^{R.} SIR,

Your moft obedient faithfull
humble Servant,
ALEX^{R.} McGILLVRAY.

COISHAVILE, 2 ffeb^y 1746.

Permitt the bearer, Duncan Campbell, to pafs to Blair of Atholl un-molefted.

ALEX^{R.} McGILLVRAY.

To all concerned.

CC.

ADAM FERGUSSON MINISTER OF MOULINE[1] TO COL ROBERTSON
OF DRUMACHINE.

SIR,

I had Information from two different Hands, about four or five weeks fince, that a party was to be fent to my Houfe, from Blair or Logierate, to fearch or riffle at large; the Informers could not diftinctly affure which or if both. I would not allow myfelf to beleev the laft; and had nothing to object to the narroweft fearch. Nor could I have excepted to the forfeing of Horfes, Arms, Horfe furniture, or things of that fort, as being a fufpected perfon. But nothing happened till yefternight, about eight a'clock, that a party of a fergeant and eleven or twelve men, who firft called themfelves Brae Athol men, but afterwards acknowledged they were Camerons, came from Blair Athol, where they have been for two or three Dayes before; alleadgeing a written order for violence againft my perfon and effects. And indeed they exercifed it upon both. They did not indeed fhow any order, and I cannot beleev they had any fuch one as they executed. They plundered and carried off my filver watch, all the monney I had (q̃ch was but litle) fome of the moft valueable of my wife's filks and other cloaths, all the belt and fineft of our Table Linnen, Bed Linnen, and Body Linnen, of all which we were very well provided. We have not had Time yet to draw out a Note of the particulars; only in generall my Wife fayes, They have carried off to the Value of between thirty and fourty pounds fterline. If it is poffible they have had, (I dont fay orders) but even allowance of any Generall Officer for this behaviour, I have nothing to fay, and will not complain. And if they had not, I hope it will not be impracticable to order and inforce reftitution of the moft valueable effects: and this I prefume will be the eafier effectuated, that they have I am told returned to Blair. If they had con-

___

[1] The father of Dr. Adam Fergufson, author of the Hiftory of the Roman Republic, &c.

tented themfelves with what Cheefes, Beef, Honney, Ale and Whifky, they confumed and carried off; or even with Body Linnens, Shoes, Stockens, it might have been thought tolerable, but to go the Length they did fhowed an over rapacious difpofition, and is what I am well convinced Lochiell would as litle allow or approve of as any man alive. I am much of Opinion That no Prote&ion would have availed anything with people in their way. But as they have begun violence not only againft my effe&s, but perfon, I beleev I muft applay, and fhall be obliged to you for a pafs to travell out of the countrey, to where I may be more fafe, till the prefent troubles be at an end. It is like if I am out of the way my Wife and children may meet with fome Indulgence upon the Score of her Friends, and that they will look more after her fafety, Whatever happen, I hope and have hitherto felt, That God who in his wife and good providence fees meet to meafure out to me fome fhare of Sufferrings, will enable me to bear them with chriftian patience and refignation.

I beg you make my compliments acceptable to Mrs. Robertfon, whom I heartly wifh well. My wife, who goes to make her moan to the Duke of Athol and you, will deliver her own to your Ladye. I am, with fincere Eftcem and Affe&ion,

SIR,

Your moft humble Servant,

MOULINE, *Feb^y* 3, 1746. ADAM FERGUSSON.

P. O. There was upwards of ten ells uncutt cambrick, and feveral other Things not named, carried of in ye plunder.

CCI.

LORD GEORGE MURRAY TO THE DUKE OF ATHOLL.

DEAR BROTHER,

It is very dificult to offer advice at fuch a jun&ure;—by fome fatall miftake a very precipitat retreat was made from Stirling, which incourages our Enemys, and difpirits our friends. I goe with a colom by the foot of the mountins northward, and his Royal Highnefs goes by Dalnacardoch. Gladly would I have had a ftand made in Atholl, and offered to do it with two thoufand men. I own, in your cafe, I think if you have two or three hundred men of your own, you might ftay at Blair Caftle till a very great body of the Enemy, (which I fupofe would not be in healt,) were in your neighbourhood; and without cannon nothing could hurt you. The roads near Dunkeld, and the pafs of Gillycrancky and fome other partes could be fo demolifhed in a few honres that cannon could not pafs for fevrall days;—at worft you could make your retreat the hill way to Ruthven, and join your friend without danger, fupofe the enemy were very near you. This, I think, would be honourable for you, and of ufe to the fervice; but it is with great fubmiffion I offer my opinion. I take my batalion with me; you will have Lord Nairn's, and as many of your other men as you can. I ever am,

DEAR BROTHER,

Your moft affect. Brother,

& faithfull humble Servant,

GEORGE MURRAY.

Indorsed, "Letter from Lord George Murray dated Perth, & Rec^d by Glasclune at Blair, 4th Feby. 1746."

CCII.

MR. SCOT TO MR. WILLIAM FLEMYNG.

Feby 4th [1746.]

DEAR SIR,

Laft night I had yours amidft a great throng of very unwelcome guefts; our houfe was then like a beehive, as it is now. My heart is like to break, but grieved for none fo much as my dear mafter the Duke, whom God Almighty fupport and protect. I gave Johnie Fence's Mafter

2 A

as ufual, my kind refpects to the D^{r.} and tell him I only got his of Feb. 1st at fix laft night, but had no time to write. I believe the horfes were fent off in time, and I fuppofe the groom carried w^t him your faddle. I bid the carrier take only 1 peck or 2 of falt. I paid Mrs. Murray her £12, who gave the Duke a thoufand bleffings, and was to write a letter of thanks in French with her own hand. I have paid about £4 to fervants, for q^{ch} I fold malt. I hope to be foon in a condition to give up my accounts, tho I'm much afraid of feeing our old neighbour this very night, of whom I expect little friendfhip. The Duke's houfe and ftables were throng laft night, as was all our town. You and all with you have a large fhare in my good wifhes, and may God direct and pre-ferve you all. Adieu.

I juft now hear there's a young lafs of our place kill'd accidentally by a Highlandman's gun.—Pray deftroy this line.

CCIII.

LORD GEORGE MURRAY TO THE DUKE OF ATHOLL.

Coupar [Angus,] *5th Feb^{r.}* 1746,
early in the morning.

Dear Brother,

I'm forry to let you know that there is great defertion amongft your men; had fome examples been made at home it might have been prevented. I fhall be glad to hear from you, which you may do by fending thro Brea of Marr to Aberdeen or Strathbogie. I wifh we had made a ftand near Crieff, for I fcarfe think the enemy would have atempted any thing this winter had we done fo. I always am,

Dear Brother,
Your moft affect. Brother,
and your moft humble Servant,
GEORGE MURRAY.

CCIV.

JAMES ROBERTSON OF KILLICHANGIE TO THE DUKE OF ATHOLL.

MAY IT PLEASE YOUR GRACE,

In obedience to your Grace's orders I have gather'd together ſome men, but, hearing of this retreat, they are all diſperſed, and the will of man will not carrie them out without ſtrangers to raiſe them, and till further orders from your Grace I can doe nothing, ſo I hope your Grace will acquaint me how to behave.   I am,

Your Grace's moſt obedient

and humble Servant,

KILLICHANGIE, 5*th February,* 1746.   JA: ROBERTSON.

CCV.

THE EARL OF KILMARNOCK TO THE DUKE OF ATHOLL.

MY LORD DUKE,

At my arrival here, I found the order your Grace was ſo good as to ſhew me at Blair for your people to riſe and attend you.   Robertſon, who is landlord here, and well-affected both to your Grace and his Royal Highneſs, is ſending about the copys, but aſſures me that they will not have near the Effect that the Croſſtarie[1] itſelf will, and that the Croſſtarie muſt come from your Grace's own hands.   I beg leave, therefore, to join with Monſr· le Marquis D'Aiguille to appriſe your Grace of this, and to pray your Grace to ſend the Croſſtaries to the different proper places without a moment's delay, as the approach of the Enemy admits not of the leaſt.   That there may be none of our ſide, I have taken the liberty

---

[1] *Crosstarie,* or *Croishtarich,* the fire-cross, or signal of war, sent round for raising the country.—See Jamieson's Dictionary.

to acquaint your Grace of this the moment it comes to my ears, as in thofe cafes there muft be no difference between night and day.

I beg your Grace will believe me with the moft profound Refpeét,

MY LORD DUKE,

Your Grace's moft

DALNACARLOCH,[1] *Feby 5th*, 1746,   obedient humble Servant,
   7 in the evening.   **KILMARNOCK.**

CCVI.

THE DUKE OF ATHOLL TO THE EARL OF KILMARNOCK
AT DALNACARDICH.[2]

MILOR,

Je n'ay pas eu l'honneur de votre Lettre datté d'hier au foir jufqu'à une heure aprés midy, celluy qu'il la rendue à difparu fur le Champ, ainffy il a falut trouver un autre perfonne pour Envoyer à votre hote Mr. Robiffon avec la Crofftarré, qui part d'ycy a trois heures; ainffy dans le cas, n'etant que fept milles d'ycy, je compte quelle fera rendue ce foir, felon les ordres prefentes qu'il a receu, pour que cela puiffe produire tout l'effet qu'on attend d'une tel ordre. Le Prince n'arive que ce foir ycy.

Je vous prie Milor de vouloir bien mes refpeéteux compliment à fon Excelence Monfeur le Marquis D'Aiguilles Embaffadeur de Roy tres Chretien auprés de notre jeune Maitre. J'efpere que Milor aura la bonté d'excufer fi je ne pas pû ecrire de main, etant Milor, avec les Refpeétes le plus parfait,

MILOR,

Votre tres obeiffant et humble
ferviteur.

AU CHATEAU DE BLAIR,
ce 6 Fevrier vieux stil, 1746.

[1] Dalnacardoch.

[2] This anfwer to the preceding Letter of Lord Kilmarnock seems to have been written by a French secretary.

CCVII.

MR. SCOT TO DR. COLVILLE.

DUNKELD, 6*th* *Feb^y.* 1746.

H: S^R,

Yours of the 2^d with one inclofed to M^r. Guthrie, came to my hand about 2 a clock, and 'tis now 3; I had difficulty to get one that would undertake to run Exprefs, but have now got it fent off, and gave the ten fhill: with one to bear the lad's charge till his return, when I promifed to reward him to his pleafure.

I have it from a good hand that a good body of the Enemy lay laft night at Crief, and were thought would take the weft road. Cumberland was laft night at Perth, and he, Duke James,[1] &c., were to dine this day at Huntingtowre. There has been feveral platoons heard, q^ch 'tis faid were made as the forces were pitching their tents on the moor near Nairne this day. God make all well.

ADIEU.

Pay the Exprefs.

Thursday afternoon.

CCVIII.

PATRICK ROBERTSON OF TRINAFOUR TO MUNGO MURRAY.

DALNACARDOCH, 6*th* *February* 1746.

SIR,

I received yours with the Crofftarie, and have fent it to my next

---

[1] Of Atholl, younger brother of the Marquis of Tullibardine.

nightebours, according to the ufull way.   I never met with fuch a confufion as I have this day met with.—I am,

Sir,

Your moſt humble Servᵗ·

PAT: ROBERTSONE.

CCIX

CHARLES MᶜGLASHAN TO NEILL MᶜGLASHAN, WRITER AT CLUNE.

Dᴿ Uncle,

This moment I received an order from my Lord Duke defiring me to
fend all the meall I have in readyneſs to Blair Caſtle, and to meall all the
corn I have threſhcn, and fend it likeways ; pleafe know that I have litle
or no meall fucken, and the litle meall I get from them, it does not maintain my ffamily ; wherefore you'll be fo good as tell His Grace I have
not a Boll by me of what meall multure I got this winter.   I have a
few Bolls oats by me, which I intended for feed, and if I fhould meall
them, my miller affures me that a Boll of them would not give three firlots
meall.   If you can prevail with His Grace not to infiſt on my making
meall of them, it will be confiderablie in my way ; if oyʳways, rather than
his Grace fhould be in the leaſt difoblidged, I fhall, on recept of your's,
meall them, whatever lofs I may fuſtain thereby.   I offer my complyments
to my Aunt, & am

Dᴿ Uncle,

Your affectʳ Nephew & Servᵗ·

CHA. MACKGLASHAN.

Inver, 6ᵗʰ *Febʸ* 1746.

I hade all their oats befpoke for feed, & was to get £7 the Boll, fo that
you'll eafily know my lofs.   I beg you'll write me wᵗout lofs of time if I
be to mcall them.

CCX.

THE LAIRD OF GLENGARY TO THE DUKE OF ATHOLL.

My Lord,

 I had the honour & pleaſure of your Grace's moſt kind affe&c&tionat Letter of condolence. I ſhould be the moſt ignorant creatur on Earth, were I not moſt ſenſible of your Grace's Repeated favors don me, and as for the friendſhip the Family off Atholl honoured my poor ffamily with, and the Remarkable good offices they have offten don it, is manifeſtly knowen even to the meaneſt of my ffamily; and I aſſur your Grace (as far as I know myſelfe) my greateſt ambition is to merite the continuance of that friendſhip wᵗ· the ffamily of Athole, has ſo long ſubſiſted twixt our ffamilys; and that if in my power to ſerve your Grace or ffamily off Athole, your Grace think me ſo far worthy as honour me by Laying your commands upon me. The Youth your Grace deſires will ſoon have the honour of waiting of you; he is happy if your Grace honours him by taking him under your patronage. I am ſincerely wᵗ the greateſt Eſteem, Zeale, due Reguaird, and ſtrongeſt attachment,

My Lord,

Your Grace's moſt faithfull, moſt obedient,

and moſt oblidged humble ſervant,

JOHN M'DONELL OFF GLENGARY.

Fort Augustus, *Febʸ·* 7ᵗʰ, 1746.

CCXI.

DUKE OF ATHOLL TO GRIGOR MURRAY.

Sir,

 Herewith is ſent a general Croſſtarie order for raiſing all the able bodied men in Glenamond: this order is executing through all Atholl with yᵉ outmoſt exactneſs & Expedition; and providing you have a mind to efface yᵉ three different times you have forſook me, you'll, without loſs of time, come here, & bring at leaſt fifty good men with you. I am well aſſured there are arms for that number in the Country, ſo that I ſhall reckon you greatly wanting in your Duty if you do not bring them all arm'd.

The Bearer being choſe out as a truſty expeditious perſon, this is earneſtly requiring of you to get inſtantly all the Accounts & Intelligence you can of yᵉ Enemies motions, & without loſs of time ſend it me by this Expreſs, which ſhall ever be remembered to your advantage.

After you have made uſe of yᵉ Croſſtarie order, if you can find a truſty Perſon, pray ſend it directly to Donald Macklairane, Drover in Balquhidder, as an anſwer from me to what Jaˢ· Steuart of Clunes heard of his hearty Diſpoſition towards our preſent honeſt Concerns from Tuch, dated Janʸ· 26ᵗʰ, it will alſo be a valuable ſervice rendered our King & Country at this critical Juncture. If you intend to oblige me in earneſt, you will no leſs faithfully than diligently execute what is here required, & juſtly expected of you by one who ſhall ever accordingly be found in the moſt agreeable manner,

SIR,
Your affectionate humble Servant.

BLAIR, 7ᵗʰ *February*, 1746.

CCXII.

WILLIAM DUKE OF ATHOLL, &ᴄᴀ.
UNDER THE PRINCE REGENT,
COMMANDER-IN-CHIEF OF HIS MAJESTIE'S FORCES,

To all the worthy Gentlemen and people in Atholl, Health and Happineſs.—Theſe many years paſt, the unnatural ſecond ſon of my family, from a narrow felfifh difpofition has let himfelf be feduced both as to publick and private concerns, in fo much that he has moft unfairly become the creature of long declared enemies to our King and Country, whereby they make ufe of him as a tool, not only to ruin all valuable fentiments amongft many in this Country, but alfo he endeavours to root out the known principles of honour and honefty, which formerly appeared amongft thofe who were friends and wellwifhers in thefe parts, to both truth and right reafon. Such a pitiful Brother of mine amongft rebellious Britons, headed by ungenerous foreigners, is now barefacedly coming with fome of our fubtle neighbours to force me out of my juft inheritance, that you may be unworthily made fubmit to their no lefs artful than dangerous defigns, which makes me pofitively require all of you, from the age of fixteen to that of fixty, who regard true fafety, and whatever is dear to the pofterity of undaunted forefathers, without lofeing a minute to fet every where about the Crofftarie, that all of you may be fufficiently warned to come here diredly and join me for the defence of your houfes, wifes, children, and Country. All which Fafkeily and Blairphety have trufted to your care and mine, by generoufly going North with my bold Brother George, who with our young mafter the Prince, goes foon to bring up a powerful army from thence. In the meantime, with equal Courage will not brave Atholl men here ftand by me to fave yourfelves from ignominious devaftation and ruin. Let us then with firm unanimity maintain ourfelves againft all affaults may be made on us by the ufurpation of fome impofing weftern neighbours, and perjured people who ftick at nothing to obtain their ambitious proud ends. Therefore, once more I fay, without delay on fight of this my earneft requeft and order, forthwith come and join me here, as before God and man you will be anfwerable. For the doing of which, this fhall be to you and all concerned, a fufficient warrand: Given under my hand and feal, at Blair Caftle the eighth day of Feb^ry 1746.

(Indorsed,)—" M. of Tullibardine's Declaration, Feby 8, 1746."

2 B

CCXIII.

THE DUKE OF ATHOLL TO GLENKILRIE & STRALOCH.

As the Campbells are come into Atholl, to the number of between 4 and 500, and that all the people of the Country are refolved to go along with me, that they may be quickly repulfed, This is pofitively ordering and requiring you, according to what was demanded two or three days ago by the Croſſtarie, to fend out all the fencible men, with the beſt arms in the Country, and join us to-morrow by mid-day, or at fartheſt, two or three hours after at Mulinarn, as you regard every thing ought to be dear to us, which muſt forever make me have a fingular eſteem for you, who am,

GENTLEMEN,
In a moſt affectionate manner,
Your moſt humble Servant.

BLAIR CASTLE, *8th February* 1746.

To Colonel Spaldane of Glenkilrie, or any other Commanding Officer of the Strath- ardale men who is in the Country.

Since writing what is above, I was prodigiouſly furprized at Mr. Rt. Stuart, Adju^t of Lord George Murray's Reg^t's arrival, who was fent with a party of the Appin men to raife the Country; but it moſt furprifingly appears that none amongſt you have thought fit to obey the moſt pofitive preffing orders that could be fent. Therefore, without ufing further rigour, This is requiring you, on your allegiance and the duties due from you to King & Country, that you forthwith fend to join us, at leaſt the 200 men who have received both his R. H. arms and pay ; which at your peril you are immediately to perform, without waiting for any other advertiſement, as you will be anſwerable both before God and man.

To Mr· Spaldane of Glenkilrie, and
Mr· Robertson of Straloch, with all the
other honest people in Strathardle.

CCXIV.

DUKE OF ATHOLL TO INNERSLANY, CROFTMORE, AND DALVOREST.

As the Campbells are come into Atholl, and that all the people of the Country are reſolved to go along with me, that they may be quickly re-pulſed, This is poſitively ordering and requiring you, according to what was demanded of you two or three days ago by the Croſſtarie, to ſend out all the fenſible men, with the beſt arms in the country, and join us to-morrow by mid-day, or at fartheſt two or three hours after at Blair, as you regard every thing ought to be dear to us ; which will make me forever have a ſingular eſteem for you, who am, Gentlemen, in as moſt affeƈtion-ate manner,

Your humble Servant.

CCXV.

DUKE OF ATHOLL TO KYNACHINE.

Sir,

This is to acquaint you that the Campbells, to the number of 4 or 500, are come into Dunkeld, which has ſo animated and raiſed the ſpirits of all our people who have heard of it, that they want at any rate to go and drive them out of the Country. As I hope your men are fully ready before this time, this is earneftly entreating you will not lofe a minute's time in bringing them here, or rather down through the Glen of Fincaftle, as the fhorteft way to meet me; who, as foon as I can get any fmall number gathered in thefe parts to go down as far as Moulinarn, this night in my way to meet thefe particularly ancient enemies of this Country. Therefore without lofs of time, pray make all the difpatch imaginable to join us, as you are inclined to render a confiderable fervice to your King and Country, as well as fingularly oblige,

SIR,

Your moft affectionate humble Servant.

BLAIR CASTLE, 8 *February* 1746.

After perufal, pray let this Letter be fent to Shian, without a minute's lofs of time, who I hope will have the fame regard for the contents as if it were particularly addrelfed to him ; and if his fhorteft way to meet us, in going down the Country be by Strathtay and Logiereat, I hope he will take that road as early as poffible to-morrow morning, and that with the utmoft expedition.

CCXVI.

DUKE OF ATHOLL TO KYNACHIN.

SIR,

This morning I fent you an exprefs, telling that as the Campbells are come into the Country, It was believed that our people would incline to drive them out of the Country, but befides fome other reafons for not going down the Country to meet them, it feems our people are from being fo hearty as was imagined. Therefore at this time it is thought convenient that we fhould give up fuch a worthy undertaking, which makes it unneceffary for you to think of coming down the Country, as was defired by what I writ you, fome hours ago, fince every body thinks it beft you fhould come directly here as foon as poffible, without lofeing a minute's time. Be fo good as to advertife Shian of this laft refolution with no lefs expedition, than poffibly you may have done the former. So hoping to fee you with all your men, and their beft arms againft to-morrow night, I need add nothing further here, but that I am entirely,

SIR,
Your moft affectionate,
Humble Servant.

BLAIR CASTLE, *8th February* 1746.

CCXVII.

STEWART OF KINACHINE TO COL ROBERTSON.

DEAR SIR,

This moment I have an Exprefs from the Duke telling of 4 or 500 Campbells being come to Dunkeld, & wants that I fhould, with all the men I can raife, meet his Grace this night att Moulin, or thereabouts; and defires me to fend to Shian to meet him likewife with his men. Shian is here, & not a man about him, having only ordered them to meet him fomewhere about Bonrannoch to-morrow. I have as few about me, having fent them to the moft tardy corners to recruit. It is now near 3 o'clock afternoon, and have neither officer nor fergeant about me, being all employed elfewhere, fo cannot, tho' I fhoud do my beft, raife, when it is dark, a dozen men; meantime Fincaftle, Ballechan, Kinnaird, Garth, & Balnacree, have their companies in the way from this to Dunkeld. I hourly expect Bohaly from Blair, who went laft night from this for orders.

I do not know what to do; if I go without men, (as I certainly muſt, if I ſhould go immediately,) then the recruiting of this country will be ruined; if I ſhould not go, but ſet about the raiſing the men, I may be reflected on. What ſhall I do? I expect to have my mind relieved when Bohaly comes, and am, in heaſt,

DEAR SIR,

Yours moſt affectionately,

DAVID STEWART.

KYNNACHAN, 3 o'clock,
Saturday afternoon.

As I judge from his Grace's letter that he may be gone before this can reach Blair, I have given you this trouble, which I intreat you 'll notify.

(*Indorsed*,)—" Letter from Kynachin to Col. Robertson,
dated Kynachin & received Blair 8 February, 1745."

CCXVIII.

MR. GRIGOR MURRAY TO MR. MUNGO MURRAY.

S.R.

I received his Grace's orders and immediately ſent ane expreſs for the officer, who lives four miles diſtance from this place, and on his way ſpoke to ſo many of the tennents, for we durſt not make uſe of the Croſſ-tarie for alarming the enemie, for there is above two hundred of them laying at Crieff and Monzie, and a trup of horſe at Drummond Caſtle, beſides a partie of the Camphols, who comes up the King's road every day for information. By all the accounts, the enemey who marched to Perth on Thurſday laſt is reckend to be twelve thouſand men, foot and horſe, and I hade ſertain information this evening that a part of the enimie was to be at Dunkeld this night.

As our frindes marched through this countray on Munday and Tuefday laſt, they both plundered and carried of a great many horfes, and feverals of them is not returned as yet.

If the officer and I can gett the men raifed, we ſhall come ſtraight to Blair or wherever his Grace ſhall be. —I am,

S^{R.}

Your moſt humble & obedient Servant,

GRI: MURRAY.

CURYHUN, *Febry.* 8th, 1746.

P.S.—We are every night within four miles of the enemie in the Waſter Glen, and the Eaſter Glen within two miles of them; you may confider what fituation we are in. I fent off the exprefs to Ballquidder juſt as the berar went from this, be four a Clock in the morning.

CCXIX.

STEWART OF KYNACHIN TO THE DUKE OF ATHOLL.

MY LORD,

Att three o'clock this afternoon, I had the honour of a letter from your Grace, the anfwer whereof I fent to Coll. Robertfon. I ſhall, with the utmoſt expedition, raife the men of Bonrannoch, Bohefpich, and all of both fides of this water. I have fent an exprefs this night to forward Glenlyon's fon with the folks of Fortingall; I'm hopefull, once to-morrow, to have them together, fo as to march Monday. Shian is here, and fets out very early for Rannoch, where he expects to have all his men to meet him, from whence he has a very ſbort cut to Badenoch, if he is

allowed to go that way. I fhall fend to-morrow for further orders, and
am, with much efteem and refpeﬅ,

My Lord,

Your Grace's moft obed^t Ser^t,

to ferve you,

DAVID STEWART.

Saturday, near 8 o'clock att night.

(*Indorsed,*)—" Letter from Kynachin, dated 8,
received Blair 9, February, 1746.

———

CCXX.

THOMAS BLAIR OF GLASCLUNE TO THE DUKE OF ATHOLL.

My Lord,

In the execution of the orders with which your Grace was pleafed
to honour me, I have hitherto fucceeded tollerably, tho' in a manner
very contrary to my inclination, being often obligded to ufe the greateft
extremeties, vizt. that of burning, which nothing but the Prince's intreft
and your Grace's commands cou'd allow me to infliﬅ, but, as the rule of
my conduﬅ is to promote the one and obey the other, (which are infe-
parable,) I affure your Grace nothing confiftent with a man of honour
fhall be left undone to the beft of my judgement.

Yefterday I fent up, under Gourdie's command, upwards of forty men,
(fome of whom, I underftand, are fince deferted,) and this day I have
above fixty more, who are juft now in this place and the nighbourhood,
but, when on their march for Blair, were ordered back by Mr. Warren;
they are but an unarm'd mob, and fit to proceed on nothing till better
provided, but in that cafe I can venture my perfonallity with them, (and

the Prince's caufe much more valuable,) any where to behave nighbour-like.

This quarter I judged fafeft for men in their condition, and refolve to keep them here till your Grace's further inftructions, which I prefume to expect, and at fame time have the honour to fubfcribe myfelf,

My Lord,

Your Grace's

Moft obedient and humble Serv.

LOGIEREAT, 8ᵗʰ *Febrʸ* 1746.

THO: BLAIR.

P.S.—The party belonging to the Appin Regmᵗ was this day recalled, fo if I'm to continue this courfe, another party of ftrangers is abfolutely neceffary to obtemperate my orders in their full extent.

CCXXI.

COLONEL ROBERTSON TO DR. COLVILL.

Sir,

I hear this moment that it is thought neceffary to cut the Bridge of Tumble; I fhould think proper to deftroy the paffage boat at Kenloch-Rannoch alfo, for there a great number of foot may pafs in one night, and if they fhould take the route of Dalinfpidal, which they may do in abfo-lute fafety, and is but a few hours march from Kenloch-Rannach, they might prove very troublefome.

I'll be wᵗ you foon; meantime you may communicate this.

I am,

Sir,

Your moft humble Serᵗ

LUDE, *Febʸ* 9ᵗʰ, 1746, *wᵗ in a quarter of two afternoon.*

D. ROBERTSON.

If Shian is in Rannoch, he wou'd be proper perfon to execute this.

2 c

CCXXII.

COLONEL ROBERTSON TO DR. COLVILL.

SIR,

This moment, upon my arrival here, I found a fervant from Kille-chaffy, who tells me, he faw the enemy to the number of 500 foot and 12 dragoons, on this fide Tay-bridge, about 12 o'clock this day. He fays, there came an exprefs to acquaint the Prince of this, but, not being abfolutely fure of that exprefs, I thought it proper to fend Killechaffy's man, w^t whom you may converfe.—I am,

SIR,

Your moft obed^t,

D. ROBERTSON.

LUDE, *Feby. 9th, 1746,*
20 minutes after 7 at night.

Give the bearer 6 pence.

CCXXIII.

STEWART OF KYNACHIN TO LORD NAIRN.

MY LORD,

Bohaly told me that my Lord Duke had fome arms keeping for our men here, which I entreat you 'll fend by the bearer without lofs of time.   Ld Glenurchy came, attended by a few gentlemen, thro' night to Taymouth; we hear fome hundreds of the Campbells are betwixt Teyin-drom and Killin.   Shian is gone from hence this morning to Rannoch, where he expects to meet all can be got of his men.   I have expreffes and parties every where raifing the men in this country, and hope to have them ready to march fometime to-morrow; and, fince there can be neither meat nor quarters att Blair, I think we fhould be allowed to march ftreight from this to Dalnacardoch, being a full day's journey in our way.—Pray write me fully when and what way the Prince marches, that we may exactly take our meafures accordingly. If there is any intelligence from Ld George or the enemy, pray acquaint me, who am, with utmoft efteem and fincerity,

Your Lo^p's moft obed^t·
humble Ser^t,

KYNNACHAN *Sunday,* 11 *o'clock.*   DAVID STEWART.

(*Indorsed.*)—" Letter from Kynachin to Lord Nairn, dated Kynachan, and rec^d· Blair, 9 February 1746.

CCXXIV.

STEWART OF KYNACHAN TO DR COLVILL.

SIR,

Juft now I'm favoured with yours & another from Coll. Sulivan, ordering me with all our men hereabouts to repair to Blair to-morrow morning; I am hourly expecting Killiehaffy & Garth with their men, & Glenlyon's fon with his; I and all about me have been, & are as throng recruiting as poffible. I expect to have them affembled att Bohefpick fometime to-morrow morning, which place being within 4 miles of Dalnacardoch, by going the high road, & being at leaft 15 miles by going about by Blair, befides being obliged to wade the waters, will, I hope, induce his Grace to allow us to take the fhort road fo as to meet his Grace at Dalnacardoch. We hear that fome of the Dragoons, & about 5 or 600 Campbells, are come this forenoon to Appin Dull. I have fent Expreffes three different ways, to know their numbers and their motions, that they may not catch us napping here. I am defired by M^r· O'Sulivan to get the Bridge over this Water [1] cut down, but as I have neither mafon nor tools, all the men I have would not do it in a week, which, pray, 'tell, that if it is thought neceffary to have it cut there may be mafons & tools, without lofs of time, fent here from Blair. I heartily wifh us all a happy meeting, & am fincerely,

DEAR SIR,

Your moft humble Ser^t

DAVID STEWART.

KYNNACHAN, SUNDAY,
40 *minutes after* 5.

(*Indorsed.*)—" Letter from Kynachan to D^r· Colvill, dated Kvnachan 9, received Blair, 10 February 1746."

CCXXV.

Dr. COLVILL TO THE DUKE OF ATHOLL.

MY DEAR LORD DUKE,

As it is my outmoft wifh and defire to contribute to our Dear Prince's Intereft, I cannot help informing your Grace that I have certain intelligence of the Bridge of Kynnachan being yet entire; that I hear every wellwifher to the caufe, who knows the fituation of the country, fay, the breaking of it would be of very great confequence, & that (which furprifes me greatly) it might have been in ruins before now had his R. H. orders been obeyed. My informer told me he faw the Mafons deputed by your Grace, begining to demolifh it, and that they were actually ftopt by a Major Vis, fo I humbly think the only remedy will be another meffage from the Prince backed with a fufficient Force.

[1] The Tummel.

I have the Honour to be, with the moſt affectionate Eſteem and Reſpect,

> MY DEAR LORD DUKE,
> Your Grace's moſt obedient
> and moſt faithfull humble Servant,
> GEORGE COLVILL.

BLAIRFETTY, MUNDAY,
half-an-hour after eight at night.

I am to ſtay here all night, & ſhall have the Honour of ſeeing your Grace to-morrow morning.

Pleaſe cauſe mind the Boat of Kinloch-Ranach.

(*Indorsed.*)—" Letter from Dr. Colvill, dated Blairphety the 10th [February], received Dalnacardich 11, at one in the morning."

CCXXVI.

MAJOR McLACHLAN TO THE DUKE OF ATHOLL.

MY LORD DUKE,

No doubt but your Grace admires my long abſence, occaſioned by the place where my charge landed, beſides was the moſt of the time lick and under the care of a Surgion, and that from place to place for fear of my enemies. Thurſday laſt I got the moſt of my charge ſafe landed, and ſeenring it the ſafeſt way I can untill I get people to eſcort it. I have been dealling with the McLeans all the time, and got their faithfull promiſe to come how ſoon I would be in power to ſerve them with money, arms, and ammonition, which now I can doe. I ſent them ſome money, and ſhall have what they want upon their arrival, which I expect ſoon; and then have the pleaſure to come to his Highneſs with what I have of my charge, with McLeans and all other people I can get together. I was overjoyed to hear of your Grace being in perfect health after coming from England:—God grant your Grace long life and happie days, and for ever am,

My Lord Duke,

Your Grace's moſt obliged and

moſt obedient humble Servant, while

ALEX^{R.} M^CLACHLAN.

[Borradeal in Arrasig,]¹
 Febr^y 11^{th,} 1746.

I refer the berrare to tell the place.

CCXXVII.

Dr. COLVILL TO THE DUKE OF ATHOLL.

My Dear Lord Duke,

I had the Honour to ſee our Dear Prince at the Quarters at Caſtle-hill, he deſired me to make his compliments to your Grace. Mr. Murray, &c. &c. bid me offer their moſt humble ſervice to your Grace; all at the Quarters ſeem hearty & in full ſpirits. I ſaw the Quartermaſter, who told me your Grace's Quarter is at Culloden Houſe, where the E. of Kilmarnick, Ld. Luis Gordon, & Ld. Nairne are likewiſe quartered. The only piece of news is, that there are eight or nine hundred of the Loyaliſts to ʿcroſs the Ferrie this evening, to purſue the Enemy; they conſiſt of the Frazers, McDonalds, and Camerons. I ſaw the Frazers aſſembling, & my Couſine Inneralachie, who commands them, told me what they were going about. The Preſident is gone along with Lord Loudon, McKloid, &c. &c.; McIntoſh is with them; they went ſtreight to Brand Caſtle.

¹ So indorsed.

I am juſt now with two ſiſters, who I have not ſeen theſe eight years paſt, they are very earneſt I ſhould ſtay with them all night; in which caſe I hope your Grace will excuſe me. I went to Cullodden Houſe & ſpoke to the Maſter houſehold, (a Stewart,) who told me your Grace's room ſhould be ready; the cellers are pretty well pleniſhed, and plenty of proviſion of Horſes:—I ſhall go there to-morrow & order a good fire in your room.

I beg leave to aſk your Grace will pleaſe offer my moſt humble ſervice to the Heroine[1] & the other Ladies, in which my Landladies heartily join; they long very much to have to honour of your Grace for a lodger. The Secretary told me they had a letter from Lord George laſt night, when his Lop. would be at Elgin, & this night at Forres. I have honour to be, with the outmoſt Eſteem and Reſpect,

MY DEAR LORD DUKE,

Your Grace's moſt obedient and

moſt affectionate humble Servant,

GEORGE COLVILL.

INVERNESS, 19 *Feby.* 1746, *six at night.*

The ſtreets here are much expoſed to the Caſtle, from whence they fire ſeveral ſhot, & wound[ed] one of the Loyaliſts (a private man) this forenoon.

CCXXVIII.

ROBERTSON OF DRUMACHINE TO THE DUKE OF ATHOLL.

MY LORD DUKE,

I give your Grace the trouble to introduce four young Lads from

[1] Lady Mackintosh, who, a few days previously, had, by a very extraordinary ruse *de guerre,* defeated Lord Loudon's attempt to surprise Charles Edward at Moy Castle.—See Home's Hist.; Scott's Tales of a Grandfather, &c.

Atholl for L^{d.} G's Regiment; they fay more are following. As I had a very bad night, I can only add, that I am ever, & with the greateft refpect & affection,

MY LORD,
Your Grace's faithful
Servant,

CORRYBROCH, *Feb:* 20th. 1746.   D. ROBERTSON.

P.S. As thefe Lads left the Country Monday afternoon, their Intelligence will add to the laft.

CCXXIX.

SPALDING OF ASHINTULLY TO THE DUKE OF ATHOLL.

MY LORD DUKE,

I wrote Dr. Colvill of the fuccefs I would have had with ye Strathardle men, were not ye camp removed from Stirling fo foon; and altho' I could not have ye ufe of a partie, the vaffals and tenants of Afhintilly agreed to give me fourfcore and ten men (a part of which is in Bleaton's company) and altho' there was no men left in Blair Caftall, I would have prevealed with a good maney, providing I had not been obliged to flay under night, from a ftrong party of the Ufurper's men that is juft now in that Country; it is now a hardfhipe if ye Prince will not alow me a reafonable fubfiftance, being fo fituated as I have it not myfelf. I humblie prefume to lay this my condition before your Grace, on whom I wholely depend, and am, with ye greateft refpect,

MY LORD DUKE,
Your Grace's moft faithfull and
obliged humble Servant,

INVERNESS, 24*th Feb*^y. 1746.   DAN. SPALDING.

MEMORANDOME FOR DOCTOR COLVILLE.

THAT it may be demanded of a great many of Bleaton's company, how many went home and followed after Glenkilrie, after he had conveyed the Duke of Atholl to Edin.—

Secondlie, it may be afked of John Spalding and Andrew Rattray, Lieutenant and Enfign to Bleaton, if it was by his interift fuch of my men as are there was raifed.

It may be alfo afked, whither John Spalding was prefent when Peter Ayfon and his Brother Alex., told how they were advifed home ; they can tell by whom themfelves, &c.

If the Duke of Atholl were once in Atholl, it may be afked of Mormount, whither he was prefent when Glenkilrie his brother faid, had he been Bleaton he would have keept a guard for himfelf, but that he would have returned home the reft.

It may be alfo afked Alex. White, whither Glenkilrie propofed to produce ye Letters he had, offering commiffions to him by Lord Geo. &c.

And it may be afked y^e faid Alex^r. and Donald McKenzie in Kirktown if or not there was a Joint Letter wrote by fo maney Gentlemen in y^e Country, to Lord James Murray, who are belived to be friends here.

CCXXX.

ROBERTSON OF DRUMACHINE TO D$_R$. COLVILLE.

SIR,

The Inclof'd came to me this Evening, under Cover from Lady McIntofh. As the Gentlemen for whom the Letters are addreffed are not at hand, I did not fcruple to fee what they contained. It feems y^e

Invernefs Poffe is not fo ftrong as reprefented fometime ago, and that 3 days ago, the intelligence of H. R. H.'s motions had not reached thofe parts.

I have been in great diforder all this day, and cou'd not get out of bed 'till 5 this Evening, elfe I had been at the head Quarters. I wifh Malcolm Stewart in Sheerglafs, who is Funcaftle's Lieut., was called for to attend clofe at Blair Caftle ('till relieved by fome other officer) to command a fmall piquet of this Country people, to furnifh Expreffes, &c. as the Duke of Atholl fhall have occafion. I defir'd Funcaftle, w^t his Company to attend this day, for I fee no pretence they have to abfent themfelves; but all the people on this fide of Garry have the army quarter'd upon them, and are order'd befides to be ready with their Horfes to march w^t the Prince's Baggage, both which the Funcaftle people are free of.

Pray be fo good as prefent my duty to the Duke of Atholl. I'm forry it was not in my power to attend his Grace this day, tho' I cou'd have done but little fervice, for I find by repeated Experience that I can bear no exercife. I am alwife,

D^r. S^r.

Your moft obed^t. humble Ser^t.

D. ROBERTSON.

LUDE, *Feb.* 27th. 1746,
after 7 *at night.*

CCXXXI.

SPALDING OF ASHINTILLIE TO DR. COLVILL.

KEPAC, *March* 18th, 1746.

SIR,

Altho' my friends ftood by ye Campbels when Lord James and they were in competition about ye eftate of Afhintillie, I did not, untill Commiffary Biffet, who managed his Lordfhipe as he had a mind, was

like to trifle me out of yᵉ Eafes obtained from yᵉ Creditors for fupporting my Father's famillie, &c.; my love is more extencive towards yᵉ Duke,
who has yᵉ true right; and as I always had, and has, my whole dependance
on yᵉ noble Famillie of Atholl, and haith no farther to fay in any petition
I can give in to yᵉ Secretary, than to tell I had a commiffion from yᵉ Ufurper, he therefore may negleƈt to mention my name to yᵉ Prince, if his
Grace the Duke of Atholl will not fpeak in my favours himfelf, which
would do yᵉ affair at once.

Sir, I forgot to tell yᵗ it was not fo Eafie for me to raife men when
Glenkilrie was takeing money from fuch as fhould have given me men,
To witt, from Clerk Chalmers five pound, which yᵉ clerk told me in prefence of witneffes; and I told him he behooved to git a man to me however; and as he told me he would not, I confes I buffed him. He got money
from oyʳˢ alfo, as well as from yᵉ clerk.

I would willingly reward your trouble, if you would preveall with his
Grace to do for me out of bygone arrears at Leat, and think it well Laid
out, my Enemies are fo many, altho' I have a right, I have none. I am,
with refpeƈt,

SIR,
Your much obliged humble Ser.,
DAN. SPALDING.

P. S. I hear my Lord George and yᵉ McPherfons are gone to Atholl.
I hope I will git money in order to go home at any rate.

CCXXXII.

DUKE OF ATHOLL TO ROTHEMURCUS.

SIR,
As the late Rothemurcus, your father, fhowed me particular friendfhip & kindnefs on juft fuch an unfortunate occafion as the prefent, makes

Servants and fome baggage, which I fend you rather than it fhould fall.
into enemies hands ; fo that if you cannot keep it, and get it fent me in
time & place convenient, it may be of fome ufe to yourfelf, who I efteem
on your family & father's account ; tho' we have not had the occafion of a
perfonal acquaintance, which I hope may yet agreeably happen, in whatever bad Situation our affairs may appear at prefent, then I may agreably
be able to return you fuitable thanks for fuch an obligation as will for
ever oblige,

SIR,

Your aff: Humble Servant and Coufin.

18th March, 1746.

CCXXXIII.

CO^{L.} WARREN TO DR. COLVILL.

I am very impatient, Dr. Doc^{r.} to hear of your perfect recovery ;
pray indulge me with a line, or if not yet able, let Mr. Murray tell me
how you do.

I muft alfo beg it as a particular favour that you fend me by the bearer
your Journal (if not already done) as I want to pick out fome dates &
names of places of great ufe to me. I fhall return it to you moft faithfully by the ambaffador who is to come down to fee me.

I hope to be ready for the fea by Saturday or Sunday.

I have now the pleafure to tell you that I affembled here thefe 2 days
paft, all the boats of Nairn, Broghhead, Caufie, &c., and fent them off laft
night, wth 4 men in each boat, of Stoneywood's and Sr Alex^r Banner-
man's, wth orders to proceed to Portmahamoch in the frith of Dornoch.
Lord Cromartie has orders to have all his men ready there, to be ferried

over by them to Sutherland, to furprife L$^{d.}$ Loudon, who'l probably little expect fuch a thing, and I hope in God will be entirely routed. I hope they are got over fafe, as not one of them appeared this morning, and they are out of the reach of 3 m. W.[1] now cruifing in our fight at a great diftance. If this fucceeds, ce fera un Coup de partis. My duty to his Grace, wth this acct, wch was kept as fecret as poffible.

My hearty refpects to your loving Sifters, and believe me, Dr Doc^r moft fincerely your affec^t humble Servant,

WARREN.

FINDHORN, *Wednesday,*
18 *March* 1746.

Pray, fay a thouf^d fine things for me to the heavenly Lady McIntofh, Sifter, &c.

CCXXXIV.

MUNGO MURRAY TO COL: WARREN.

SIR,

All of us here are much obliged to you for the account of the boats which are fent from Nairn, &c^a. into the frith of Dornoch; God fend they may have the fuccefs which is hoped for. Doctor Colvill is ftill at the point of death, therefore, no ways in a condition to fend you any thing regards his Journal, which you require of him; but my Lord Duke who defires me to give you his affectionate Service, fends you here inclofed a copy of M^r· Dumont's Journal fince we left Edinb^r·, that you may be able to find out certain dates and names of places, which is all feems to be required at prefent. At the fame time, he, and every one of your friends amongft us, wifh you all fuccefs and expedition, in fo good an errand as you are going. In Doctor Colvill's ftead, I fhall fay from you all the

[1] Men of War.

fine things poffible to the valuable Lady McIntoſh, her Sifter, &c^a. Being
with perfeét regard and efteem,

Sir,

Your moft affeétionate
Humble Servant.

No doubt you have heard of the indefatigable Expedition of Lord
George Murray into Atholl, who has furprifed and taken all the regular
troops and Campbells at Blair, and every other garrifon they had in the
Country thereabouts, which can't but produce good effeéts for the Prince's
Service.

CCXXXV.

LORD GEORGE MURRAY TO THE DUKE OF ATHOLL.

Blair, 24th March 1746.

Dear Brother,

I hope you will excufe my not writing to you fince we camè here,
for as you would hear of every thing I wrote to Sr. Thomas[1] or Mr. Murray, and indeed I have not had one fpare moment; our Duty here is
conftant and fatiguing, but we grudge nothing that is for H: R: H: fervice and the good of the Caufe. Coll: Mercer, with 150 men, is at Dunkeld, and fecured the boats, but I have ordered him to retyre to the Paſs
if a Body of the Enemy fhould come near to that place, which they can
do by paffing the river at Perth. All here defire to make you their compliments, and I always am,

Dear Brother,
Your moft affeétionate Brother
and humble Servant,
GEORGE MURRAY.

[1] Sheridan.

The people in the Caſtle[1] have not ſet out their heads ſince we came, and are living on biſket and water. If we get the Caſtle, I hope you will excuſe our demoliſhing it. Adieu.

CCXXXVI.

DUKE OF ATHOLL TO LORD GEORGE MURRAY.

BROTHER GEORGE,

Since, contrary to the rules of right reaſon, you was pleaſed to tell me a ſham ſtory about the expedition to Blair, without further ceremony for me, you may now do what the Gentlemen of the Country think fit with the Caſtle; I am in no concern about it. Our great-great-grandfather, grandfather, and father's pictures, will be an irreparable loſs on blowing up the houſe; but there is no compariſon to be made with theſe faint images of our forefathers and the more neceſſary Publick Service, which requires we ſhould ſacrifice every thing can valuably contribute towards the Country's ſafety, as well as materially advancing the Royal Cauſe. Pray give my kind ſervice to all valuable friends, to which I can add nothing, but that in all events you may be aſſured I ſhall ever be found, with juſt regard,

DEAR BROTHER,
Your moſt aff. Brother,

INVERNESS, 26 *March* 1746.   and Humble Servant.

At the upper end from the door of the old ſtable, there was formerly a gate which had a Portcullis into the Caſtle: it is half built up and boarded over from the ſtable ſide, with a hollow large enough to hold a horſe

---

[1] Blair Castle, at that time garrisoned by a party under the command of Sir Andrew Agnew.

at hack and manger. People that know the place imagine it may be much eafier dug through than any other part of the wall, fo as to make a convenient paffage into the vaulted room, which is called the Servant's Hall.

CCXXXVII.

DUKE OF ATHOLL TO SIR THOMAS SHERIDAN.

DEAR SIR,

Mr. James Murray, wounded at the action of Inverury, a gentleman of my name, born in Sicily, whom the Ambaffador took the trouble of introducing to the honour of kiffing H. R. H.'s hands, is refolved, by his Excellencie's protection, to raife a company for the fervice amongft the new men that are raifing, provided he can obtain the Prince's commiffion. This is, therefore, defiring you will be fo kind as to intereft yonrfelf with his R. H. for that end, being only afked in fo far as it may be for the Royal fervice, which will alfo be taken as a particular favour done to,

DEAR SIR,
Your moft obedient
& moft humble Servant.

INVERNESS, 28 *March* 1746.

With this I entreat you'll give my duty to the Prince, who, I am extremely glad to hear, is perfectly recovered of the cold with which he was troubled for fome time paft; I long much to be in a tolerable fituation to pay my dutiful refpects to H. R. H. I beg you'll excufe the not writing with my own hand, which really cannot be done in a hurry.

CCXXXVIII.

SIR THOMAS SHERIDAN TO THE DUKE OF ATHOLL.

My Lord,

I have juft now received the honour of y Grace's letter, dated this day, in relation to M^r. James Murray. It was a thing to wch I was entirely a ftranger, but, coming from your Grace, I coud not but fhew it to the Prince, who told me that he had refolved to grant no more fuch commiffions, the few he has already given being at leaft enough to give employment for all the men he can hope to raife by that method, and to exhauft the fmall fund he can afford to lay out upon them. Were not this the cafe, y^r Grace might be affured that y^r recommendation woud be fufficient without any other.—I have the honour to be, with all poffible refpect,

My Lord,
Yo^r Grace's moft humble &
moft obedient Servant,
THOMAS SHERIDAN.

Inverness, *March y^e* 28th, 1746.

CCXXXIX.

LORD GEORGE MURRAY TO THE DUKE OF ATHOLL.

Blair, 29th *March*, 1746.

Dear Brother,

I received your letter of the 26th. I'm forry you feem to think I told you a fham ftory (as you exprefs it,) about our expedition here. I told you we were to indeavour to take poffeffion of Caftle Grant, and try

2 E

to hinder that clan taking party againſt us; this was done ſo far as in our power. I alſo told you, if we could contrive to ſurprife any of the partys in this country we might attempt it, but that depended ſo much upon infidents, that my very hopes could not reach ſo far as we performed. Secrecy and expedition was our main point, once we refolved upon the thing, which was not till I met Clunie and Sheen in Badinoch. If the greateſt fatigues, dangers, and hard dutys deſerve aprobation, I think ſome thanks is due to us, and from non more ·than yourſelf. For my own part, I was at one time ſeventy honres without three of ſleep; but we undergo all hardſhips for the good of the common cauſe.

You will ever find me,

Dear Brother,

Your moſt affect· Brother,

& faithful Servant,

GEORGE MURRAY.

I am ſo ill ſuported with men, money, and every thing elſe, our people here have no pay, that, after all our endeavours, I 'm afraid we muſt abandon this country without the Caſtle.

CCXL.

THE DUKE OF ATHOLL TO LORD GEORGE MURRAY.

Brother George,

This evening I had yours of yeſterday's date. As to any difference betwixt you and I, without prejudice to paſſed expedition and ſecrecy mentioned, at meeting it muſt be difcuſſed the beſt way we can, ſince lately behaving according to dutiful ſentiments, no body is more ſatiſſied than I am of your indefatigable activity for the publick ſervice. Had you ſent me your letters to the Secretary, who, I am very ſorry to ſay, is at Elgin dangerouſly ill, or any other of the miniſtry to whom expreſſes were addreſſed, I ſhould have directly endeavoured getting the moſt ſatiſfactory anfwers could be fent your preffing reall demands, which are not well underftood if much regarded by every body here; I am informed by Mr. Hay and Cruben, who were juft now with me, that all the men who were with you have been fully paid till Wednefday laft, and that, with fome neceffary forefight and pains, you might have had a good deal of provifions from below the Pafs, whilft that expedient was practicable, fince you might have naturally known that money cannot be foon fent from hence, but on an abfolute neceffity, you know meal can be ftill brought you from Kiliwhimen. With what I wrote you the 26th, in cafe the enemy could not be otherwife forced out of my houfe, I gave Sir Thos Sheridan an account to be fent you of a fecret paffage into it, which is here again tranfmitted, in cafe making any advantageous ufe of it has been hitherto neglected: was it not hoped, by this time, you have near got the better of thefe obftinate intruders into the Caftle, at any rate I fhould go myfelf and try if I could not ufefully help towards reducing them to a fpeedy furrendering of fuch unfortified tho' thick old walls as it is compofed of. Pray continue your accuftomed vigilance on fuch a valuable occafion as will render you dear to all honeft men, as well as particularly giving me an opportunity of fhowing with what efteem I am,

DEAR BROTHER,

Your moft affectionate Brother,

& moft humble Servant,

INVERNESS, 30th *March,* 1746.

CCXLI.

SIR THOMAS SHERIDAN TO THE DUKE OF ATHOLL.

MY LORD,

Here are two letters found in a packet dropt fomewhere on the Spey, & faid to have been found on board the Hazard Sloop. As I met with y^r Grace's name in them, I have thought it beft to tranfmit them to y^r Grace. I hope this will find you in good health. I have the honour to be, with all poffible Refpeᴄt,

MY LORD,

Y^r Grace's moft humble and

Moft obedient Servant,

THO. SHERIDAN.

INVERNESS, *April* 11th, 1746.

CCXLII.

DUKE OF ATHOLL TO SIR THOMAS SHERIDAN.

SIR,

Juft now I have the honour of your's, with the two inclofed letters for me from M^r· L'Abby De Preville, for which I return you many thanks, & fhall trouble you with explaining the contents at meeting, which may be foon. My rumatick pains & ftrained leg being a little eafier than hitherto, fo hopes to wait this night or to-morrow on the Prince. In the meantime I beg you'll pleafe give my humble duty to H. R. H., being, with the utmoft refpeᴄt.

INVERNESS, 11 *April*, 1746.

CCXLIII.

COPY LETTER FROM M^R. ALEXANDER M'LEOD, AID-DE-CAMP TO THE PRINCE, TO THE LAIRD OF CLUNY M'PHERSON.

D^R SIR,

You have [heard] no doubt ere now of the ruffle[1] we met with this forenoon. We have fuffered a good deal; but hope we fhall foon pay Cum-

---

[1] The Battle of Culloden !

berland in his own Coin. We are to review to-morrow, at Fort Auguſtus, the Fraſers, Camerons, Stewarts, Clanronalds, & Keppoch's people. His R. H. expeᒼts your people will be with us at furtheſt Friday morning. Diſpatch is the more neceſſary that his Highneſs has ſomething in view which will make an ample amends for this day's ruffle.

I am,

DEAR SIR,

Your's

ALEXANDER MᶜLEOD.

GORTLIG, *April* 16,
9 *at night,* 1746.

We have ſent an exprefs to Lord Cromarty, Glengyle, & Bariſdale, to join us by Bewly. For God's ſake make haſte to join us; & bring with you all the people can poſſibly be got togither. Take care in particular of Lumiſden and Sheridan, as they carry with them the Sinews of War.

Friday.

Dᴿ SIR, Mʳ· MᶜLeod's letter ſeems to be a ſtate of politicks I do not comprehend, tho' I can gueſs it is wrote the day of the Battle; and, in-ſtead of ſending any word to us, every body are ordered from Lochaber to Badenoch to cover H. R. H. from being purſued, which I wiſh it had taken effeᒼt. Adieu. I wiſh we may ſoon ſee better times.

Your's,

G. M.

I obſerve the rendezvous was to be as yeſterday at Fort Auguſtus, but thoſe who came from that laſt night, ſay H. R. H. was gone for Clan-ronald's country.

This is Lord George Murray's anſwer to what was wrote to Cluny on the other ſide.

APPENDIX.

APPENDIX.

I.

COMMISSION BY THE PRINCE TO THE DUKE OF ATHOLL.

CHARLES PRINCE OF WALES, &c. REGENT OF SCOTLAND, ENGLAND, FRANCE, AND IRELAND, AND THE DOMINIONS THEREUNTO BELONGING, TO OUR RIGHT TRUSTY AND WELL BELOVED WILLIAM DUKE OF ATHOLL.

We repofeing efpecial truft and confidence in your loyalty, courage, and good conduct, do hereby conftitute and appoint you, in terms of your former Commiffion from his Majefty, to act as Commander-in-Cheif of the King's forces, (we finding it neceffary to remain in the fouthern part of the kingdom,) benorth Forth, fo long as we fhall continue on this fide; and hereby authorifes you to do whatever you fhall think moft condufive to his Majefty's intereft, and requiring all his Majefty's officers to obey you.

Given in our Camp, att Pinkey, this 22d of Septr. 1745.

CHARLES, P.R.

II.

LORD EDWARD MURRAY TO THE MARQUIS OF TULLIBARDINE.

BLAIR ATHOLL, *Septemb^r y^e* 26, 1715.

My Lord,

I am ordered by my Lord Duke to accquent my Dear Nephew that he thinks it proper to fend me to waite of you, and my Brother, Nairne, to difcourfe you of matters of gratest concequence and laft importance to you and your fameleys; foo that I have your word of honour to goe and come faffeley. I am, with all maner of refpect,

My Lord,

Y^r moft faithfull humble Servant,
EDWARD MURRAY.

III.

LORD JAMES MURRAY TO THE MARQUIS OF TULLIBARDINE.

Dear Brother,

Mr. Duncan Stewart carries you the meffage that Lord Edward Murray was to do, if you had fent him word that he might meet you; all I can fay by this bearer is, that however you relifh this propofall, that you will returne for anfwer, that you defire that you may fee me upon this head, that I fhall have your anfwere, and have leave to returne; this is the only method I can propofe to fee you, and I defire it very earneftly on many accounts, particularly that I may have ane opportunity to convince you how much I am,

Dear Brother,

Your moft affectionate Brother,
and moft humble Servant,
JAMES MURRAY.

BLAIR ATHOLL, *Sept.* 28th, 1715.

IV.

COMMISSION—THE MARQUIS OF TULLIBARDINE IN FAVOUR OF LORD NAIRNE.

WILLIAM DUKE OF RANNOCH,[1] MARQUIS OF TULLIBARDINE, &c., COM-MANDER-IN-CHEIF OF HIS MAJESTY'S FORCES IN SCOTLAND, TO THE RIGHT HONOURABLE WILLIAM LORD NAIRN.

By verteu of the power given me from the King, as Commander-in-Cheif of His Majefty's Forces in Scotland, I doe hereby conftitut and appoint you, William Lord Nairn, a Major-Generall of His Majefty's Forces, as weell foot as horfe. You are therefor to take upon you the faid command, and to difcharge the duty aforfaid, by doeing and performing every thing which to the office and truft of a major-generall does apper-tain ; and all and fundry the officers of His Majefty's Forces are hereby requir'd to obferv and obey you as fuch ; and likeways your felf to obferv and follow all fuch orders and directions as you fhall from time to time receive from the King, the Captain-Generall, myfelf, or other Commander-in-Chief of His Majefty's Forces, for the time being, or any other your fuperior officer, according to the rules and difciplin of war, in purfuance of the truft hereby repofed in you.

Given at the Ifle in Lochmorer, this fecond day of November 1719, in the eightien year of His Majefty's reign.

By his Grace's Command,

WILLIAM MURRAY.[2]

Lord Nairn, a Major-Generall.

[1] This dukedom seems hitherto to have escaped obfervation. It had apparently been created by the Chevalier in favour of the Marquis of Tullibardine during his father's life-time, but the date of the patent has not been ascertained. The above commission to Lord Nairne had been granted about the time of the affair of Glenshiel.

[2] This signature has been effaced, but is still legible.

APPENDIX.

                              V

LETTER [FROM THE MARQUIS OF TULLIBARDINE] TO THE KING.

SIR,

  I had the comfort of what your Majefty is juft now gratioufly pleafed to write in anfwer to mine of the 18th of this laft January, which, by accident, is dated above two years agoe; and tho' for fome time paft, as yet your Majefty gives no direct return to feverall confiderable points that my indifpenfible duty obldiged me to lay before you, neverthelefs, this letter of Feb[ry] the 15th, which I am honoured with a few days agoe, neceffarly requires I fhould again prefume to fay fomething more of the plain truth, feeing non can ever have a deeper fence of your Majefty's inherent compaffion, with extreme regaird and condefention, towards your faithfull afflicted fubjects, who are diffintereftedly miferable by fairly afferting your Majefty's and their Countrey's juft rights. Neather is it poffible for any who is moved with true principalis of loyalty, but to have the gratefulleft fentiments of the extraordinary care your Majefty always fhowed to fupply their reafonable neffefitys, which ftill made me endeavour all that was poffible to want no other fubfiftance then what might bairly fupport one in really executing what appeared abfolutly requifite for difcharging your fervice, even from one in my low fphear; as the matteriall effects are ftill fo obvioufe, that the grateft oppulency of any who have been fince tampering, has not yet produced fuch confiderable things; and the indifferent condition I am in after all, will prove how little concern I ever had about any profite, except advancing the undoubted reputation of your fubftantiall affairs in earneft; and am content to fee, by the prefent meafures, that they have now fmall occafion for fo mean ane inftrument, which, as matters ripen, muft ftill deminifh accordingly; yet had I been a little more polietly in the felfifh mode, perhaps one might been valued

_____
[1] A small town about three miles West of Paris.

by finding how to merite amongft thofe who cliverly employ their utmoft
fkill, at any rate, to carry all fort of darke projects without controll; but
fince it feemes people are of no other confequence with them then as
blind tooles, it may be evident by what ever becomes of me, that as I
never had the leaft advantage under any adminiftration, and brought my
felfe to the prefent condition, only through hopes of contributing, in fome
mannour plainly, towards advancing your Majefty's and the publick fervice; fo at laft finding I can be of no particular ufe for inteligibly pur-
fuing any follid chife aime, what ever has been innocently laid out, by
faithfully regarding the common caufe, and is unaccuntably made to ferve
the bay ends[1] of fome fellow-fubjects, that likeways accufe what themfelves
occafioned, fhall to the utmoft be made up and fairly clear'd, as occafion
offers; whereby, according to capacity, ones liberall inclinations need not
appear unfrugally miffplaced, when only turned to anfwer the unavoidable
functions of life, as either by a privat condition or publick, muft in the
event be obvioufly known to all who diftinctly has ane impartiall notion
of the various neffefitys, and perpetuall irregular accidents attending
humain affairs. Thefe 7 or 8 long years has fufficiently fhowen how unfitt
I am for meddling with the deepe concerns of State, which even, after the
utmoft demonftration of attatchment to the publick wellfaire, makes the
well-affected in Britain, or elfewhere, cautious of fuch fufferers, that of
cource ought as more reafonably to underftand who they allfo daile with;
and fince Providence has given me the grace to fee through and diftin-
guifh artfull practifes or oblique infinuations, that may be really detrimen-
tall to your facred caracter and intereft, fo I muft own, that the per-
plexed obfcure practifes of thofe who, through privat vews, makes ftrange
partys, in menefeftly drawing very differently from the common good, unavoidably creates fuch pernitious confufion as ever brought things to the
loweft pafs, efpecially in thefe laft generations, which are notorious ob-
ftackles, impofing meddlers, have fadly put to the publick happinefs, making every honeft endevour prove in vain, by unheard contrivances, to irecoverably fupprefs the beft inclined countrymen, that they may univerfally

_____
[1] By-ends.

infulte, even to the enflaving our clear nattural judgements, inftead of pretended reafonable liberty and property; fo all honefty muft go to ruine, reather then every thing fhould not be throughly moddeled to their elabourat inquifition of confounding fkeames, that at laft loads fuch as have fairly ventured to affift them with their oun miffcariages, fo as the wortheft people may unextricably miftake their trueft old friends. Here has ftood the main ftrength of your open enemys, and hitherto does fecure them againft all your Majefty's valuable attemps, that are feconded by the carneft defires of many well-meaning fubjects, at home and abroad, which fome of us has proved by fuch undifguifed actions, as occafions we are now brought to be univerfally criticifed, having left no refourfe to fuftain us from falling under the worft of injuries, when depending for the meaneft things on their caprice, who arives at greatnefs through fubtilly defaming every body they have gott in their clutches, refpecting no fort of merit or condition, even of the higheft natture, when ever fo eafy found facrifices are imagined ufefull for any imediat turne.   This is a cafe I have conftantly lamented beyond expreffion, that cruell fattality fhould ftill drive your faithfulleft fubjects, who are of any honourable confequence, from rendering neffefary fervice to our Soverain; for they can be no friends to the Royall Familie, and their Countryes juft caufe, that is any way inftrumentall in fuch cunning projects, as mifreprefenting, or other ways underhand difguifing the plain truth, in fo good and right a claim, as your Majefty's, which certainly requires you fhould, by all juft means, be truly helped in feeing plainly what may prove moft for your lafting fatiffaction and glory, through fair endevours towards reftoring the Croun and your unhappy nations to their lawfull privilidges in Church and State. Long before appearing openly in what was belived for your Majefty's fervice, which, by fad experience, has too irecoverably ruined feveralls of your beft fubjects, and many of my, every way, poor unfortunat friends, that were intierly devoted, for fupporting the true intreft of our anfhent Royall Familie with me, who, as I fay, a great while before your Majefty's leat fifter dyed, ere there was thoughts amongft afpiring ftatefmen of going to armes, had avoided all occafions of eftablifhing myfelf, fo as no

engagement might in the leaft retarde acting when neffefary fome figni_
ficant part; but fince irefiftably every good endevour has come to nought,
I hope it will not be found at laft, after fo many years unfpekable dif_
afters, and unprofitably weafting the vigorous floure of age, that there
wants giving honourable proofes of reall courage, or that now any can be
prefipetantly defperat, by regularly meaning to preferve themfelves in
fome meafure, for being gainft a right occafion ufefull as formerly at home,
feeing it's too evident we are of no juft confequence abroad. In garding
from a ftorm, it's not fo materiall to looke where the calamity falls, as
obferving whence it comes; and in faving people from wrongs, it's not
allways fo fignificant to mind the ftone that's thrown as the hand that fent
it, which, till this time, has too remarkably made the greateft attempts
for delivery from injuries, and fettling all on the old foundation, prove in
vaine; yet if a right ufe can be made of fuch repeated fbokes, every thing
through fympathifing, unconftrained refignation, to all mighty difpenfa-
tions, may ftill take a good turn, fo as the undoubted conftant endevours
your Majefty magnanimoufly perfhues, will at length produce the bliffings
are referved for thofe whofe unfhaken loyalty hitherto moves in no other
fphear then being teribly incapacitated for any reall buffinefs, by the un-
fuportable perfecution of them that have exorbitantly affumed the property of what, in fome meafure, flows from many others fincere dealings;
which I queftion not your Majefty may fully obferve, when all your well-
inclined fubjects can have right accefs to ftate every thing humbely, as they
really ought, before the impartiall penetration of your confumat wifdome,
that our Mafter's unprejudifed inclinations may be in a true condition to
fecure himfelf and affectionat people from being hereafter monopolifed
through any precedented factions calamitys, which utterly fupprefs all
plain virtue, by fkillfully nurifhing moft deftructive vices, that unbridles
every kind of immorality, and dangeroufly inftilles the moft leveling fentiments amongft unwary eafey multitudes, to the anarchicall diffolution of
all true lawfull government. So there's occafion for no weighter obftakles
which I know, or belive that fuch as pourefully declaire againft eftablifhing the anfhent conftitution, wifh, nor otherways imagine, they need be

at much paines about pitifull manuvers, with a mean fett of unregairded
fugitives, who are too fenfibly become defpicable every where. Thus I
have once more endevoured, as unavoidably nceffefar, at all hazards to difcharge my incumbent duty, which, in the worft events, no fort of earthly
torture ought to difpence amongft true-hearted men of juft refolution,
efpecially when things are brought to the prefent condition, tho' one fhould
ireparably fall under the greateft miffortune in not being able to procure
any anfwerable countenance, whileft giving the utmoft proofe of the
ftrongeft fidelity, by even venturing to lofe your Majefty's indulgent favour,
which I conftantly valued more then life, but that one muft efteem more
the unqueftionable advantage of your lafting intreft and fervice, as cannot
faile one time or other to appear confpicuoufly, fince one patiently en-
counters all fort of imaginable tryalls, in the hardeft maner, both before
God and man for the naturall veneration [that] was unalterably infufed with
my birth towards your Majefty's moft facred perfon and Royall Familie.
But what ever happens me from ane unmercifull world, a good confience
may fufficiently comfort and protect one, through inward fatiffaction, that
no fublunary practifes is able to deftroy, fince given from above, as the
earneft of fully making up all imediat loffes, fo muft intierly recompence
every difafter to him, whos reafonable ambition has ftill been dedicated
towards the end of our creation, for the honour of my native Prince and
ruined Countrey, which cannot be demonftrat further, then by being thus
expofed through the greateft markes of unfaned fterving fubmiffion, in
him that will in earneft rejoice while worthy of difgrace, for fubftantially
fhowing how unviolably I have ever been,

Sir, &c.

I am right thankefull for both your Majeftys being pleaf'd to thinke
of me, who am very glad the Queen and Prince are well; and again begs
leve to offer my humble duty to Her Majefty.

My Lord Panmure and Airly, with others who have feen your Majefty's
letter, find this according to their fentiments.[1]

[1] Printed from the original scroll in the Marquis's hand-writing.

VI.

A LETTER FROM A GENTLEMAN OF UNDOUBTED CREDIT IN ANGUS SHIRE.

SIR,

As your friends here heartily fympathized with tbe City of Ed^r· & the Country around, during the unhappy Time the Highlanders were with yow; the many Roberies, oppreffions, & numberless Hardfhips to q^{ch} yow were then fubjected, filled us w^t equal Concern for your diftreff'd Situation, & Indignation at your oppreffors, we expect the like Sympathy when now reduced to the fame Melancholly Circumftances, by this 2^d gathering from the North.

Perth & Dundee, & tbe Country around, are one Scene of Horrour & oppreffion; Roheries are perpetual, & many of them in open day, in the publick ftreets, in the fight of all men, & even of their own officers. Multitudes in the Town are obliidged to leave their bufinefs & their Families, by which the Diftrefs, tho' not fo vifible, is yet exceeding great. They have fallen now to Houfe breaking too, q^{ch} puts us into the moft dreadfull apprehenfions of the worft. In Strathmore they have attacked many of the Clergy & robbed them, with great Infults, of Confiderable Sums. The whole parifhes in Angus are diftreffed by preffing, (or forcing men) or, which they love better, a Compofition in money, that falls beavey upon the poor Tennants. They have invented a new & unheard of Demand on the Gentlemen, cefling them fome two hundred, fome 100, fome 50 £ Ster. & he is a great favourite q^o efcapes. It is intended to raife a 100 £ each from 15 merch^{ts}· in Dundee, who 'tis believed muft forfake their famelys whilft Rebels are there in Power, if they would fhun this Tax, q^{ch} we doubt greatly will not do, for this new army are very hungry & rapacious.

In a late rejoicing at Dundee, for a French landing at Montrofe, it was by authority proclaimed, that every houfe fhould teftify their Joy by illuminating their windows, or be fubject to a fine of 20 £ Scots;—a notable way (purpofely intended) to point out to the Highland Executioners the families who would not rejoice on this happy Event.

The Prefbiterian Min^rs. it feems, could not on that occafion temporife w^t them. The Effect was like to be unhappy. Their windows are broke, innumerable ftones thrown violently into one of their Houfes, & at laft they fired fharp fhot. The family had retired into the moft diftant parts of the Houfe, & violent attempts were made to break in. No man could have anfwered for the Confequences, if fome Neighbours had not come by a back door & begged the family to efcape w^t them. The aged Min^r. remarkable for calmnefs, confcious of being in the way of his Duty, & having been long ufed, under the happy Revolution Government, to think his houfe was his Sanctuary, would not move; at laft, it is f^d, he wrote to one of their principal People, his acquaintance, q^o was gracioufly pleafed, after much entreaty, to call them off.

In fhort, our Cafe grows worfe & worfe, & almoft intolerable. The Inftances of cruel oppreffion are fo multiply'd, that People grow weary of complaining, or of even repeating the prolog, the leaft of q^ch, under K. George's Goverm^t, & by his Soldiers, would fill City and Country w^t noife for many days. And if an end is not foon put to thefe diftreffes, the Calamity thro' loffe of Trade, of money, and credit thro' Infults, fcattering of Familys, Robbery, Bloodfhed, & no body knows what demands, will ruin us altogether.

Yow may make thefe things as publick as yow pleafe. The facts are true, & the publifhing of them may tend to ftir up all forts of men to exert y^mfelves to the utmoft in ftopping y^s unjuft & unhappy Rebellion, raifed and Supported by the Enemies of mankind, who, by thefe beginings ar fhewing how proper Inftruments they would be to fulfill the unhallowed will of an arbitrary, perfecuting, & bloody Goverm^t

I am Sir, your

moft humble Servant.

VII.

LORD LOVAT TO CHARLES ERSKINE, ESQ. OF TINWALD, LORD ADVOCATE, AFTERWARDS LORD TINWALD.[1]

My Dear Lord,

I think it is an age fince I had the honour to fee you, or hear any wayes from you ; but I am glad to know, by others, that you are in good health, and that you kept your health while you was at London. And I beg leave to affure your Lop. and all your lovely family, of my moft affectionate humble duty, and very fincere attachment, to your perfon and concerns.

As I am now out of the world and forgot, I neither enquire after nor meddle with any politicks. I have been in a very fickly and dangerous ftate of health fince the begining of winter till within this month. I was feverall times near my exit, but I blefs God I am pretty well recovered now, and in condition to ferve the government, and fpeak boldly to the Spaniards and French in their own language, if they dare invade us; and my patrons will find, that I alwayes will have a fincere attachment to their perfons and intereft, notwithftanding of the ill ufage that I have met with of a long time.

I now, My Dear Lord, beg a favour of you that will coft you but a few lines writing, and the granting of it will hurt no man, and infinitly oblige me. It is this,—the parifh of Fern, in Eafter Rofs, is vacant by the death of one Mr. Hugh Duff, and I have a relation, one Mr. Donald Frafer, who now attends my eldeft fon at Edin[r.] that affifted Mr. Duff for two or three years, and preached for him the faid parifh. He is a very honeft man, and a very capable man. The parifh is very fond to have him their minifter, and the beft gentleman in that country have a great regard for him. The King is patron of the parifh ; fo I moft humbly intreat that your

---

[1] The directions of this and the two following Letters from Lord Lovat, have not been found, but it appears, from internal evidence, that they were addressed as here printed.

Lop. will be fo good as to write for a prefentation to my coufin, Mr. Donald Frafer, to be minifter of the parifh of Fern; for I know your Lop. can as eafily do it as give me a botle of the extraordinary good wine that I uf'd to get from you.

I truly long to have the honour to kifs your hands, and I am, with the utmoft attachment and refpect,

MY DEAR LORD,

Your Lop^{s.} moft affectionate

coufin, moft obedient, and

obliged humble Servant,

LOVAT.

BEAUFORT, 24th *Aug^{t.}* 1739.

VIII.

LORD LOVAT TO LORD TINWALD.

MY GOOD LORD,

I hope this will find your Lop. in perfect health, it is my fincere wifh, and I beg leave to affure your Lordfhip of my moft affectionate humble duty.

I have not prefumed to trouble your Lop. with my letters fince you went to London, becaufe I knew that you would be every day very much taken up with the affairs of the publick, fo that I thought it ill manners to take up your time with a letter that cou'd have nothing of moment in it, nor nothing worth your while, except you would think it worth your while, that I fhould, from time to time, affure your Lop. of my affectionate friendfhip, and my unalterable attachment to your perfon and intereft, which I humbly and moft fincerly do by this letter, and that is the chief defign of it; and I hope that your Lordfhip's being an officer of ftate in the King's fervice, and my being out of employment and in difgrace, will not alter the conſtant friendſhip that has been betwixt us for many years, without any flaw or alteration. But, my Dear Lord, when I conſider that no man in the iſland ſerv'd the Earle of Ilay and Sir Robert Walpole with more zeal, fervour, aſſiduity, and diligence, than I did, ſince ever they had the management of affairs, and that I never offended them in thought, word, or deed, and yet have been abandon'd by thoſe two great men in an open and mortifying manner, how can I be ſure of any great man's friend-ſhip after that? But as there is a great difference betwixt your Lop.'s ſituation and that of thoſe great men, I believe, likewiſe, there may be a difference betwixt your friendſhips; and in all events I am reſolved to re-ſpeᴄt and honour your Lop. with a faithful friendſhip, and will allways let you know it, till you forbid me to have any correſpondence with you.

I told you, my dear Lord, before you went to London, that I was per-ſwaded that my diſgrace wou'd augment, becauſe it began without any juſt reaſon or foundation. I find that I gueſſed right; for the ſhirriffſhip of Inverneſs is taken from me in the ſame manner that my company was taken from me, and that is without attributing any fault to me, and the countrey is ſurpriſed with the one as they were with the other, and really ſtrongly offended and affeᴄted; all I ſhall ſay of this part of my diſgrace is, that the King's ſervice will ſuffer a great deall more by it than I will, for I can freely ſay in face of the ſun, that I was fitter to be ſhirrief of that great and troubleſome ſhire, to keep it in peace and good order, than any one man beyond the Grampions; nay, I may ſay than any man in Scotland, for, beſides my own intereſt in the ſhire, all the principall Gen-tlemen who has eſtates in it, are my near relations, and upon my account were more diligent than ordinary to keep their country and people in peace, ſo that except private theft, which can never be curb'd and extin-guiſh'd without a particular aᴄt of Parliament for that purpoſe, during the many years that I was ſhirrief, there were neither riots nor publick quarrells, and there were few ſhires in the North that could ſay the ſame; I can likewiſe ſay that I was more than one hundred pounds a-year out of pocket by the ſhirriffſhip, and all thoſe that know my family know that it was no feather in my cape, for my anceſtors were ſherriff of Inverneſs and

Murray, *fimul & femul*,[1] above three hundred years agoe, which appears by the charters of feverall gentlemen in both thefe fhires, fo that I fhould now borrow the motto of Barron Kenedy and his family, Fuimus. And what advantage the adminiftration has by taking it from me, is more than I can comprehend.

I remember I beg'd your Lop., when you was going to London, if you found a proper occafion to tell the Earle of Ilay, who was for many years my Patron and warm friend, that whatever wrong impreffions his Lop. got of me, they were only the product of lyes and calumnys; for I defy the Devil, and all the men on earth, to prove that ever I fpoke a difre-fpectfull word of his Lordfhip, but, on the contrary, as I really was his faithfull and zealous partifan, and not an ufelefs one, I profeff'd it openly wherever I was, even in prefence of his greateft enemies; and what I have done to fall into his difpleafure, I declare faithfully I do not know it, nor can it have any other foundation than an unhappy prejudice founded upon calumnys and lyes.

And, notwithftanding that the hardfhips that I have met with are beyond example in any army or country in Europe, yet I do fincerly declare, that I have ftill a refpectfull friendfhip and attachment for the Earle of Ilay, not only as my worthy protector's fon, but likewife for the warm appearances his Lop. was pleafed to make for me; and it has been allways my principle, that no after difappointment will make me forget the good that I have received; I think that fhoud be a ftated point of gratitude with all honeft men; and as to Sir Robert Walpole, as I received particular marks of favour from him, I fhall allways remember them gratfully; and as I was his faithfull partifan, and never gave him occafion to be angry at me, I truly attribute the great hardfhips that he put upon me, or allowed to be put upon me, meerly to the effect of calumnys and lyes; but it was hard to receive and entertain bad and falfe impreffions of me to my hurt, without letting me know, by himfelf or any other, what grounds were for it. You will fay, that the firft min[r.] is not oblidged, nor cannot let men know the reafon why he turns them out of the King's

---

[1] i. e. *Semel*, but sic in orig.

Service; but I fay, and all the world muft own it, that a firft min^{r.} ought to let any man, whom he knew to be a faithfull ffriend and partifan of his own, know the reafons that were for difgracing him, and fhoud tell it before his difgrace that he might have time and occafion to vindicate himfelf; and when that is not done, and that a man is hurt by a hidden lye or calumny, when he thought himfelf fecure by the protection of his great ffriends; a difgrace or a fuffering, in that cafe, is a vaft hardfhip and an uncommon miffortune, that no man can be proof againft. However, I blefs God, that whatever I fuffer, or may fuffer, no power can take away the comfort that I have of a clean confcience and upright heart, that never betray'd a private man, nor a publick caufe; and I believe thofe two great men have had feverall Partifans, whom they heap'd with riches and honours, that even abandoned themfelves and fometimes betray'd them. I coud name feveralls of them that they cannot have forgot; and while I was their Partifan for many years, I defy them to have the leaft ground of fufpicion of my fidelity and zeal for their perfons and intereft, and now the world fees my reward, but no difappointment, of whatever kind, can alter my upright way of thinking. There is one thing that I cannot comprehend, how the Earle of Ilay, the fon of the great Duke of Argyle, and who himfelf knows very well the intereft of his family, can prefer the Laird of Grant, or indeed any Laird or Lord in the north of Scotland, to the Lord Lovat and his family, fince he cannot but know, that the Lords of Lovat and their kindred loft many times their blood and their lives in the quarrell of the family of Argyle againft the McDonalds, Gordons, &c.; and I blefs God they are as capable to ferve the Family of Argyle, as any that is beyond the Grampions, in any fhape except in Gafconading, for indeed I coud not promife as the young Laird of Grant fays he coud, to bring five members of my family to the Parliament, to ferve an adminiftration. I coud, without vanity, allways affure them of one member for the fhire of Invernefs, becaufe my intereft in that county will always caft the ballance as to member of Parlia^t. I did really diffwade the Laird of McLeod, thefe three years paft, to fet up for member of Parlia^t., and never confented to it, till he preff'd me fo ftrongly in October laft, otherwife Sir James Grant would not have a vote in that fhire but himfelf, his fon, and other two Grants; and as it is, McLeod will have twelve to fix, notwithftanding of the commiffions, &$^{ca.}$ &$^{ca.}$; and the Laird of Grant, after his vaft promifes, will have difficulty enough to bring one member to the next Parliament; fo that great men, who believe thofe that have a vaft deal of Irifh affurance, are often impofed upon, and miftaken in their oppinion of mankind, and of their intereft in the countrey.

I beg your Lo$^p.$ a thoufand pardons for this long Letter, but I cannot end it without telling your Lordfhip, that all your friends and acquaintances were much pleaf''d, and did very much applaud and approve of your kind and friendly behaviour towards your coufin who liv'd for fometime too cooly with you,—I am affured that he is very fenfible of the extraordinary friendfhip that you have done him, and that he never will forget it; and I can fincerely affure your Lo$^p.$, that I never will forget the reall efteem, and the faithfull zeal and refpect with which I am, while I live,

MY DEAR LORD,

Your Lordfhip's moft obedient,

moft oblidged, & moft faithfull

humble fervant,

EDIN$^R.$, *March,* 1741.   LOVAT.

P.S.—I am glad that our ffriend, Sir Robert Munro, is out of the ougly fcrape, in which his enemies malice and hatred appear'd moft violently ag$^{st.}$ him; I was fo lucky as not to be call'd to the agreement or arbitration, tho' my Lord Royftoun defired that I fhoud be one of the peacemakers; fo I fhall fay nothing of it fince Sir Robert's relations feem to be very angry at it, but it is very naturall to think, that the Gentlemen, to whom Sir Robert gave Carte Blanche, did what they thought beft for his intereft; but it muft be own'd by all men, who know the affair, that Sir Robert has fufficiently paid for any concern he had in that riot. I was told this day, that there is a mifunderftanding betwixt Sir Robert and his arbiters upon what has happen'd; but as I was entirely ignorant of what paff'd betwixt them, it is none of my bufinefs now to meddle

with it, only that I am forry to fee that our countrey is full of jarrs, dif-
putes, and quarrels, from Dan to Bafheba; and where all that will end,
God only knows; for my own part, as I am now old and valetudinary,
and entirely free of ambition, my greateft defire, and moft ardent wifh
woud be, to live at home in peace, and come once a-year to fee my
ffriends in this place; but where is there a man on earth that has his wifh?

IX.

LORD LOVAT TO LORD TINWALD, THEN LORD JUSTICE-CLERK.

My Very Dear Lord,

The only defign of this letter is to give your Lordfhip my moft
humble and fincere thanks for your goodnefs towards me, for William
Frafer, Writer to the Signet, has informed me that your Lordfhip has
been fo very kind as to write to the glorious young fellow your fon, who
is an honour to his country, in as preffing terms in my favour as you could
do for a brother, this is an inftance of generofity very uncommon and
rare to be found in this age.

It is true that your Lordfhip and I lived for many years in as intimate
friendfhip as if we were brothers, and communicated freely our fentiments
to one another, yet I thank God there is never a word that paffed between
us that ever was heard of without your Lordfhip's apartment. You have
now, my dear Lord, given proof that you are what I allways believed [you]
to be, that is, a man of the beft fenfe and judgment of your country, a man
full of goodnefs and affection for your relations, and a man of reall friendfhip for thofe that you profefs friendfhip to; I have the honour to have
a claim to your Lordfhip's goodnefs and affection as a relation, and you
know, my dear Lord, that I have fome claim to your friendfhip,—but
what would all that fignify if your Lordfhip's generous foul did not oblige
you to put it in execution. I have, my Lord, done great and effential
fervices to thofe of the firft rank in Scotland who now abandon me as if

2 H

I had come from Turkey with the plague upon me, but, as the Scripture
fays that ingratitude is next to the fin of murder, let them anfwer for it.
I blefs God I am fitter to appear before the Judge of all the earth than
they are; and, tho' my family feems to be now in a very low and defpe-
rate condition, yet I hope, by God's mercy, before this age is at an end,
that it will be more flourifhing than theirs, and then they will fee their
fhame as well as ingratitude. Your uprightnefs, my dear Lord, has put
you above this, for you neither abandon nor forfake your friend becaufe
he is unfortunate and in diftrefs.—May the God of Heaven reward you,
my dear Lord; may you live many years in perfect health, and may your
pofterity flourifh with honour and wealth more than any that wore the
gown in Scotland.

I molt humbly beg of your Lordfhip to recommend me once more to
your lovely fon, whom I expect to be the hero of my caufe, and who, perhaps, may fave my grey head from the block; but, whatever come of
me, I am fure he will gain great honour to himfelf, fince he has a large
field to walk upon.—I have the honour to be, with the utmoft gratitude,
attachment, and refpect,

My Very Dear Lord,

Your Lordfhip's moft obedient and moft
obliged humble Servant,

Tower of London, 20th Jan^y, 174⅔.   LOVAT.

X.

LORD JUSTICE-CLERK'S REPORT TO THE EARL OF HOLDERNESS,
HIS MAJESTY'S SECRETARY OF STATE.—*Novem^r*, 1752.

Report.—To the Right Honourable the Earl of Holderness, one
of his Majefty's Principal Secretaries of State, by Charles Are-
skine of Tinwald, Lord Juftice-Clerk.

In purfuance of your Lordfhip's defire, fignify'd to me by your letter dated at Whitehall the 30 June, 1752, having, with the zeal and dilligence which you recommended, examin'd into the truth of the facts therein fpecify'd, I take the liberty to lay before your Lordfhip the refult of my enquiry, which I fhall ftate in as few words as is confiftent w^t taking notice of ye variety of matters y^erin contained, referring to feveral vouchers, letter'd or number'd, hereunto annex'd.

The firft objection ftated in your Lordfhip's letter is general, namely, ^{1st class complain} "That non-jurors, and other difaffected perfons, meet with countenance and fupport, while many loyal and good fubjects have been remov'd from their imployments, or neglected, fince the Rebellion."

I fincerely affure your Lordfhip that, in the courfe of my enquiry, I have not been able to difcover any folide foundation upon which this complaint can ftand.

The Removes and Preferments in the Excife and Cuftoms have been examined into by the feveral Commiffioners appointed by his Majefty for the managment of thefe revenues, in confequence of the orders they received from their fuperiors; and I take it for granted a report has been made by them, and for that reafon I did not enter upon any enquiry concerning them. That there have been removes in the more confiderable offices fince the Rebellion is true, but the fprings and caufes of fuch removal were not a proper fubject for my enquiry. To be fure they were well weigh'd and canvaff'd before his Majefty was mov'd to make them; and I may venture to fay, that their fucceffors, as far as I have been able to obferve or learn, have ferv'd his Majefty with honour, and fill their offices with reputation.

It has been faid, that perfons zealoufly affected for the good of his Majefty's fervice have been difcourag'd to give intelligence, their names having been made known by perfons employ'd under the Government; but having ufed all probable means to inform myfelf concerning this fact, I met with no evidence to fupport it. The fact may be true, but, till I had the honour of your Lordfhip's letter, I never heard it furmif'd. I can anfwer for one, and that is all I can fay upon this fubject, fince no particular fact has been fuggefted.

Your Lordſhip has likewiſe been inform'd, "that vexatious law-ſuits have been carried on againſt officers of the army, for having done no more than their duty required of them during the time of the Rebellion; and, in particular, againſt Co^{ll.} Howard, Capt. Hamilton of Mordaunt's, Capt. Coneille of Herbert's, Lieut. M'Lachlan of Hulk's, and Capt. Moleſworth of Guiſe's regiment."

With regard to the proſecutions brought againſt theſe gentlemen, I have laid before me by Mr. William Alſton, agent for the Crown, a perſon of known warm affection to his Majeſty's Government, of integrity and confeſt ability, a ſhort but particular account of them, from which your Lordſhip will ſee whether there was any probable cauſe for proſecuting the officers, and whether they met with injuſtice before the Courts. And, if any complaint lyes on this head, I ſubmit it to your Lordſhip if it does not reſt ſolely upon the particular plaintiffs who believ'd themſelves injur'd.

laſs of plaints.

It is alſo objected, "that perſons of the Epiſcopal perſuaſion in Scotland, of ſuſpected characters, and even non-jurors, are made Sheriffs-ſubſtitute. In particular, the Sheriff-ſubſtitute of Clackmannanſhire, Forbes, Subſtitute of Aberdeen, and Mr. Campbell of Carſgowrie, Subſtitute of Angus, Mr. Young, Subſtitute of Mearns, and Mr. Grant of Aberdeenſhire, who were appointed to theſe offices in the year 1745."

It is farther ſaid, "that the Sheriffs-depute diſcharge perſons taken up and put into their cuſtody bv the troops, for wearing, contrary to law, the Highland dreſs, carrying arms, ſtealing cattle, and other crimes, under pretence that they have no means of maintaining theſe priſoners in gaol, and other frivolous pretences."

If this objection cou'd be ſupported, it was ſtrong, and the manadgment of theſe gentlemen, appointed lately by his Majeſty to the offices of Sheriffs-depute, muſt have been not only unaccountable, but of very pernicious conſequence to his Majeſty's Government and to the ſubjects of this part of the United Kingdom.

It was for this Reaſon, that, tho' the charge was general, I endeavour'd to try if it cou'd be enquer'd into in the Detail; and upon Application to

General Churchill, I received from him Abftraĉts of all the Returns made by the feveral officers for the years 1749, 50, 51, & 1752, herewith tranſmitted & mark'd, from which your Lordſhip will obſerve, that in the ſpace of four years, in carrying a new Law into Execution in a wild Place of the country, the complaints of the Military are few, and the greateſt part of them relate not to ſheriffs-depute or their ſubſtitutes, but to inferior Magiſtrates or Juſtices of the Peace. Your Lordſhip will likewife obſerve from thefe Returns of the officers, that their Accounts were founded only upon the Repreſentation of non-commiſſioned officers & ſoldiers, whoſe Relation of the Faĉts could not intirely be depended on, as may appear from ſome of the Returns hereafter to be particularly mentioned.

I take the Liberty further to obferve, that from examining both the Sheriffs-depute & the Military, I find that the chief occafion of the diſputes between them aroſe from a new form of dreſs contriv'd by ſome of the Highlanders, which could not be ſaid to be the Highland Dreſs prohibited by Law, or any Part of it, and yet was not altogether the Low-Country Dreſs; and if a ſheriff-fubſtitute allow'd his Doubt to carry him ſo far as to admit them to Bail untill he was advif'd by his Principal, it does not feem to be unreaſonable in itſelf, or detrimental to His Majeſty's fervice; efpecially when effeĉtual care was taken by the Principals to have even that new Form of Dreſs fuppreſſed, as appears from the Extraĉts of the Returns ſent to the General, wherein there are no complaints poſterior to the few Returns from the officers upon this fubjeĉt.

The moſt glaring of the complaints contain'd in the Returns, is that made by Captain Hughs, 1 Sept. 1749, ſet furth in Page 3ᵈ of the Extraĉts.

As to this, It appears the Captain's Repreſentation was founded only upon the Relation of a corporal, by which he was mifled. The fubſtitute to whom the complaint relates, was Duncan Campbell, Brother to the late unfortunate Glenure, nominated to that office as the Perſon moſt capable to ſerve his Majeſty in that part of the country by Mʳ· James Erſkine, Sheriff-Depute of Perthſhire.[1]

[1] Son of the Justice Clerk, and afterwards Lord Alva.

The General tranfmitted a copy of the Return to the Sheriff-Dep^{t.} In confequence whereof he, in concert with Co^{ll.} Crawford, who then commanded at Perth, made enquiry into the truth of the Facts fuggefted by the Corporal to Capt. Hughes, the Progrefs and Refult whereof is fully fet furth in two Letters, dated the 14 Auguft & 3 October 1749, written by him, and directed to Capt. Coalzier, then General Churchill's Aid-de-Camp, and in a 3^d Letter addreft to me, Copys whereof, marked are herewith tranfmitted; and in them he appeals to Co^{rl.} Crawfurd for the truth of his Reprefentation of the Facts, very different from that made by the Corporal.

Of Mr. Erfkine's Zeal & Activity in the fervice of the Government, it wou'd be indecent for me to fuggeft what I believe is the general opinion in this Part of the Kingdom. His Character is well known to the General and all the Officers who have commanded and refided at Perth.

Here I have refer'd to the Letters themfelves, not to incumber this Report with long Narrations. In thefe letters mention is made of a Difficulty the Sheriffs-Depute were under, in that there was no fund allow'd them for the Maintenance of Prifoners thrown into Goal on account of Wearing Arms or the Highland Habite; and a Fear is expreft, that if fome Remedy was not found out for this Defect, the Service might fuffer, and Sheriffs-Depute poffibly be tempted to difmifs Prifoners upon Bail, if they were to be maintain'd not by the Publick, but out of their own Pockets. This probably has given occafion to that part of the complaint mentioned in your Lordfhip's letter, that " Prifoners were difmift under frivolous Pretences, fuch as that the Sheriffs-Depute had no means of maintaining thefe Prifoners in Goal." But upon the ftricteft fearch and enquiry I do not find that ever any one prifoner was difmift upon that or any fuch Pretence, either by that Gentleman, or by any other of the Sheriffs-Depute or Subftitute, tho' he avers he has paid out about £100 upon that fervice, which he has never yet recover'd, for the Reafons fet furth in his Letter; and if the complaint has no other Foundation, he thinks it is at leaft unkind, that a Reprefentation to the General of a real Hardfhip the Sheriffs lay under, honeftly meant not only for their relief,

oners put custody
eriffs-
· dismist
er pre-
e that the
iffs or
r substi-
no
ns to
itain
e pri-
rs in
l.

but for His Majefty's Service, fhou'd be turn'd upon him or his brethren as a Reproach.

As to what relates to Prifoners for other Crimes, fuch as Theft, as far as I can gather from the Excerpts, it is founded upon the Return made by Capt. Proby the 15th Septemr. 1751, fet down in the end of the 7th Page of faid Extracts; and the Reafons affign'd by the Sheriff-Depute of Invernefs for his Procedure, which I fubmit to your Lordfhip's Judgment, are fet furth in his Letter to the Captain, bearing Date the 7th Septr 1751, of which your Lordfhip has a copy in the 8th Page of faid Extracts.

I fhall not trouble your Lordfhips with making any further Obfervations upon the Returns, the copy whereof is certify'd by Capt· Stewart, Aid-de-Camp to General Churchill, & authenticated by the Genl's letter, bearing date, Aug. 19, 1752, marked   , fo that the whole of them are therein contain'd, but leave this fubject with one Obfervation, that a Doubt did arife to fome of the Subftitutes, Whether the New invented Drefs fell under the fanction of the Law; and as the Crime was not capital, they judg'd the Perfon accus'd might be admitted to Baill, notwithftanding the Words in the Act of Parliament that they were to be imprifon'd without Baill or Mainprife, which relate to Perfons convicted, & not to fuch as are only to be brought to Trial.

To proceed next to the Sheriffs-Depute & Subftitute particularly mentioned in your Lordfhip's letter, in order to deliver the Report from immatterial circumftances, I fhall firft mention what relates to Mr· Grant of Aberdeen-fhire, & Mr· Young, Subftitute of the Mearns. The firft neither is, nor was, Sheriff-Dept· or Subftitute in Aberdeen-fhire fince the Jurifdiction Act, in confequence whereof Mr· Grant was turn'd out of that office, and Mr· David Dalrymple, Advocate, was named by his Majefty.

Mr. Gran: substitut Aberdee shire, an Mr. You substitut the coun Mearns.

As to Mr· Young, he was Subftitute named by Mr· Gordon, the Sheriff-Dept· of Mearns, & acted fome little time in that character, but he is fince dead, and therefore I judg'd it unneceffary to inquire what Part he or Mr· Grant acted in creating Impediments to His Royal Highnefs the Duke's March to Culloden.

As to what is reprefented in Relation to Mr· Graham, Subftitute of

Clackmannan-fhire, I wrote letters not only to the Sheriff-Dep.^{t.} who appointed him, but alfo to fome of the Gentlemen of the county who are of confeft Loyalty & Affe
ction to His Majefty's Perfon & Government; and particularly to Mr. Abercrombie of Tillibodie, a Perfon whofe chara
cter for veracity as well as Loyalty, is above all exception; and I find no founda.^{t.} for the charge againft him: but on the contrary, dureing the Rebellion, he correfponded with Gen^{ll} Blackney, who then commanded at Stirling, giving him all ye intelligence he could gather, and doing him all the fervice in his power, and had his approbation of his condu
ct, as appears more fully from Mr. Abercrombie's letter, marked
to which I hereby refer.

Bryce, iff-sub-te of Stir-fhire. As to what refers to Mr. Bryce, fheriff-fubftitute of Stirlingfhire, appointed by Mr. Walker the fheriff-depute, I find it is true that he granted a commiffion to take the oath of James Stirling of Craigbarnot, as a witnefs, who was excepted out of the A
ct of General Pardon, and againft whom a bill was found within the three years.

The truth is, in proceffes in this part of the country when a witnefs is fummoned, if both the plaintiff and defendant agree to the examination of a witnefs upon a commiffion, the Judge feldom or never interpofes, but the commiffion goes in courfe; and whether Mr. Bryce refle
cted upon Craigbarnot's particular cafe, I do not know; but Mr. Walker, the fheriff-depute, in his letter marked   fays, with fome affurance, that he is perfuaded he neither is diffaffe
cted himfelf, nor a favourer of diff-affe
cted perfons; nor have I heard of any inftance to found a fufpicion againft him, except his granting the above mentioned commiffion, wch very probably might proceed from inadvertency. But upon this head I muft refer myfelf to his letter dire
cted to me, marked   herewith alfo tranfmitted.

Campbell arsgourie, riff-sub-ite of the e of For- It is alfo obje
cted that Mr. Campbell of Carfgourie was nominated by Mr. Brown, fheriff-depute of Forfarfhire, notwithftanding that feveral well-affe
cted perfons of Angus aud Mearns join'd w^t the Synod of the Clergy in a reprefentation to the faid Mr. Brown, defiring him not to appoint him a fubftitute, becaufe he was a nonjuror. It is likewife faid,

that Mr. Campbell has been complain'd of to the Judges of the Circuit, as exercifing his office with great partiality, and that he has been feverely reprimanded on that account by them from the Bench.

As to the firft part of this complaint, I muft refer your Lordfhip to a letter bearing date the 1ft Auguft, 1752, fign'd by Mr. Brown, wherein a particular account is given of the applications made to him concerning the nomination of a Subftitute, in which he refers to a great many letters from gentlemen and minifters of the gofpel, recommending Carfgourie to him as a proper perfon to be Sheriff-Subftitute, a lift of whom is herewith tranfmitted, marked   Moft of the gentlemen I am well acquainted with, and the letters I have feen, and they are in the terms reprefented by Mr. Brown; and, I verily believe, that the other facts fet furth by Mr. Brown are true, as he is a gentleman of honour and integrity, and intirely well affected to his Majefty's perfon and government.

I have alfo feen the letters from eleven Prefbyterian minifters, mentioned in the lift, all of that county, and feveral of them of that prefbytery in which Mr. Campbell refides, recommending him as a perfon fit to be his Subftitute. But it is improper to trouble your Lo^p by repeating what is at great length fet furth by Mr. Brown himfelf in the faid letter.

As to the 2^d part of the complaint, I apply'd to the Lords Elchies and Kilkerran, who were the Judges upon the Circuit at the time when the Subftitute is faid to have been feverely reprimanded on account of partiality in his office, and I found that the complaint offered againft Mr. Campbell was no other than that Mr. Doeg, provoft of Montrofe, was fummoned as a juryman, as feveral other magiftrates of incorporans in the Shire of Fife were alfo fummoned by the Sheriff of that county, when the Circuit Court was to be held at Perth in Autumn 1751, and that he and other well-affected heritors in the county were call'd upon that duty out of courfe. Mr. Campbell anfwer'd, that in returning the lift of jurors he had always obferv'd a regular rotation round the inhabitants of the fhire, in tranfmitting the names of forty-five jurors to the Court of Jufticiary, from among whom a quorum of the Court named fifteen to be fummoned. That he was not anfwerable for a regular rotation in the choice of the fifteen, which was done by the Court of Jufticiary. That, as for Mr. Doeg's being a provoft, he did not know that magiftrates of burghs had any exemption by law, and that when the lift was made up, it did not occurr to him that the Circuit Court and the elections of Burghs cou'd interfeir.

The Court upon this gave orders to the Provoft and all the magiftrates of royal burghs to return home in order to attend their elections, and therefore difmift Provoft Doeg and all other fuch officers, but without any rebuke to Mr. Campbell, and only recommended to fheriffs to obferve certain rules concerning that matter, then laid down, in all time coming.

This your Lordfhip will fee more fully reprefented in a narrative of this fact written with Lord Elchies's hand, which being read in my prefence before Lord Kilkerran, he agreed that the narrative was full and juft. This narrative is marked

orbes, of eenshire. With regard to Mr. Forbes, fubftitute of Aberdeenfhire, I received a letter from Mr. David Dalrymple, the fheriff-depute there, wherein the facts charged upon him are aver'd to be falfe and groundlefs; and a very particular narrative is given of his education and principles, and his behaviour in the difcharge of the dutys of his office. It is marked

This letter I have fhown to feveral of the Judges of the Jufticiary, who, in their circuits, have occafion to receive complaints of fheriffs-depute and their fubftitutes, and alfo to other well-affected gentlemen; and I have no reafon to fufpect the facts are unfairly fet furth by Mr. Dalrymple.

Francis len, she-epute of rns, and John it, sheriff-ite of El-nd Nairn. It has been furmif'd, that feveral of the fheriffs-depute are advocates depute, and are thereby oblig'd to attend the circuits, which is hurtful to His Majefty's fervice; fince they cannot be fuppof'd to attend fufficiently to the difcharge of the dutys of fheriff-depute and advocate depute, efpe-cially as they are engaged in other bufinefs before the fuperior Court.

The fact is true that Mr. Francis Garden is fheriff-depute of Mearns, and Mr. John Grant of the countys of Elgin and Nairn, and, at the fame time, are both deputed by His Majefty's Advocate to ferve upon the circuits.

As this was a matter that chiefly related to Lord Advocate, his Lordfhip in his letter to me, marked   has touched upon this point among feveral others to be aftermentioned, to which therefore I refer. If thofe gentlemen do not refide during the fpace mentioned in the Act of Parliament, they are fubject to be removed upon a complaint. If they do, I can fee no great danger of hurting the fervice by their being imploy'd as advocates-depute during the circuits. The Lord Advocate has fufficiently fet furth the merits of Mr. Garden, his nephew; and I only take the liberty to add, that Mr. Grant is a young gentleman very capable of difcharging with reputation the offices he now holds.

Mr Martine Lindfay is faid to have collected the cefs in Perth, for the ufe of the Rebels during the time of the late Rebellion; and, notwith-ftanding, has been allow'd to purchafe a place in the Court of Seffion of the value of £40 per annum, viz. Extractor in the King's Office. As alfo, it is fuggefted, that William Elliot, conjunct agent for the Crown, and principal clerk to Lord Advocate, attended a nonjurant meeting houfe before the Rebellion, and continues to fhow marks of difaffection. That as he is agent for the Crown, it is his bufinefs to find evidences againft Rebels and other offenders, and to manadge the defence for the Crown againft the claims enter'd upon the forfeited eftates; all which, it is faid, he performs with partiality.

As to Martine Lindfay, I call'd upon two of the principal clerks of the Court of Seffion, namely, Mr. Gibfon and Mr. Pringle, in whofe office the faid Martine Lindfay had been appointed a priviledged Extracter long before the late Rebellion; as alfo upon a Gentleman mentioned in your Lordfhip's letter, who was imploy'd in taking Depofitions about the Rebels, and as Sollicitor at Carlifle when the prifoners were try'd there for treafon; and I find that the faid Martine Lindfay was taken into cuftody at Edinburgh after the Rebellion, carried to Carlifle, and try'd and acquitted.

I have feen no evidence that he collected the cefs at Perth for the Rebels, and I am apt to believe that particular fuggeftion is not true; for there is a procefs now depending againft another, namely, David Car-michael, for repetition of the cefs levy'd by him as collector. But upon

Mr. M⋅ Lindsay William conjunc for the and prin to Lord cate.

this head, I fhall refer myfelf to a memorandum put into my hands by the before-named Mr. Gibfon, from which your Lordfhip will fee what the faid Mr. Lindfay fets furth for himfelf, marked   ; and only in a word obferve, that in appointing extraƌers in the feveral clerk's offices, the Judges have no concern, they having their commiffion only from the principal clerks; nor do the Judges fo much as know who they are, or when they are put in.

After his being acquitted, he continued his bufinefs, as being a privileg'd extraƌer in the forefaid office; but the clerks would not allow him to aƌ, as having been *fufpeƌed* of acceffion of fome kind or other to the Rebellion, untill he had qualify'd himfelf by taking the oaths to the government, which he did accordingly.

The faid Martine Lindfay never was appointed extraƌer in the King's office, that having been poffeft by one Robert Low, fince July 1743, untill his death; and upon his deceafe, Peter Low, his fon, was appointed in his place, and ftill continues to difcharge the dutys of that office, with a fallary only of £10 a-year, as appears from the Records of Exchequer. However, what probably has given rife to this fuggeftion, is, that two or three years after the Rebellion, the faid Martine Lindfay purchafed a trifling office, namely, the Keeping of the Regifter of Bonds, recorded by thofe two clerks only, from the perfon who then held it, and upon whofe dimiffion Martine Lindfay was appointed by the aforefaid two clerks to fucceed him.

As to William Elliot, clerk to the Lord Advocate, I muft refer myfelf to his Lordfhip's letter herewith tranfmitted, wherein the merites of his cafe are amply fet furth. I have good reafon to believe that fince the late Aƌ of Parliament, he never attended a nonjuring meeting-houfe; nor do I know or have I heard of his having fhown any marks of difaffeƌion to the government, or that he perform'd his duty, as agent for the Crown, with partiality. Mr. William Alfton is conjunƌ agent with him, very able in his profeffion, and of undoubted loyalty; and from my own knowledge, I can take upon me to fay, that with regard to proceffes that depended before the Court of Seffion, the manadgment of the perfons in-

trufted with the defence for the Crown againft the claims entered on forfeited eftates, has been irreproachable, and if any defect of that kind had
been there, the Judges muft have feen it; and I hope your Lordfhip will
do them the juftice to believe they were not inattentive to the intereft of
the Crown in cafes that came before the Court. For the reft that refers
to this gentleman, I refer to the forefaid letter put into my hand by the
Lord Advocate.

As to Mr. Gabriel Napier, it is faid, that he was Regifter to the Barons 4ᵗʰ Clafs
of Exchequer before the late Rebellion, but fince has been left out, and Complai
it is not known upon what account he has met with his difgrace. Napier.

I call'd upon Mr. Napier, and upon fome of the officers of the Court of
Exchequer, and I find that Mr. Napier was imploy'd as clerk to the
Mafters of Reference, under the Commiffioners of Enquiry upon the
Eftates forfeited in Scotland by the Rebellion in the year 1715. That on
the determination of that Commiffion, by an act in the 13ᵗʰ year of His
late Majefty's reign, all the papers and records relating to thefe Forfeitures
were ordain'd to be lodg'd in the Court of Exchequer, and the Barons
were to fell fuch of thefe eftates as remained unfold, and to determine
all matters relative thereto. Mr. William Bowles, the Deputy King's
Remembrancer in Exchequer, imploy'd one Mr. Henry Norton, who had
been a clerk to the faid Commiffioners, to affift him in that branch of
bufinefs; and upon Mr. Norton's death, the end of the year 1728, Mr.
Bowles in 1729 imploy'd Mr. Napier to affift him. That on the 21ˢᵗ·
October 1735, Her late Majefty Queen Caroline, then Guardian of the
kingdom, gave a fign manual for paying Mr. Bowles at the rate of £100
p. annum for fix years, from Midfummer 1728, to Midfummer 1734;
Mr. Philp, as Auditor, at £80 p. annum for faid time; and Mr. Napier
at £50 p. annum, for five years, from Midfummer 1729, to Dᵒ· 1734—
and there have been no more fallarys warranted or paid on that head
fince; but Mr. Napier ftill continued to have the cuftody of thefe Papers
and Records under Mr. Bowles; and for whatever bufinefs was done,
there were confiderable fees attending the fame: and when Mr. Bowles
went to London in 1738, Mr. Napier was ftill imploy'd to have the

charge of thefe matters under Mr. Bogle, and now under Mr. Moncrieff, and has his fees on any bufinefs done relating to thefe forfeitures; fo that Mr. Napier's complaint is not that he was turned out of any office he had, but that after the mannadgment of the late Forfeited eftates was committed to the Court of Exchequer, that fuch office was not erected by the Court with regard to the laft forfeitures, as he was imploy'd in concerning the former. The reafons, as far as I was able to learn, why the Barons did not create fuch office were, that creditors, as well as his Majefty's fervants, murmur'd not a little at offices not neceffary and with large fallarys being eftablifhed, as hurtful, not only to the Crown, but to the creditors of the forfeiting perfons; and, therefore, the Court thought it more expedient the bufinefs fhou'd be carried on by y⁰ ordinary officers.

Mr. Napier's zeal and fervices, during the late Rebellion, are fully fet forth in a letter he wrote to me herewith tranfmitted, marked

William y of New- 1.
As to Mr. William Gray of Newholm, he was indeed imploy'd in taking Depofitions about the Rebels—attended a great number of prifoners to Carlifle—acted on the road as Commiffary—and at the feffions as Affift- ant Sollicitor; and as far as I have been able to inform myfelf, difcharged that duty very faithfully. What was the amount of his incomes from his bufinefs before the Rebellion, or how much it has decay'd fince upon account of his fervices to the Government, I can report only from his own reprefentation. Nor do I know what the value of the Commiffariot of Rofs was reprefented to be of, nor by whom; but I have ground to believe that it will not return above £12 or £14 a-year. In all this, if there is any blame, or upon whom it ought to ly, I really do not know, but this I can fay, that as far as was in the power of feveral of the King's fervts here they have endeavour'd to ferve him.

hn Trigg.
As to John Trigg, he is faid to have been very ufefull during the late rebellion in feveral particulars, and was rewarded by a place in the Fifhery, but fince has been turn'd out, and his arrears of fallary not paid.

Upon this head I apply'd to the Secretary of the Commiffion appoint- ing the Truftees for manadging the money appropriated for the encourage- ment of Manufactures and Fifherys, and from him have received extracts from the minutes and books of the fᵈ Commiſſioners, whereby it appears that Mr. Trigg was difmiſt from their fervice becaufe he would not comply with the orders and directions given by them. All his fallarys preceding the year 1750 were paid to him, and, as to that year, the Truſtees having order'd him to ſhow caufe why he had not comply'd with their orders, he alfo faill'd to give obedience in that particular, and on that account they order'd that fo much of his fallary for that year ſhou'd only be allow'd to him as was fufficient for defraying any charge he had been neceſſarily put to in that period, but no account was ever given in by him, and there that matter reſted. But, for the greater certainty, I humbly refer to the fore-mentioned excerpts from the Truſtees' minutes, herewith tranſmitted, marked

The forefaid excerpts from the minutes of the Truſtees contain alſo Alexand what relates to Alexander Hay, from which it appears that the Truſtees did all that was in their power to provide and encourage him in their way, but it was impoſſible to do him any good; they tried him in feveral ſhapes, but he could not be prevailed upon to give any attention to the bufinefs, and under thefe circumſtances they believed it would have been a mifbehaviour in them to have continued a fallary on him out of the moneys intruſted to their manadgment by his Majeſty for purpofes fo beneficial to the kingdom. What is above is vouch'd by the faid excerpts, which are faithfully taken from the records keept in the Truſtees' office.

As to what relates to Adam Gordon, your Lordſhip will be informed of Adam G his cafe very fully, by caſting your eye upon the letter above referred to from his Majeſty's Advocate, who was arbiter for the faid Adam Gordon, and who, in conjunction with Mr. Robert Craigie, pronounced a decreet arbitral whereby the faid Adam Gordon received £100, tho' Mr. Gordon fays he was fruſtrated in his fuit. I confefs it would require ſtronger proofs than his own aſſertion to gain creditt that the two gentlemen above mentioned, arbiters in the caufe, would give an award whereby injuſtice was done to him, to favour the Laird of Meldrum.

How he has been treated fince by the country I cannot take upon me to fay, nor am I at all acquainted with him or his character, but if it is such as is suggested in the foresaid letter, there is some cause to suspect it may be possible that want of prudence may have given occasion to his not being treated kindly in his own country,—but as to this I intirely refer to my Lord Advocate's letter.

As to the Rev^d. Mr. Davidson, minister of Navarr, his case, as it has been represented to your Lordship, is extremely singular, and deserves to stand in a class by itself.

It is said, that his parishioners having declared openly for the Government during the Rebellion, they guarded the passes in the lower part of the country, incommoding the intelligence of the Rebels; and that in consequence of an appointment by His Royal Highness the Duke, they continued in that duty till they were suppress by the Justices of Peace.

That these people were afterwards summoned criminally for wilfull fire-raising, because they had made bonefires upon his Royal Highness the *Duke's birth-day*, and that the minister complain'd they were still perse-cuted on account of the Loyalty they had shown.

This complaint was so new to me, and carry'd with it such a contempt of all Government, that I was amaz'd I had never heard of it, therefore I was resolv'd to come to a certainty concerning it; for that reason I wrote to the minister himself, and a copy of the letter sent to him is herewith transmitted, marked   To which letter I received the answer likewise herewith sent, marked   , which affords a strong instance how complaints sent from a distant place blow up and diffigure facts in order to their support. Mr. Davidson says, that a guard of his parishioners, wch was of use during the late Rebellion, continued in arms without any interruption untill they were disarmed by the Act of Parliament. That the prosecution for the fire-raising amounted to no more than this, that a tennant in the neighbourhood on a hill, at a distance from any house, had by his servants pulled some heather, for the purposes to which that long heath is apply'd in that country; and this heather, upon the eve of the King's birth-day, was set on fire, which the tennant suspected had been done by the people of Navarr, who had gone to a neighbouring parish of Edziell, and solemnised his Majesty's birth-day; and for that reafon he brought an action in his own name, and (according to the form) in the name of the Procurator-fifcal ·of Court, againft feveral of them, for damage by the lofs of his heather, and had this damage occurred by them, fuch wantonnefs cou'd not well have been juftyfy'd under colour of being a bonefire, no more than if they had fir'd his houfe or his hay-ftack; and in this procefs the facts being refer'd to their oaths, they fwore that the heather was not burnt by them, whereby the procefs ended.

The only complaint the minifter makes, and indeed in a very modeft manner, is, that the profecutor was not decreed in cofts; but having order'd an extract of the procefs to be laid before me, I find that no cofts were demanded, as there was no litigation, and that they had no further trouble than to appear in Court and to give their oaths; and as to other oppreffions, either he or his parifheners are laid under, he fays he can mention nothing in particular; fo that the complaint has not been made by the minifter, who very candidly fets forth the true ftate of the cafe. But the tale dreft up in odious colours, has been tranfmitted to be fure with no very good intentions, and the flauderer has acted under fome kind of affurance that, at fo great a diftance, it could not be contradicted, and thus the truth of the facts, and the ignoble whifperer, might remain cover'd in perpetual darknefs.

Hitherto I have touch'd at all the fpecial facts mentioned in vour Lord-fhip's letter. As to what is faid only in general terms, when a mifbe-haviour is fo charg'd, and particulars are fpecifyed in fupport of what is advanced, if, upon examination, the facts inftanced in are found not to be true, or unfairly reprefented, the judgment to be form'd as to the whole lump is plain; and I leave your Lordfhip to judge how far upon the vouchers refer'd to, what feems to be fo generally aver'd, has any founda-tion upon which it can ftand.

It is poffible I may have committed fome miftakes in this enquiry; I'm fure they are not willfull. And give me leave to obferve, that the law with regard to the Highland Drefs has taken fooner place than could well have been expected; and that fince the Act abolifhing the Here[ll][1]

[1] Heritable.

CPSIA information can be obtained
at www.ICGtesting.com
Printed in the USA
LVOW04s1023101115

461863LV00019B/232/P